D1567725

Knowledge on Trust

Knowledge on Trust

Paul Faulkner

OXFORD
UNIVERSITY PRESS

OXFORD
UNIVERSITY PRESS

Great Clarendon Street, Oxford OX2 6DP
United Kingdom

Oxford University Press is a department of the University of Oxford.
It furthers the University's objective of excellence in research, scholarship,
and education by publishing worldwide.
Oxford is a registered trade mark of Oxford University Press in the UK
and in certain other countries

© Paul Faulkner 2011

The moral rights of the author have been asserted

Reprinted 2015

All rights reserved. No part of this publication may be reproduced, stored in
a retrieval system, or transmitted, in any form or by any means, without the
prior permission in writing of Oxford University Press, or as expressly permitted
by law, by licence or under terms agreed with the appropriate reprographics
rights organization. Enquiries concerning reproduction outside the scope of the
above should be sent to the Rights Department, Oxford University Press, at the
address above

You must not circulate this book in any other binding or cover
And you must impose this same condition on any acquirer

British Library Cataloguing in Publication Data
Data available

Library of Congress Cataloging in Publication Data
Data available

ISBN 978-0-19-958978-4

Acknowledgements

I am grateful to the Arts and Humanities Research Council for awarding me matching leave to complete the second draft of this book. I thought that would be it, but the present text is draft four. Or it might be five, I lose track. And whilst there is no doubt this draft could benefit from more work, the time has come to stop here. Over this period what I have wanted to say about testimony has slowly metamorphosed, and it has so in a significant part in response to exposure to criticism. I have accumulated a lot of intellectual debts, and I fear I will not be able to acknowledge them all. My greatest debt is to Mike Martin, who supervised my doctorate on testimony and put a lot of effort into trying to get me to think about things to a sufficient depth, and then took the time to read an earlier draft and show me where I went wrong. Then thanks are owed to the participants of the Sheffield reading group that worked through the very first draft: Chris Bennett, Chris Hookway, Rob Hopkins, Joe Morrison, and Bob Stern. To Matt Nudds and Matt Soteriou who have discussed these issues with me since graduate school. To David Owens who organised the Telling and Trusting workshop, and the British Academy who funded it, that has provided much excellent discussion. And to some OUP and CUP referees who produced some truly outstanding comments. Ted Hinchman and Ciara Fairley have identified themselves as two of these. Many others there is only space to list: Jonathan Adler, Keith Allen, Matt Bevis, Sean Cordell, Tom Crowther, Don Fallis, Miranda Fricker, Alvin Goldman, Peter Graham, Dominic Gregory, Arnon Keren, Max Kobel, Jennifer Lackey, Guy Longworth, and Jenny Saul. Finally, I must thank Claire Ryan who has helped me through each and every draft.

To my parents
Ray and Sue

Contents

1

The Epistemology of Testimony

Knowledge is something that can be shared. If I have seen what lies over the ridge, I can tell you what is there, and so put you in a position to know what is there. I know what is there because I went and looked and you can know what is there because I told you what I saw. So we can both know what is beyond the ridge, and share this knowledge. The aim of this book is to provide some explanation of this phenomenon; it is to explain how it is that we get to know things on the basis of testimony.

Our dependence on testimony for knowledge, and more broadly belief, is very far-reaching. We frequently suffer what Bernard Williams calls *purely positional disadvantage*: we can only be at one place at one time and this limits what facts we can be aware of.[1] This limitation can be shallow and accidental, as when it just so happens that I reach the brow of the ridge first, but it can also go deep. It is so much easier to consult geographical records than attempt personally to establish the height of the highest peak in the Carpathian Mountains (and the difficulties involved in personally establishing this should not be underestimated). But dependence on historical records is forced if we want to know the number of Popes the Medici gave to the Church: with a life-span rarely over four score and ten it is impossible for any living person to remember these events. And something similar is true with respect to our beliefs about other people's mental states: whilst another's displeasure might be visible, that they feel indignant requires they communicate this fact. Then in some fields, such as natural science, results can require more time and expertise to achieve than any single person could bring to bear. Here there is both positional

---

[1] Williams (2002), p. 42.

disadvantage—experiments can require too many man-hours for one lifetime—and what might be termed *epistemic disadvantage*: no one person could possess all the knowledge necessary for the experiment. This disadvantage is equally common: we frequently depend on experts and take ourselves to know things that we have only the sketchiest comprehension of. And even on matters where we are an authority, we can still depend on testimony; we are an authority on our own mental states but some self-knowledge requires observations of our own behaviour, which others are equally in a position to make and may be more perceptive than us in making.

Our epistemic dependence on testimony for much of what we know and believe is remarkable. Here are two simple cases where it is plausible to say that an audience depends on a speaker for knowledge.[2]

Case 1, being told another's observations: with his view of the information board obscured, the husband impatiently asks his wife whether their flight is boarding yet and she tells him that no, they must still wait in the lounge.

Case 2, reading an account of facts and events: whilst skimming the Sunday papers, the reader learns that the distance to the Sun was first accurately calculated by bouncing radar waves off Venus and doing trigonometry, and that this distance is now calculated to be 149,597,870.69 kilometres.

In case 1, the husband does not need to get up and look at the information board to know what it says about their flight; his wife telling him that their flight is not boarding yet puts him in a position to know this. And in case 2, in reading that the Sun is such a distance from the Earth, the newspaper reader is informed of this fact about our universe. The question, then, is how is it, in cases such as these, that testimony can make knowledge and justified belief available to an audience?

What is beyond doubt is that testimony can make knowledge and justified belief available; that by means of testimony we learn everyday facts about our environment—what is over the ridge and whether our plane is boarding—and more arcane or theoretical matters such as the distance of some celestial body. Once the extent of our epistemic dependence of testimony is properly appreciated, testimony could be defined as a *fundamental* source of knowledge, or a source for which to deny that the source yields knowledge would be to assert a form of scepticism. In this

---

[2] To aid clarity I'll default to making speakers feminine and audiences masculine.

respect, testimony can be compared to perception and memory: all are fundamental sources of knowledge.

What obviously differentiates testimony from perception and memory is that it ordinarily involves other people. Ordinarily, testimonial belief is based on another person's testimony.[3] As a way of acquiring belief, testimony necessarily involves two roles—that of the *speaker* and that of the *audience*—and paradigmatically these roles are taken by two agents. The acquisition of knowledge and justified belief from testimony involves action and reaction. This distinguishes testimony and pushes it into the practical sphere, or that sphere concerned with the interaction of agents.

As speakers, giving testimony is something we do. We choose what we say and we choose how we say it, and we have reasons for these choices. These reasons determine the practical rationality of our testimony. Our motivation in telling someone something can be the desire to influence their thoughts and so how they feel and act. In telling you what I can see over the ridge, for instance, I might want to motivate you to climb the ridge too, maybe because I want to share the great view with you, or maybe because I think you need the exercise. How others think, feel, and act is something that is a matter of interest to us. So we think about what we say and how we say it. And whilst our purposes, as speakers, can often be to inform an audience of something, our purpose need not be this, or just this, and it can be much else besides.

As audiences, accepting testimony is likewise something that we do. Since we know that people tell us things for all sorts of reasons, we often reason about what someone's testimony indicates about themselves and the world. And when we do accept a piece of testimony we can be motivated by both practical and epistemic considerations. One can accept what a speaker says just to keep the conversation going, or for the sake of argument as well as because one believes, or presumes, that what the speaker says is true. However, if acceptance issues in belief—if we take a bit of testimony to inform us of some fact—then our reason for accepting that bit of testimony must be a reason for belief. And our interest in

---

[3] The exception which demands the qualification is the possibility that one might become so psychologically disconnected from oneself that one's preserved earlier utterances offer a basis for knowledge; for instance amnesiac cases could be imagined and one's childhood diaries can put oneself in a position to know what is described even if they fail to awaken memory.

testimony as audiences derives primarily from the fact that we take testimony to be informative.

This feature of testimony—that it paradigmatically involves the engagement of two agents—then institutes a practical and theoretical difficulty. This is the problem of cooperation.

1.1 The problem of cooperation

The problem of cooperation can be introduced by way of the 'Trust Game'.[4] In this game there are two players: a trusting party or 'investor' and a trusted party or 'trustee'. In the simplest version the investor has a certain endowment, say £10, and the option of keeping this or transferring part or all of it to the trustee and keeping whatever remains. What gets transferred gets multiplied, say by a factor of 4, and the trustee then has the option of keeping the sum or making a back-transfer of part or all of it and keeping the remainder. In this case, the best the investor could do would be to give the trustee everything and hope the trustee splits his £40 windfall. If the trustee does share, both do well and the game has resulted in a cooperative outcome. But why should the trustee cooperate? How would it be in his interests to return anything?

Suppose, first, that it is a subject's individual beliefs and desires, or in economic terms the subject's preferences, that explain how the subject acts; and, second, that rational action aims at the satisfaction of the actor's individual preferences. Given this background, it does not seem rational for the investor to make an initial transfer since it seems fair to presume that the trustee will prefer to keep the multiplied sum whilst he would prefer some money to none. For the investor to be acting reasonably in making a transfer, he needs to think, for whatever reason, that the trustee will make a back-transfer. This game then illustrates how cooperation can be problematic because it is arguable that we often lack grounds for thinking this, but make transfers nevertheless. We trust and yet appear to be unreasonable in doing so.

The Testimony Game is the parallel of this. It has two players: an 'audience', or potentially trusting party, and a 'speaker' or potentially trusted party. The situation is a conversation whose ostensible purpose is

---

[4] Fehr, Fischbacher, and Gachter (2002), cited in Elster (2007), p. 350.

the giving and receiving of information. This situation presents the audience with a choice as to whether or not to trust the speaker, or accept what the speaker says. Before arguing for the parallel, it might be illustrated with the case of purchasing a used car from the pages of *Exchange and Mart*. Consider then, case 3, the position of a nervous buyer who asks about a particular car's history and is told in reply that the car has had one previous lady owner. And she mostly left it garaged. The buyer wants to buy a car but would rather buy nothing than a wreck. So if the buyer thinks that the salesman would prefer to sell his worst stock, then the buyer recognizes that the salesman has some motive to lie to him. So it seems that if the buyer is to believe what the salesman says, he needs to believe, for whatever reason, that the salesman has told him the truth. As with the Trust Game, to trust without a particular reason for doing so would be to act irrationally.

An immediate concern might be that this case is peculiar. Clearly one should not adopt a credulous attitude when purchasing a used car, but this could just be down to the fact that this is a communicative situation where the buyer believes that the vendor has some motive for deceit. And this is not true of all conversations whose ostensible purpose is the giving and receiving of information. However, there are two things driving the demand for a rationalizing belief to the effect that the vendor has told the truth. First, the buyer would rather not buy anything than acquire a wreck, which is to say that acquiring a false belief (trusting the vendor when he lied) would leave the buyer in a worse position than ignorance (not forming any belief about the car's history). This is true to the extent that an audience's interest is epistemic; as *enquirers* we have in interest in believing the truth, but would rather remain ignorant than believe falsely. Second, the buyer recognizes that the vendor's conversational purpose *might* be at odds with his goal of learning the truth. This possibility is equally the presumption for any conversations whose ostensible purpose is the giving and receiving of information. This is because speakers and audiences have different interests in such conversational exchanges.

Engaging in conversations as to the facts is to our advantage as audiences because our ability to individually gather information about the world is limited and by believing what others tell us we can be informed of the facts. Our interest, qua audience, is learning the truth. Engaging in conversations as to the facts is to our advantage as speakers because it is a means of influencing others: through an audience's acceptance of what we say, we can get the audience to think, feel, and act in specific ways.[5] So our interest, qua speaker, is being believed, and it is this because we have a more basic interest in influencing others. This can be argued by way of an analogy: Eliot Sober's example of Viceroys and Monarchs.[6] Although they are good for Blue Jays to eat, Viceroys look like Monarchs, which are not. This mimicry is an evolutionary lie. The Monarch signals truly that it is a poor meal; the Viceroy mimics this signal to communicate something false. The purpose of both signals is to influence the Blue Jay to make it less likely that the signalling butterfly will be eaten. Of course, liars and truth-tellers are not different types of person, like Viceroys and Monarchs are different types of butterfly, but the liar and truth-teller as speakers have the same underlying interest in being believed.

Consider now how the Testimony Game is parallel to the Trust Game. In the Testimony Game the choices for the audience are to trust or not. The best outcome for the audience is to trust when the speaker is trustworthy. In wanting the truth, say as to whether p, an audience wants to be told that p if p and to be told that not-p if not-p. A trustworthy speaker is one who will do this (and not tell the audience anything if they are ignorant as to whether p).[7] This trust–trustworthiness combination is the cooperative outcome. Whilst the cooperative outcome would be best for the audience, the commitment to telling the truth would not be best for the speaker. The best outcome for a speaker would be to receive an audience's trust and yet have the liberty to tell the truth or not given the shape of the speaker's interests on the occasion. However, telling the truth when it suits one is not a way of being trustworthy. So the best outcome for the speaker would be the trust and untrustworthiness combination. Since this is the worst outcome for the audience, the Testimony Game has the same structure of pay-offs as the Trust Game.[8]

What this parallel implies is that one can equally draw the conclusion that it is not reasonable to trust without a *supporting reason* that rationalizes trust. *The acceptance of testimony must be backed by reasons if it is to be reasonable.*

---

[5] Sperber argues that communication has evolved and stabilized only because it can serve both these purposes. See Sperber (2001).

[6] Sober (1994).

[7] Similarly, Williams argues in wanting the truth an enquirer wants to arrive at a state where he believes that p if p and believes that not-p if not-p. Williams (1978), pp. 37–8.

[8] Compare Adler (2002), p. 155, and Pettit (1990), p. 319 who observe the resemblance between the receipt of testimony and the prisoner's dilemma.

The *problem of cooperation* is then the problem of giving an account of the satisfaction of this condition. It is the problem of explaining the rationality of testimonial cooperation. This is then *problematic* to the extent that this condition cannot be satisfied; that is to the extent that we lack reasons—or have a psychological tendency to trust that outstrips our possession of reasons. For the moment I will leave it open whether, if at all, testimonial cooperation is problematic. And I will use the designator *the argument from cooperation* to refer to the argument of the previous paragraph that concludes that the acceptance of a bit of testimony must be supported by reasons.

1.2 Theoretical positions

In the simplest terms the theory of testimony I want to argue for endorses the conclusion of the argument from cooperation: we need reasons to be justified in accepting a bit of testimony and forming a testimonial belief. However, by means of accepting testimony we get to form beliefs whose epistemic status is determined by social facts, paradigmatically the epistemic standing of the speaker with respect to what she gave testimony to. For example, consider case 1 where the wife can tell her husband what the information board says because she can see it, whilst he cannot. She tells him that their flight isn't boarding and they are instructed to wait in the lounge. His wife telling him this then puts the husband in a position to know that the information board instructs wait. He can know this, according to the theory I will advance, because he has reasons for accepting his wife's testimony. But in so doing he acquires a belief whose epistemic standing derives from the fact that his wife can see the information board. Her knowledge, I will say, is transmitted to him. The detail of this theory is then given along two axes: first, its account of our reasons for accepting testimony; and, second, its account of how testimony works to transmit knowledge, and epistemic standing more generally.

This theory I would contrast to *reductive* and *non-reductive* theories of testimony. A non-reductive theory of testimony regards testimony to be epistemically similar to perception and memory. Considering perception, James Pryor offers the following characterization of a 'dogmatist epistemology':

The dogmatist about perceptual justification says that when it perceptually seems to you as if *p* is the case, you have a kind of justification for believing *p* that does not presuppose or rest on your justification for anything else, which could be cited in an argument . . . for *p*. To have this justification for believing *p*, you need only have an experience that represents *p* as being the case. No further awareness or reflection or background beliefs are required.[9]

A non-reductive theory of testimony is dogmatic in this sense; it proposes that when an audience has the experience of understanding testimony to *p*, the audience has a kind of justification for believing *p* that does not presuppose or rest on the audience's justification for anything else that could be cited in an argument for *p*. This could be broken into two claims.

First, testimony to *p* gives its recipient a unique 'kind of justification for believing that *p*'. Perception, the 'dogmatist' would claim, is a source of knowledge and justification in its own right, and the non-reductive view of testimony is the same: testimony is likewise a source of knowledge and justification in its own right. As with perception, appearances can be misleading, but if they are not, then a testimonial belief is justified (amounts to knowledge) merely by virtue of the fact that it is based on the testimony it is based on. This first positive claim I will refer to as the claim that *testimony is an epistemically distinctive source*, or as the claim that testimonial knowledge and justification are *epistemically distinctive kinds*.

Second, testimony to *p* gives its recipient a justification that 'does not presuppose or rest on anything the recipient could cite in an argument for *p*'. The 'dogmatic' view of perceptual beliefs is that they do not need the support of further beliefs in order to be justified, and the non-reductive view holds that the same is true of testimonial beliefs: they do not need the support of further beliefs in order to be justified. In particular, a testimonial belief that *p*, acquired through accepting a bit of testimony to *p*, does not need to be supported by further beliefs about testimonial appearances, or beliefs to the effect that the bit of testimony was sincere and competent, or otherwise likely to be true. As with perception, all that matters is that the recipient of testimony does not believe (or ought not to believe) that these things are false. This second positive claim I will refer to as the claim that

---

[9] Pryor (2000), p. 519.

we have *default entitlement* or a *general entitlement to believe testimony other things being equal.*

Different non-reductive theories of testimony are then produced by different interpretations of these two claims. The idea that testimonial knowledge and justification are epistemically distinctive kinds can be expressed as the idea that testimonial knowledge and testimonial justification are *transmitted knowledge and justification.* Different accounts of how testimony works to transmit knowledge and justification then give different expressions to the idea that testimony is an epistemically distinctive source. It has been claimed, for instance, that testimony transmits justification because it makes a speaker responsible for justifying an audience's belief.[10] And it has been claimed that testimony transmits knowledge and justification because it offers an audience a way of basing his belief on someone else's evidence (paradigmatically the speaker's evidence) for belief.[11] The theory of testimony this book argues for likewise holds testimony to be an epistemically distinctive source. So the correct account of transmission is something I will be at pains to work out.

Non-reductive theories of testimony are, second, also distinguished by how they interpret and argue for the idea that we have a general entitlement to accept testimony. This entitlement is not an epistemic sanction of credulity, although the historical advocate of this epistemological principle—Thomas Reid—gave it the label 'a principle of credulity'.[12] It is possible to argue that the entitlement requires that an audience exhibit a reliable ability to monitor testimony for falsehood.[13] However, what is important, indeed definitional, of the entitlement is that it *does not hold by virtue of* an audience's ability 'to cite an argument' for truth of the bit of testimony accepted. It could hold, for instance, by virtue of the intelligibility of testimony, or by virtue of the rationality of speakers, or the nature of communication.[14]

The contrary reductive position denies both the claim that testimony is an epistemically distinctive source and the claim that we have general entitlement to accept testimony. First, we do not have a general

---

[10] See Moran (2006).
[11] See Burge (1993).
[12] See Reid (1764).
[13] See Goldberg and Henderson (2007).
[14] See, respectively, Coady (1992), Burge (1993), McDowell (1980).

entitlement to accept testimony: the mere fact that an audience is the recipient of testimony to *p* does not justify the audience believing that *p*. Knowledge or justified belief is yielded only when the acceptance of a bit of testimony is supported by further beliefs about testimonial appearances, or when it demonstrates a reliable sensitivity to the truth of these appearances. Thus, in principle, the reductive theory could be either *internalist* requiring that an audience be able to cite an argument for the truth of *p* in order to be justified in accepting testimony to *p*; or it could be *externalist* merely requiring the audience to be reliable in the bits of testimony accepted. However, unless I make clear otherwise, I will understand the reductive theory to be internalist. The reason for this is that I think the best motivation for the requirement that an audience have some capacity to discriminate true from false testimony comes from the argument from cooperation. And this argument institutes the demand that acceptance be backed *by reasons*. On this internalist reductive theory (hereafter just 'reductive theory') an audience is justified in accepting testimony to *p* because other things the audience believes can be cited in an argument for *p*. Call this claim the demand that acceptance be (*individually* or *subjectively*) *reasonable*.

Second, the reductive theory denies that testimonial knowledge and justification are unique kinds. Rather, testimonial knowledge and justification reduce to knowledge and justification from other sources. Confronted by testimony to *p*, an audience does not have a unique kind of justification for believing that *p*: the audience's justification for belief is simply that argument the audience could cite for the truth of *p*. Since this argument determines the justification of the audience's testimonial belief, testimonial justification and knowledge are ultimately *inductive in nature*. Just as our experience has established that smoke is a reliable sign of fire so we have established that testimony, on occasion, is a reliable sign of truth. So it is the goodness of our reasons for believing a bit of testimony that explains our possession of knowledge on its basis. This is the *reductive thesis*, which given an internalist interpretation, is the view that it is those considerations an audience can cite in an argument for *p* that explain the audience knowing that *p* on the basis of believing testimony to *p*.

The theory this book will argue for agrees with the non-reductive theory that testimonial knowledge and justification are epistemically distinctive kinds. What testimony does is that it transmits knowledge and justification. However, it disagrees with the non-reductive theory over the claim that we have a general entitlement to accept testimony. We have no such entitlement. In this respect the reductive theory is correct: the acceptance of testimony must be individually reasonable. However, whilst this demand is correct—I think it is instituted by the argument from cooperation—the reductive theory goes wrong in its account of what renders acceptance subjectively reasonable. It goes wrong because the reductive thesis implies an overly restrictive account of what can count as a reason for accepting a bit of testimony. This reductive thesis is wrong, however, because testimonial knowledge and justification are epistemically distinctive kinds.

The theory this book will argue for thereby combines a central claim of the non-reductive theory of testimony (testimony is a *sui generis* source of knowledge and justification) with a central claim of the reductive theory of testimony (the acceptance of a bit of testimony must be individually reasonable if it is to be justified). I will refer to this hybrid theory as the *trust theory of testimony*.[15] In its superficial structure the trust theory is the same as the recent 'dualist' theory advanced by Jennifer Lackey.[16] However, Lackey's dualism does not really take testimony to be an epistemically distinctive source. The non-reductive element in her theory is no more than the claim that testimony can be reliable as a source. Consequently, I will argue in 2.1.3 that Lackey's dualism is best represented as a sophisticated reductive theory, and that the structural similarities to it and the trust theory are superficial.[17]

On the face of it, it might seem contradictory to combine the claim about the distinctiveness of testimony as a source with the demand that the acceptance of testimony be subjectively reasonable. For recall Pryor's characterization of dogmatism, 'when it perceptually seems to you as if p is the case, you have a kind of justification for believing p that does not presuppose or rest on your justification for anything else, which could be cited in an argument . . . for p'. So if it is sufficient for testimonial justification that an audience base his belief on a bit of testimony, then it cannot also be necessary that the audience be able to cite something in favour of the truth of this bit of testimony.

---

[15] See Faulkner (2000).
[16] See Lackey (2008).
[17] See also Faulkner (2009).

However, Pryor characterizes an epistemological theory of perception, and testimony is different from perception. Testimony paradigmatically involves two agents. So, to paraphrase Pryor, 'when it *testimonially* appears to an audience as if *p* is the case, the audience has the kind of justification for believing *p* that *does not rest on anything the audience could cite* in an argument for *p*'. What is epistemically distinctive about testimony as a source of knowledge and justification is that it is a way of resting on *other people's epistemic standings*. However, inheriting this standing does *presuppose* something of an audience. It presupposes that accepting the bit of testimony to *p* is reasonable for the audience, or that the audience can cite something in favour of the truth of *p*. This demand is equally instituted by the fact that testimony paradigmatically comes from another person because its doing so initiates the argument from cooperation. However, the epistemic role of these reasons is to ensure the audience's belief is based on the speaker's reasons; it is to make the distinctive testimonial justification available, rather than to constitute this justification.

Working out the details of these claims amounts to working out the details of the trust theory. At the heart of this theory will be a claim about how the attitude of trust provides a reason for accepting testimony. Getting this attitude right will then show why trust, and so cooperation, are not problematic.

1.3 Key concepts

In the remains of this chapter I outline my understanding of the key concepts that structure the trust theory of testimony. Whilst I offer some motivation for understanding these concepts as I do, what follows is largely a statement of the theoretical starting point, so it is a little shy on argument.

1.3.1 Knowledge and justification

In giving a theory of testimony it is possible to discriminate between knowledge and justification. Here is Robert Audi:

If I do not know that the [Professor] lost his temper, you cannot come to know it on the basis of my attesting to it. . . . Justification is different: even if I am not justified in believing that the [Professor] lost his temper, I can be credible in such a way that you *can* become justified in believing this on the basis of my attesting to it.[18]

He continues,

It is natural to say that in the first case [where I do know the Professor lost his temper] you would gain knowledge *through* my testimony, whereas in the second you would gain justification *from* my testimony, but not through it.[19]

Call these cases 4 and 5. Since the speaker is not justified in belief in case 5, this observation strikes me as correct. It can be explained in the manner Audi proposes: by giving a non-reductive theory of testimonial knowledge, and a reductive theory of testimonial justification. But as I propose it a theory of testimony should not bifurcate in this way.

It is not that I am insensitive to the differences between testimonial knowledge and justification, these differences are a focus in 7.4. Rather, there are two considerations that militate against dividing the theory of testimony in this way. First, it seems plausible that justification, like knowledge, does transmit. Case 5 is one where the speaker was not justified in belief, where the speaker, we might imagine, was engaging in a bit of slanderous gossip. In this case, it is natural to say, as Audi does, that an audience can gain justification from the speaker's testimony but not through it. But what of a third case where the audience spreads the gossip but does so thinking that it is true? In this case, the audience now as speaker does not know the Professor lost his temper but is he justified in this belief? So it seems plausible to say that the person who is then told about the Professor gains a justified belief *through* this telling.

The first reason why the theory of testimony should not make the distinction between knowledge and justification theoretically fundamental is that it seems plausible to claim that justification, like knowledge, can be transmitted. The second reason is that explanations of why knowledge transmits will be good in very many cases as explanations of why justification transmits. For example, according to one explanation, in telling an audience something a speaker takes on the epistemic responsibility for the audience's believing what he is told. This explanation can happily account for the transmission of knowledge (the speaker possesses a knowledge

---

[18] Audi (1997), p. 409.
[19] Audi (1997), p. 410.

supporting justification) or mere justified belief (the speaker possesses a justification that is not knowledge supporting).

The trust theory of testimony does not provide different theories for knowledge and justification. It does employ a particular notion of both knowledge and justification. It presupposes an externalist concept of knowledge. This is not because of the factiveness of knowledge but because what explains an audience's knowing on the basis of testimony will not be other things the audience believes but, paradigmatically, other things the speaker believes. For the same reason the concept of a transmitted justification is an externalist concept of justification. Again, because what explains an audience being testimonially justified is not other things the audience believes but, paradigmatically, other things the speaker believes.

However, consider again case 5 where the audience is justified in believing that the Professor lost his temper from the speaker's testimony even though the speaker is not justified in believing this. In this case the audience's justification is determined by other things the audience believes, primarily the audience's belief that the speaker is sincere and competent, and this bit of testimony is credible. This internalist conception of justification is important to the trust theory since it is just this kind of justification that renders the acceptance of testimony reasonable. To keep clear these two concepts of justification I will follow Tyler Burge and restrict 'justification' to the narrow internalist sense:

> Justifications, in the narrow sense, involve reasons that people have and have access to. These may include self-sufficient premises or more discursive justifications. But they must be available in the cognitive repertoire of the subject.[20]

And I will use the term 'warrant' to refer collectively to justifications in this sense *and* those justifications that are transmitted by testimony. The reference is collective because an audience can be either warranted in belief through testimony or gain a warranted belief from testimony.

Given this understanding of justification, there is one more distinction that will prove important. Return again to case 5 where the speaker is engaged in a bit of slanderous gossip but the audience believes what he is told about the Professor nevertheless. The audience can be justified in this

---

[20] Burge (1993), p. 459.

belief, Audi correctly observes, on the basis of believing the speaker to be sincere and competent in this matter. Two situations can then be distinguished. First, suppose this belief about the speaker's sincerity and competence is quite false. In this situation the audience's justification explains why the audience believes as he does but it is not an objectively good justification. Knowledge cannot be based on a false premise.[21] Second, suppose the audience knows the speaker to be sincere and competent. In this situation the audience's justification is not merely explanatory it is also an objectively good justification. It would be knowledge supporting if the supported belief were true and there were no Gettier-type accidents. Thus the distinction is between merely explanatory justifications and genuinely justificatory justifications, or, simply put, between *explanatory and justificatory reasons for belief*.[22] This distinction is important because the reductive theory will require an audience's reasons for accepting testimony be justificatory; whereas all the trust theory will require is that an audience have an explanatory justification for acceptance.

1.3.2 Testimony

Testimony is a way of acquiring belief. As a way of acquiring belief it differs from perception in that it does not start with registrations on the bodily surface but starts externally with a speaker producing a bit of testimony. What is testimony? It is something produced by a speaker whose acceptance by an audience can be the acquisition of belief.

Here are some examples of testimony. Case 1 described above: with his view of the information board obscured, the husband impatiently asks his wife whether their flight is boarding yet and she tells him that no, they must still wait in the lounge. The wife telling her husband this is testimony. Case 2 also described above: whilst skimming the Sunday papers, the reader reads that the distance to the Sun is now calculated to be 149,597,870.69 kilometres. This written statement is testimony. Both these cases arguably satisfy Coady's narrow definition of testimony as a statement that p which 'is evidence that p and is offered as evidence that p [by someone with] the relevant competence, authority, or credentials to

---

[21] Gettier (1963).

[22] Compare Pettit and Smith's distinction between motivating and justifying reasons, Pettit and Smith (1990), p. 566. And see Moran (2001), p. 128.

state truly that p'.[23] This definition is sufficient for a statement to be testimony, but it is not necessary. This is shown by case 6: a student writes in the course of a history exam that the Medici gave three Popes to the Church. The student's statement that p is offered as evidence that she knows that p, not as evidence that p. However, that it was not intended to be evidence that p would not prevent a third party—someone other than her teacher—reading it and acquiring a belief about the Medici on its basis. An illicitly read diary could be testimony in the same way.

We can also be circumspect and sophisticated in (intentionally) telling others what we know. Consider case 7: asked the time, S looks at her watch and then draws a clock face in the sand with the hands pointing to twelve. In this case, S's testimony is neither spoken nor written but is a series of actions that together form an utterance in Grice's extended sense: by means of them S means something.[24] Case 8: asked for an academic reference, Professor A writes that the candidate's 'command of English is excellent and his attendance at tutorials has been regular'.[25] This is similar to case 7 in that the Professor's testimony is not what his utterance means but what he means by this utterance. And we can make a mistake in what we say but be well understood.

However, not all intelligible utterances are testimony. Statements made in jest or uttered as part of a theatrical performance are not. This is because these statements do not present their contents as true. For the same reason a question is not testimony, though we can learn from what a question presupposes. For instance, case 9: S asks A, 'Did you shut the window?' From this question A can acquire the belief that the window is open, but S did not give testimony to this fact. This case shows that Jennifer Lackey's definition of testimony is too broad. According to Lackey, an utterance is testimony to p if a speaker intends to convey the information that p by means of it or if a hearer 'reasonably takes [it] as conveying the information that p (in part) in virtue of [its] communicable content'.[26] In case 8, A can reasonably take S's question as conveying its presupposition, but S's question is not testimony to this.

---

[23] Coady (1992), p. 42. Coady adds a third condition: the testimony 'is relevant to some disputed or unresolved question (which may, or may not be p?) and is directed to those who are in need of evidence on the matter'. This condition is motivated: See 4.2 but it is odd to make it part of a definition of testimony: does our testimony cease to be testimony if our audience is not interested in what we say?

[24] See Grice (1957).   [25] Grice (1967), p. 33.   [26] Lackey (2008), p. 32.

Or consider case 10: a taxi driver excuses the damage to his cab's front wing with the explanation that just this morning a typically stupid woman driver pulled out of a side road without looking. In this case, the passenger could reasonably take the taxi driver's utterance to convey the information that he has a sexist attitude towards women drivers, and his utterance conveys this information in virtue of its content. So by Lackey's definition the taxi driver testifies that he is sexist. However, whilst the passenger could reasonably acquire the belief that the taxi driver is sexist from his testimony—she could reasonably acquire this belief because it could be *reasonably inferred* from the taxi driver's testimony—it is not that the taxi driver actually testifies that he is sexist! In this respect, Lackey's definition of testimony, like reductive theories of testimony, blurs the distinction between *testimonial beliefs* and *beliefs inferentially acquired from testimony*.

In light of these cases, I propose that an utterance U is testimony to *p* if and only if a speaker means that *p* by U, and presents it as true that *p*. On this account, the taxi driver does not testify that he is sexist because he does not mean this by his utterance; it is just that this can be reasonably inferred from what he does mean. The student's examination answer is testimony to the Medici giving three Popes to the Church because this is what the student means by what she states and it is something she presents as true. Professor A's reference is testimony to the poor philosophical abilities of his student since this is what he means and presents as true by what he says.

This account of the nature of testimony takes two related notions as basic: the notion of a speaker meaning something by an utterance and the notion of a speaker presenting what they mean as true. And when testimony is considered as a way of acquiring belief a third thing is taken for granted: an audience's understanding. The possibility of forming a testimonial belief arises for an audience only when the audience confronts an utterance and understands that by it a speaker means something and presents what is meant as true.

1.3.3 Testimonial belief

Not every belief acquired through communication is testimonial. We learn from *how* people say what they do in addition to *what* people say. A child's nervousness when she blames her pet for the broken vase can inform her parents that she is responsible.[27] By contrast, testimonial beliefs are acquired by accepting what someone says; they are beliefs acquired by accepting someone's testimony. This could be formed into a provisional definition: *a belief that p is testimonial if and only if it is acquired by accepting testimony to p.*

This definition is merely provisional because it is false. It is possible to accept testimony to *p*, in doing so acquire the belief that *p* and yet this belief not be testimonial. This is possible because the testimony might be *merely the cause of the belief.* For instance, case 11, if an audience forms the belief that a vocalist has a baritone voice on the basis of recognizing this quality of the vocalist's voice when he tells the audience this, then the vocalist's testimony is the audience's reason for belief but the belief that the vocalist has a baritone voice is not testimonial.[28] Or consider case 12 where a teacher gives testimony to a geometrical theorem and at the same time provides a diagrammatic proof on the blackboard. At time t_1, when the student first accepts the teacher's testimony, he believes the theorem because of the teacher's testimony. A short while later at time t_2 after working through the proof, the student believes the theorem because he understands its proof. In this case, the student's belief, which is acquired by accepting the teacher's testimony, is testimonial at time t_1 but ceases to be testimonial at time t_2 once it is based on the proof.

In both these cases, a belief acquired through accepting testimony is not a testimonial belief. The reason for this is that describing a belief as testimonial says something about its warrant. An audience A's belief that *p* is not testimonial if A's warrant for believing that *p* is *entirely independent* of the fact that A acquired the belief that *p* by accepting testimony to *p*. This is true of the former case where the audience's warrant derives from perception of the vocalist's voice; and it is true of the latter case once the student grasps the accompanying proof. This suggests that the provisional definition of testimonial belief should be updated to read: *an audience A's belief that p is testimonial if and only if it is acquired by accepting testimony to p and its being acquired in this way determines, at least in part, A's warrant for belief.*

The 'at least in part' clause is needed because of cases like the following. Suppose that I know that *q* but am ignorant as to whether *r*, you know that *r* but are ignorant as to whether *q*, and you tell me that *q&r* in the mistaken

---

[27] See Goldberg (2001), p. 512.
[28] This modifies an example from Audi (1997), p. 420, n.14.

belief that you know q and r whilst I am ignorant of both. Is my belief that $q\&r$ testimonial? I suggest that it is because it is acquired by accepting testimony to $q\&r$ and its being acquired in this way determines its warrant at least in part.

1.3.4 Acceptance and belief

Testimonial beliefs are beliefs acquired through accepting testimony. However, the acceptance of a bit of testimony should not be equated with the acquisition of belief. This equation should not be made for two reasons. First, an audience might accept a bit of testimony because the audience already believes it. Case 13: If you tell me that Scarfell Pike, which is the highest mountain in England, is less than 1000 metres high, I will accept what you tell me. I will accept what you tell me because I happen to know Scarfell Pike is measured at 978 metres. Second, even if an audience does not already believe a bit of testimony, accepting this testimony might issue in a state of acceptance rather than a state of belief. Acceptance is very much like belief: to accept that p is to reason and act *as if* one believed that p. Acceptance is differentiated from belief in that one can accept something one believes to be false. And acceptance does not have the stability of belief: what is accepted either becomes belief, or is abandoned when the context of acting and reasoning ends.[29] One context of reasoning could be a discussion had with a speaker where one might accept what the speaker says merely to keep the conversation going, or not to cause offence.

The act of accepting a piece of testimony sometimes issues in a state of belief, sometimes issues in a state of acceptance, and sometimes issues in neither but is motivated by what is already believed or accepted. In considering testimony as a source of belief the principal interest is in beliefs acquired on the basis of accepting the content of a piece of testimony. When the act of accepting a bit of testimony to p is one of acquiring the belief that p, call this the *uptake* of testimony.

What cases 11 and 12 (the baritone voice and taught proof cases) then made clear is that an interest in testimonial beliefs is an interest in beliefs that derive their epistemic status from the uptake of testimony. And testimony may be a source of knowledge and warrant even if it is not a

---

[29] See Cohen (1992) and Bratman (1999), p. 30 n.20.

source of belief. This is illustrated by a case that is the mirror image of cases 11 and 12: that is a case where a belief has a non-testimonial cause but gets to be warranted by being subsequently based on testimony. For instance, consider case 14: there have long been big cat sightings in the British Isles, and rumours of a roaming panther periodically make it into the local press and occasionally the national press.[30] Imagine a boy, much taken by these rumours, who believes himself to see a panther in his garden. In fact he sees no more than the neighbours' black cat in the lengthening shadows, but that night a panther comes and sits on the patio whilst his father is watching. Over breakfast the next morning the father excitedly tells the son what he saw. The son would accept the father's testimony because he already believes what the father says. However, though his father's testimony would not produce belief, the son could get to be warranted in his belief that there was a panther in the garden *if* he continued in this belief *because* of what his father told him. So when the acceptance of testimony results in the acquisition of belief *or* when it comes to sustain a belief already held, let me talk about the *uptake* of testimony.

1.3.5 *Warrant for uptake and warrant for belief*

In considering testimony as a source of belief there are two questions that need to be considered. First, there is the *question of the warrant of uptake*: what warrants an audience A in the uptake of a speaker S's testimony to p? Second, there is the *question of the warrant of belief*: what warrants A's belief that p and explains A's knowing that p when A does get to be warranted in belief or to know that p on the basis of uptake of S's testimony?

The question of the warrant of belief is not in any way particular to the epistemology of testimony. In the same vein, were A to believe that p on the basis of the perceptual appearance that p one would ask what warrants A's perceptual belief that p and explains A's knowing on this basis of perceptual appearances? Similarly, what is being asked is what explains A's being warranted in believing that p or knowing that p on the basis of uptake of testimony to p?

The question of the warrant of uptake, however, is specific to the epistemology of testimony. It arises from the fact that paradigmatically testimony comes from another person and institutes the argument from

---

[30] See http://www.britishbigcats.org/ (accessed 16.08.10).

cooperation. This problem of practical rationality establishes that we must have reasons for accepting a piece of testimony. Where acceptance issues in no more than a state of acceptance, then all that is needed to rationalize it is a practical reason. However, where the acceptance of testimony is the uptake of testimony, an audience's reasons for acceptance must be epistemic.

Call an audience's reasons for testimonial uptake the audience's *proprietary justification*.[31] An audience's proprietary justification must be epistemic and it plays *at least* a dual role. First, the audience's proprietary justification justifies the uptake of testimony: it justifies the audience in acquiring the belief that p on the basis of accepting testimony to p. Second, the audience's proprietary justification justifies the belief that the audience forms on the basis of accepting a piece of testimony: it justifies the audience's testimonial belief that p. Suppose it is turns out that the speaker was wrong or lacked warrant for what she said, as in case 4 (where the speaker slandered the Professor). In this case, we can agree with Audi's judgement: the speaker's lack of warrant does not imply the audience lacks warrant since the audience has that warrant for belief that comes from his proprietary justification.

If an audience's proprietary justification is deemed to *only* play these two roles, then we have a familiar epistemological picture. The audience A is propositionally justified in believing that p since other things A believes about S's testimony to p give a sufficiently good reason for believing that p is true. And A is doxastically justified in believing that p since A believes that p on the basis of these good reasons. In this case, A's testimonial belief is warranted in virtue of the way it was acquired: on the basis of good reasons to uptake S's testimony to p. This is the epistemological picture advanced by reductive theories of testimony. All that matters epistemically is an audience's proprietary justification. This, I will argue, misses what is epistemically distinctive about testimonial knowledge and warrant: it is transmitted knowledge and warrant.

On the trust theory of testimony this monograph proposes an audience's proprietary justification does not only play this dual role of rationalizing uptake and justifying belief. Moreover, the role of justifying the audience's belief is *essentially subsidiary*. Supposing a speaker S gives

---

[31] I follow Burge (1993), p. 485.

testimony to p, an audience A needs to have a reason for uptake to be warranted in believing that p, but what warrants A's testimonial belief that p, and explains A knowing that p, is essentially not this reason but the fact that S knows that p or is warranted in this belief. Call the proprietary justification possessed by the speaker, and the prior sources if the speaker's belief is testimonial, the *extended body of warrant*.[32] Then on the trust account the question of the warrant of uptake is answered by the audience's proprietary justification. These reasons, if justificatory and not merely explanatory, also determine the audience's testimonial belief to be justified, but that is not their fundamental epistemological role. The fundamental epistemological role of an audience's proprietary justification is to rationalize uptake *and thereby make the extended body of warrant available*. This extended body of warrant then answers the question of the warrant of belief.

In this respect, the trust theory is in agreement with non-reductive theories of testimony: testimony operates to transmit knowledge and warrant. So it is the extended body of warrant that explains an audience (testimonially) knowing that p or being (testimonially) warranted in believing that p. The trust theory is then at odds with non-reductive theories over how to answer the question of the warrant of uptake. Non-reductive theory answers this question with the hypothesis that we have a general entitlement to accept testimony. This hypothesis gives no substantive epistemological role to an audience's proprietary justification. We need reasons merely to defeat defeaters of this entitlement. This fails to recognize how testimony institutes an argument from cooperation, which implies the need for a substantive justification of uptake.

1.3.6 Uptake principles and transmission principles

Uptake principles state when an audience is warranted in acquiring a belief on the basis of accepting a piece of testimony. Given a speaker S's testimony to p, an uptake principle states the conditions under which an audience A is warranted in believing that p on the basis of S's testimony to p. A reductive theory would propose that A is warranted if and only if other things A believes about S's testimony justify A believing that p.[33]

---

[32] Again I follow Burge (1993), p. 486. See also Faulkner (2000).

[33] In principle, a reductive theory could propose an externalist uptake principle: A is warranted iff A has a reliable ability to discriminate true testimony (across a certain range of

A non-reductive theory would propose some general entitlement to form belief on the basis of accepting testimony.

Transmission principles state the conditions under which testimony transmits knowledge and warrant. To borrow Lackey's illustration, transmission principles think of testimony like a bucket chain established for the purposes of extinguishing a fire, where 'each must have a bucket of water in order to pass it to the next person'.[34] For non-reductive theories testimony works like a bucket chain where what gets passed down is the extended body of warrant. The moot questions are then: what are the correct transmission principles? And by virtue of what do these principles hold? Or, how is it that knowledge and warrant get transmitted? These are not live questions for a reductive theory because reductive theories regard all transmission principles as false. It is an audience's proprietary justification—maybe in conjunction with some further non-epistemic facts to do with truth and reliability—that explains the audience knowing something, or being warranted in believing something, on the basis of testimony.

1.3.7 Trust

Trusting is both something we do and an attitude that we can have and take. The *act of trusting* is one of putting oneself in a position of depending on something happening or someone doing something. The *attitude of trusting* is then characterized as an attitude towards this dependence. I trust you to turn up on time, for instance, in waiting for you at a certain place and time, and by adopting a certain attitude towards your turning up on time. With respect to testimony, we trust speakers to tell the truth and we trust testimony to be true, and we show this attitude of trust by accepting what we are told or what is said. And when acceptance is motivated by an attitude of trust—when it is a case of trusting—it issues in belief. The act of trusting testimony is the uptake of testimony. There are, however, two

---

worlds). However, and for the reasons noted in 1.2, I presume reductive theories to be internalist. I discuss this further in 2.1.

[34] Lackey (1999), p. 471. The bucket chain analogy also illustrates why the term 'transmit' is poor: it implies that when S transmits X to A, S loses X; the bucket moves down the chain. Whereas when S transmits knowledge to A, S does not lose knowledge. A better verb would be 'infect', but I persist with normal use and its infelicities.

quite distinct senses of trust so that our trusting testimony can have two quite distinct motivations.

In some cases the attitude of trust can be merely a judgement of outcome made in a situation where one depends on the outcome. Thus Martin Hollis remarks, 'we trust one another to behave predictably in a sense that applies equally to the natural world at large'.[35] We can trust one clock to tell an accurate time and another to be roughly right. We can trust a thermometer to give a true reading and in this sense we can trust a piece of testimony to be true. Following Hollis I refer to trust in this sense as *predictive trust*.[36] Predictive trust is just a matter of depending on some outcome—something happening or someone's doing something—and expecting this outcome to occur. The expectation constitutive of predictive trust is an attitude of belief.

In other cases the expectation constitutive of an attitude of trust is normative. To illustrate this contrast consider the following two ways of filling in the details of my waiting for you. First, imagine you left home this morning without some important work documents. I know your route to work, so I know that I can intercept you and get these documents to you before you reach work. In waiting for you I trust you to turn up some time soon. Second, imagine we make a plan to go for a drink after you finish work, and arrange to meet at the same corner. Again, in waiting for you I trust you to turn up some time soon. In both scenarios I depend on your turning up; I depend at the very least in that if you don't turn up my journey, time, and effort are wasted. And in both scenarios I expect you to turn up. But whilst this expectation is a matter of prediction or belief in the first case, it is something different in the second. In this case, my expectation concerns your reasons for acting: I expect you to see the fact that I will be waiting for you as a reason to try to turn up on time. This is a normative expectation: I think that you should see things this way and so should act for this reason; and if you don't do as I expect, or don't act for this reason—for instance if you find something preferable to do and then merely pass by because this is your route home—then this failure will be liable to provoke my resentment. This thicker notion of trust, with its concern with the trusted party's motivations, I've called *affective* trust.[37]

---

[35] Hollis (1998), p. 10.
[36] See Faulkner (2007a).
[37] Again see Faulkner (2007a).

'Affective' because the defeat of its constitutive expectation engenders characteristic reactive attitudes—those provoked by trust being let down—which identify the expectation as normative and not merely predictive.

To illustrate how these distinct attitudes of trust engage with testimony consider the following example, case 15, from Coady.

Consider the case of Jones whom we know to have been hypnotised by a master criminal. The criminal has programmed the unsuspecting Jones to state the criminal's arch-rival is hiding out at a certain address and . . . [w]hen Jones blurts out the information, it is reasonable for us to take it as evidence for the arch-rival's hiding-place because we know of the hypnotism and the master criminal's interest in having the information made available to us.[38]

Coady uses this case to argue that Jones is not testifying since he does not have the relevant competence. Be that as it may, Jones's utterance is still testimony on my understanding. And Jones's audience can trust this *testimony to be true* for the reason Coady states. However, for this same reason Jones's audience would not trust Jones for the truth. The distinction here is an old one. 'To *have faith in*, or *trust to*, or *beleeve a man*, signifie the same thing; namely, an opinion of the veracity of the man', Hobbes observes, 'but to *believe what is said*, signifieth onely an opinion of the truth of the saying.'[39]

So there are two ways in which we can trust testimony. We can trust in the predictive sense, depending on a bit of testimony because we believe it to be true. And we can trust in the affective sense, depending on a bit of testimony because we expect certain things of its speaker. This distinction is important because neither reductive nor non-reductive theories properly recognize that trust has a normative dimension. This normative dimension, I will argue, is important to the epistemology of testimony. The route to this conclusion is a little winding but what the trust theory ultimately proposes is that testimony is the distinctive source of knowledge and warrant it is because we have a way of life founded on affectively trusting one another for the truth.

---

[38] Coady (1992), p. 45.
[39] Hobbes (1651), pt. 1, ch. 7, p. 132.

1.4 Book outline

Chapter 2 considers the reductive theory of testimony. It aims to present a plausible reductive theory. The reductive theory is often criticized for implying scepticism of testimony; it is contended that we do not have experience sufficient to establish generalizations about testimonial reliability which could explain our knowing everything we take ourselves to know on the basis of testimony. Chapter 2 defends the reductive theory in this regard. Chapter 3 then argues that the reductive theory is nevertheless fundamentally misconceived. The problem, I will argue, is twofold. First, it gives too limited an account of our reasons for acceptance, where this limitation is revealed by the inadequacies of the reductive response to the problem of cooperation. And, second, the reductive theory is wrong to deny that testimony can transmit knowledge and warrant. Chapter 4 turns to the non-reductive theory and considers various arguments for a general entitlement to accept testimony. Chapter 5 then rejects the best of these arguments in favour of the demand that uptake be rationally supported. Chapter 6 introduces the assurance theory of testimony. It then argues that this theory needs an account of how trust can rationalize testimonial uptake. Chapter 7 then outlines a solution to the problem of cooperation: it outlines how our trusting affectively is linked to ways of thinking about trust that make trust non-problematic. And it argues that our trusting in this way has played a role in setting up testimony as the source of knowledge and warrant that it is. Chapter 8 then briefly states the trust theory of testimony.

2

The Reductive Theory

According to the reductive theory, there is no general entitlement to accept testimony: the mere fact that one is the recipient of testimony to *p* does not warrant one believing that *p*. To believe that *p* merely because one receives testimony to *p* is to be *credulous*, and credulity is an epistemic failing: if the belief that *p* is acquired by the credulous uptake of testimony to *p*, then it is unwarranted by virtue of its being acquired in this way. This is to say nothing about our *psychological* propensity to be credulous or not—though David Hume, the father of the reductive theory, thought we do have this disposition stating, '[n]o weakness of human nature is more universal and conspicuous than what we commonly call CREDULITY, or a too easy faith in the testimony of others'.[1] Rather, it is to say that to be warranted in a testimonial belief one must *not* be credulous. That is, in the testimonial situation where a speaker *S* tells an audience *A* that *p*, *A* is warranted in believing that *p* if and only if other things that *A* believes give sufficiently good reason to believe that *p*. It is thus A's proprietary justification that warrants the uptake of S's testimony to *p*.

It is equally this same set of reasons that warrants *A*'s testimonial belief that *p*, according to the reductive theory. This could be broken down into two claims. Audience *A* is propositionally warranted since other things *A* believes about S's testimony give a sufficiently good reason to believe that *p* is true; and *A* is doxastically warranted since *A* believes that *p* on the basis of these good reasons. Testimony, as such, is *not* an epistemically distinctive source of knowledge and warrant; confronted by S's testimony to *p*, *A* does not have a unique kind of warrant for believing that *p*. Testimony does not transmit knowledge and warrant, it is merely a source of belief, and whether a belief formed through the uptake of testimony is warranted

---

[1] Hume (1740), §1.3.9, pp. 112–13.

or not comes down to what else the subject believes that could be cited in an argument for it.

We thereby acquire knowledge from testimony, according to the reductive theory, in just the same way we acquire knowledge from the world more generally; 'testimonial knowledge' is no more than inductive knowledge: it is merely a species of inductive knowledge. To quote a familiar passage from Hume:

> [Our trust in testimony derives from] no other principle than our observation of the veracity of human testimony, and of the usual conformity of facts to the reports of witnesses. It being a general maxim, that no objects have any discoverable connexion together, and that all the inferences, which we can draw from one to another, are founded merely on our experience of their constant and regular conjunction; it is evident, that we ought not to make an exception to this maxim in favour of human testimony, whose connexion with any event seems, in itself, as little necessary as any other.[2]

Consequently, the reductive theory of testimony denies that there is any epistemically significant distinction between *testimonial knowledge* and *knowledge acquired from testimony*. Suppose that an audience has established one speaker to be reliably correct and another to be reliably incorrect when it comes to making predictions about tomorrow's weather. In this case, there would be no significant epistemic difference between believing that the weather tomorrow will be fine on the basis of the first's testimony that it will be so and believing this on the basis of the second's testimony that it will not be so. Indeed, there is no significant *epistemic difference* between reaching the belief that tomorrow's weather will be fine in either of these ways and reaching this belief on the basis of observing a red sky at night (supposing this to be a sign of fine weather).

Moreover, since an audience's epistemic standing with respect to a testimonial belief is determined solely by the audience's proprietary justification, together with the background non-epistemic facts, the reductive theory in effect asserts the *epistemic autonomy* of audiences. For example, suppose an audience has equally good reasons to accept the testimony of two speakers in their statements of the whereabouts of the American President. But suppose that the correctness of the first is due to his being part of the special services responsible for the President's welfare, while the

---

[2] Hume (1777), §88, p. 111.

correctness of the second is due to his possessing a mysterious clairvoyant power. On the assumption that even reliable clairvoyance is not a way of acquiring knowledge, only the first of these two speakers knows what he testifies to in giving testimony to the whereabouts of the President. However, according to a reductive theory, there is no epistemic difference in the testimonial beliefs an audience acquires by uptake of either bit of testimony. This is because what warrants these testimonial beliefs is the audience's proprietary justification and by hypothesis there is no difference between these cases in this respect. (One might suppose the speakers to be comparably reliable and the audience to have made comparable observations of the reliability of each speaker.) Thus, though we might depend on testimony for believing what we do, we are autonomous in the warrant we have for our testimonial beliefs.

In testimony, as in much else, warrant comes by way of the subject's other beliefs. Again this is not a psychological claim; in particular it is not the claim that the uptake of testimony involves reasoning. This is important because the uptake of testimony is often psychologically immediate. As Michael Dummett observes, 'If someone tells me the way to the railway station, or asks me whether I've heard that the Foreign Secretary has just resigned, or informs me that the museum is closed today, I go through no process of reasoning, however swift, to arrive at the conclusion that he has spoken aright: my understanding of his utterance and my acceptance of his assertion are one.'[3] However, the reductive account of testimonial warrant is an epistemic, not a psychological, proposal. To be warranted in the testimonial belief that the museum is closed today other things that Dummett believes must give him sufficiently good reason to believe this bit of testimony, and his uptake of it must be based on these reasons. This is not to imply that he goes through any 'process of reasoning' in coming to this belief. It does not imply this because it is possible for the beliefs that supply his reasons to be in the cognitive background; such beliefs are available to reflection but need not be psychologically occurrent when accepting this bit of testimony. It is possible, thereby, for acceptance to be psychologically immediate and epistemically mediated.[4]

---

[3] Dummett (1993), p. 419.

[4] Adler (1994), p. 272, gives the following analogy: if Grice's analysis is accepted, then our understanding of implicature is reasoned but it may, nonetheless, be immediate.

For a reductive theory (of the internalist type described) to be viable, two things must hold. First, our possession of testimonial warrant requires it to be the case that *other things we believe do give us sufficiently good reason* for the uptake of testimony. That is, and in short, it must be true that *we do possess reasons for believing things on the basis of testimony*. And, second, our possession of testimonial knowledge requires it to be the case that the beliefs, which give us our reasons, are not false. Knowledge cannot be based on a false premise; or, indeed, on an unwarranted premise. So it must be true, at least, that *our reasons for accepting testimony are justificatory and not merely explanatory*. This must be true if these reasons are to play their reductive epistemic role and be suitable for explaining our acquisition of knowledge from testimony. In the next two sections, I examine challenges to these two foundations of the reductive theory.

The main challenge will be to the first claim; it will be to idea that we possess reasons for accepting testimony. 'Most men', Thomas Reid claimed, 'would be unable to find reasons for believing the thousandth part of what is told them.'[5] And this sentiment has been echoed down the years. This problem can be successfully addressed, I will argue, either by a proper appreciation of the extent of our reasons, or by making the reductive theory partly externalist.

2.1 The observational problem

Confronted by testimony to *p*, an audience *A* is warranted in believing that *p* if and only if *A* believes that *p* is true given this testimony to *p*. And the best reason *A* could have for believing this would be the observation of the truth of past testimony. Our warrant for believing testimony ultimately comes from our observation of the truth of testimony. (This is Hume's point when he says that our judgement that a bit of testimony is true must be 'founded merely on our experience of their constant and regular conjunction', i.e. the constant conjunction of testimony and truth.) And this requires that we have observed the truth of testimony and done so enough times to warrant our body of testimonial belief. The observational problem is then the claim that our experience is too limited for this.

---

[5] Reid (1764), p. 197.

The claim that we have a paucity of observational evidence could be illustrated by reference to the following statements: 'blood circulates in many fine vessels around the body', 'box jellyfish are rare in the Atlantic', 'the venom of the North European adder is rarely fatal', 'the Nuer have fifty-four distinct adjectives for cattle', and 'the distance to the Sun is calculated by bouncing radar waves off Venus and is calculated to be 149,597,870.69 kilometres'. The reductive theory requires that we be able to personally verify testimony, but consider how one might go about this for such bits of testimony, which, after all, are the kinds of thing one might easily encounter any Sunday reading the newspapers. How would one obtain the cadaver needed to observe a body's 'fine vessels'? Without consulting a dictionary, how could one verify that the Nuer have fifty-four distinct adjectives short of tracking them down in the Sudan? If one managed to administer an adder's bite, could one be sure that this was the cause of death in those rare cases when death followed? Equally, could one be sure that personally unknown tides and currents do not influence any attempt to count box jellyfish? And how would one even identify box jellyfish? Moreover, these kinds of problem are probably insurmountable in the last case since the claim about the distance to the Sun is based on radar data whose verification would require a level of expert knowledge that few possess.

These cases illustrate that the verification of pieces of testimony can be all but impossible. The observational problem can then be presented as the claim that the difficulties one would encounter in such cases are not, in any way, extraordinary. Rather, these difficulties are representative of those one should expect to encounter if one set out to verify testimony. It is cases where we can observe the truth of testimony that are exceptional. On this basis the observational problem challenges that we are simply unable to make enough observations to ground the body of generalizations needed to warrant our acceptance of testimony.

This problem is forcefully expressed by C. A. J. Coady when he claims that the reductive theory of testimony is '"plainly false" because it seems absurd to suggest that, individually, we have done anything like the amount of fieldwork that [the reductive theory] requires'.[6] The problem is that if it is a requirement that we find reasons for believing what is told to

---

[6] Coady (1992), p. 82.

us in order to be warranted in testimonial uptake, we must have observed the truth of testimony many times. And we have just not done enough 'fieldwork' for this. So the reductive theory is 'plainly false' because it implies, as Reid observed, that we are only warranted in believing a 'thousandth part' of what we are told.

The specific shape of a reductive theory of testimony is largely given by how it responds to this problem. To respond, what needs to be argued is that limitations in what can be observed do not imply limitations in the warrant we have for accepting testimony. Specific reductive theories are then given by how this is argued. There are three ways of arguing this, and so three permutations of the reductive theory, which I want to identify. The first two responses claim that induction is more sophisticated than this objection allows. The third claims that an externalist element can be added to take up the epistemic slack.

2.1.1 Refining our observational evidence

Since the observational problem challenges that we have a poverty of reasons, a response is given by a description of our reasons which shows how extensive these reasons are. There are, I suggest, two ways in which we can bring our experience to bear in judging that a piece of testimony is evidence for its truth. First, we can reason straightforwardly from past track record. Second, we can reason by inference to the best explanation. And both modes of reasoning can be more subtle than the observational problem would allow.

First, our experience of testimony has allowed us to form generalizations about the reliability of testimonial types. We identify certain sources as particularly credible, certain topics as particularly safe, and others as not so. Thus, and for instance, we think the *New York Times* is more credible than the *National Enquirer* in its factual reporting but recognize that there might be little difference between their medium-range weather forecasts. We might take a mechanic to know a great deal about car maintenance but not be disposed to accept what the mechanic says generally. Conversely we might think that in general a friend knows a great deal but is clearly ignorant of car maintenance. Such distinctions then enable us to have some expectation of the probable truth of any given testimony. With some degree of idealization, these generalizations could be represented as statements of the observed relative frequency of truth for each type. Confronted with a particular testimony, we can then directly infer its probable truth from the generalization established by experience as to the probable truth of its type. Our inductive reasoning is straight statistical generalization.

In forming generalizations about the reliability of testimonial types, a distinction could be drawn between *stringent* and *liberal* reductive theories. Stringent theories require assessments of the reliability of testimonial types to proceed exclusively from an audience's own observations. Liberal theories allow that an audience's generalizations might themselves be informed by testimony, provided any regress of reasons entailed by the uptake of this testimony terminates in correlations that the audience has observed.[7] If reductive theories must be stringent then the observational problem looks to be insurmountable, but if reductive theories can be liberal, then this problem looks much less pressing. For example, suppose, case 16, an audience A's observations justify the uptake of the testimony of a specific individual, a knowledgeable uncle say. This uncle tells A that such-and-such Sunday paper has a highly reliable scientific column and in this column A reads that radar data have established the Sun to be 149,597,870.69 kilometres distant. Audience A could then justifiably come to believe this to be the case (on the basis of believing this column to be reliable on the basis of what his uncle tells him) without having to make any troubling observations.

The moot question is then whether liberal reductive theories are a genuine epistemic possibility. Can we be warranted in accepting testimony to another testimonial type's reliability? On the face of it, there is no reason to think not; after all, claims about the reliability of testimonial types are just claims about factual matters, and need not be particularly improbable. However, the following is an argument to the conclusion that there is indeed a problem here; it is an argument to the conclusion that liberal reductive theories collapse into stringent ones.[8]

---

[7] Compare Stevenson (1993), p. 437.

[8] Another argument for this claim is owed to Coady, who claims that reductionism must be stringent otherwise it is 'question-begging'. Coady's argument for this claim is that liberal reductionism allows that 'the experience upon which our reliance upon testimony as a form of evidence is supposed to rest is itself reliant upon testimony which cannot be reduced in the same way'. Coady (1992), p. 81. The only way I can understand this is as the claim that if we justify testimony1 by reference to our experience of testimony2, then we can neither justify testimony2 by reference to our experience of testimony3 nor by reference to experience. However, both these consequences are *non sequiturs*.

Consider, then, what an audience must do to establish the reliability of testimonial type T. According to stringent reductive theories, an audience must have (1) observed this testimonial type to be reliably true. According to liberal theories an audience must have either satisfied this same requirement, or (2) received testimony to the fact that this testimonial type is reliably true. What (1) requires is that the audience observe the truth of instances of type T. The observational problem is then the claim that we all too frequently are not able to make these observations: we are too constrained by time, space, and our own ignorance. However, according to liberal theories, if an audience cannot observe the truth of instances of type T, there is always possibility (2): that the audience have received testimony to the fact that type T is reliably true. The problem is that the uptake of this testimony must be warranted if its receipt is to be of any help. What this requires is that the audience observe the truth of instances of some different testimonial type, call it S: testimony as to the reliability of testimonial type T. In order to observe the truth of instances of type S, the audience must thereby already know the reliability of type T. So if the audience is unable to observe the truth of instances of type T, and so unable to determine the reliability of type T, appeal to further testimony does not help. Therefore possibility (2) offers no further grounds for belief and liberal reductionism collapses into stringent reductionism.[9]

Reductive theories, I think, can be defended against this criticism—being liberal is a genuine theoretical possibility—but this defence reveals a crux presumption of reductive theories. Suppose then, to illustrate the criticism just outlined, that type T testimony is the testimony of such-and-such column in such-and-such Sunday paper on scientific matters. Though audience A has not made the observations needed to establish the reliability of this type, what A does have is the testimony of his uncle that this type is indeed reliable. Now whilst A will not have established his uncle to be reliable about this particular subject—he will not have established the reliability of his uncle's testimony as type S—he will have established his reliability for some other domain. This allows A to make an inference from the fact that his uncle was reliable with respect to this other domain to the fact that he is reliable in his judgement of this column.

---

[9] This argument is based on Schmitt's argument that a key problem for reductionism is that only experts can establish the credibility of expert testimony. See Schmitt (1987).

Thus what liberal reductionism requires is for this kind of move to be possible. It requires that it *be possible to infer the reliability of testimony construed as one type from its reliability construed as another type*. Let type U be testimony on some matter, the weather maybe, and suppose that *A* has established his uncle to be reliable with respect to type U. Then what needs to be possible is an inference from the reliability of type U testimony to the reliability of type S testimony. This inference presumes that the observations that *A* has gathered are not merely representative of the reliability of the uncle's type U testimony but are representative of *his reliability more generally*. What is thereby presumed is that, for some broad but delimited range of testimonial types of which type S is one and type U is another, the uncle *is uniform* in his reliability.[10]

This presumption of uniformity is at the heart of reductive theories of testimony because it enables a direct and simple response to the observational problem. This response is: *testimony is such that we can fortunately work with whatever observations we have*. Our observations may be limited, but this limitation is not epistemically debilitating because we can just presume that the observations we have made are fit for purpose.

This is to consider our reasons for judging a testimonial type to be true. However, we can possess empirical reasons for judging that a bit of testimony is true even if its type is quite unreliable. This is because we can infer the truth of a piece of testimony from the fact that it was uttered, as opposed to inferring it from its track record. The inductive reasoning here is inference to the best explanation rather than statistical generalization. This is the reductive theory put forward by Peter Lipton.

Your decision on whether or not to accept a piece of testimony depends on how well it would fit together with the other beliefs you hold, and the notion of fit can be articulated in explanatory terms. Roughly speaking, the question is whether the candidate belief would, in the context of those other beliefs, provide the best explanation of, among other things, the informant's utterance.[11]

An audience is thereby warranted in accepting a piece of testimony if the audience's best explanation of the piece of testimony is either its truth or

---

[10] Precisely, what is presumed is that that there is no intermediary type between S and U which differs in its reliability from U. See Pollock (1990), p. 131, who labels this *non-classical direct inference*.

[11] Lipton (1998), p. 27. This is also the position of Malmgren (2006) and Adler (2002).

implies its truth.[12] This allows a response to the observational problem because it is possible to reason in this way and judge that truth is the best explanation of a piece of testimony with no prior experience of this, or any like, testimonial type. Moreover, given only a single observation of the truth of a bit of testimony, the general reliability of its type could be established as a best explanation.

When engaged in this kind of explanatory reasoning it is premises about the motivations at work in the testimonial situations, I suggest, which are key. For example, the testimony of doctors on medical matters is frequently taken to be true. However, this is a testimonial type whose reliability would be hard for a non-medically trained person to establish (at least without recourse to the kinds of indirect inference illustrated in case 16). But this need not imply an audience lacks grounds for being warranted in accepting the testimony of doctors because the judgement that such a bit of medical testimony is true can be inferred, first, from the existence of institutional controls on doctors. These controls supply a motivation to get things right since a failure to do so, if uncovered and deemed negligence, can be sanction—where the ultimate professional sanction is being struck off the General Medical Council.[13] And it can be inferred, second, from the fact that doctors adopt a duty to care, where the adoption of this duty is likewise associated with the motivation to get things right. Both these explanatory inferences then proceed from premises about the motivations at work in the testimonial situation.

There are, Bernard Williams suggests, four general motivations people can have to cooperate.[14] In the context of the Testimony Game this is four general motivations to tell the truth. Fear of sanctions is one; the others are: particular self-interest, a positive evaluation of cooperation, and a positive evaluation of friendly relations. Sanctions can be informal or formal. Informal sanctions consist in some form of social exclusion, such as loss of reputation or simple ostracism, and the further losses this causes. Formal sanctions can be anything from a fine to a prison sentence; or in the case of professionals, such as medical doctors, the loss of a legal right to practise. We are sensitive to all these motivating reasons for cooperation or

---

[12] By 'best' Lipton means 'loveliest' or that explanation which would provide the most understanding, if it were true. See Lipton (1991).

[13] See Blais (1987).

[14] Williams (1988), p. 118.

truth-telling. And their recognition can be our basis for judging that a particular bit of testimony is true, irrespective of what we think of its type. And it can equally be our basis for judging a testimonial type to be reliable, irrespective of what observations of truth we have made, since where this judgement of type-reliability has this basis the grounding observations will not be the truth of instances of testimony so much as beliefs about human motivations and the structures that determine them. This background of belief both finds and presumes 'a great uniformity among the actions of all men'.[15]

In this respect, there is a particular source of motivation that is one worth remarking on since it will figure prominently later. There is, I will argue, something like a norm of truth of telling. This social norm can be identified by the reactive attitudes that accompany its breach. Speakers who lie will frequently feel guilty about doing so, and seek to avoid lying. Audiences who are lied to will ordinarily demonstrate some resentment if they discover this fact—they will feel wronged. And the third parties who witness the lie will tend to exhibit punitive attitudes of disapproval. This set of reactive attitudes can then act as a sanction which sustains the norm. Thus Pettit observes,

> The trustee is likely to have a desire, intrinsic or instrumental, for the good opinion of the trustor and of witnesses to the act of trust. The desire for that good opinion will tend to give the trustee reason to act in the way in which the trustor relies on him to act.[16]

And for the 'Testimony Game' this can be read: 'the speaker is likely to have a desire for the good opinion of the audience and others . . .'. As such the belief that there is a norm roughly of truth-telling is a consideration that could be cited in an argument for the truth of a bit of testimony. It is a belief about our society and speakers' motivations that can thereby give an audience a good reason to believe that a bit of testimony is true, and so warrant its uptake.

This defence of reductive theory is close to that offered by Jack Lyons.[17] In parallel he claims that the observational problem shows the reductive theory does not have the resources to warrant our testimonial beliefs only if 'it shows that induction is insufficient for justifying any beliefs'.[18] And

---

[15] Hume (1777), p. 65.   [16] Pettit (1995), p. 216.
[17] Lyons (1997).   [18] Lyons (1997), p. 168.

he claims that the observational problem fails to recognize how broad our inductive base is, noting in particular that 'we can also acquire inductive evidence for the reliability of testimony by inferring it from (non-testimonially) justified folk psychological beliefs', where the most relevant folk psychological belief is 'that people generally try to tell the truth'.[19]

2.1.2 *The global reduction of testimonial warrant*

The observational problem challenges that we have not made, and cannot make, enough observations of the truth of testimony to justify our testimonial beliefs one by one. But suppose that we have made enough observations of the truth of testimony to justifiably believe that testimony is generally reliable. If we can justify this belief then, unless we have reasons not to make the inference, we can infer that any given piece of testimony is true. The reasoning here is the same: it is a direct inference from a statistical generalization. But rather than concern a narrow testimonial type, the generalization concerns all of testimony. Or the reasoning is an inference to the best explanation with the background belief about general reliability justifying holding the truth-based explanation as the 'default position'.[20]

We have sufficient evidence to justifiably believe that testimony is generally reliable, Tomoji Shogenji argues, because our evidence is not limited to observation of the truth of particular bits of testimony. In addition to these directly confirming observations, we also make indirectly confirming observations of the truth of testimony; for example, 'the report of a heavy rain . . . makes it more likely that travelers arrive late, no baseball game is played etc.' so our observation that the baseball game is cancelled provides indirect confirmation of this report.[21] Much indirect confirmation will also come by way of further testimony, and if we treat the claim about the general reliability of testimony as a hypothesis, these confirming reports add to our sum of evidence.[22] In a similar vein Jonathan Adler argues that we can empirically justify taking the truth-based explanation of utterance to be the default. We know that the acceptance of testimony is an empirically successful practice. We know that there constraints on speakers to speak truthfully. We know, I will argue, that there is

---

[19] Lyons (1997), p. 171.   [20] See Adler (2002), pp. 144–57.
[21] Shogenji (2006), p. 341.   [22] Shogenji puts this all in formal probabilistic terms.

something like a norm of truth-telling. And this background knowledge justifies us believing that testimony is generally reliable.

This is not to argue that we have a general entitlement to accept testimony. Although just as the hypothesis that we have a reliable testimonial faculty can be a premise in argument for our possession of such an entitlement, so too can this claim about general reliability. Rather it is, Adler claims, to show that we can empirically support our 'positive bias' in favour of testimony, and to show that this bias is compatible with our possession of empirical evidence in favour of our testimonial beliefs.[23] However, according to the reductive theory, this positive bias is either a justified response to testimony, because empirically supported, or it is a mere psychological tendency. It is not a bias we have some general entitlement to. And what matters, for the reductive theory, is an audience's own proprietary justification, which gives the audience's reasons for this bias towards testimony, and provides what warrant the audience enjoys for belief formed on testimony.[24]

2.1.3 An externalist reductive theory

A different strategy for responding to the observational problem is to adopt an externalist, or partly externalist, account of testimonial knowledge and warrant. This strategy is adopted by Elizabeth Fricker when she proposes that we have the capacity to *monitor* speakers for trustworthiness. This capacity takes as input an audience's perception of the testimonial situation and yields as output the disposition to believe a piece of testimony to be true or false. Monitoring is

typically conducted at a non-conscious level . . . the specific cues in a speaker's behaviour which constitute the informational basis for this judgement will often be registered and processed at an irretrievably sub-personal level.[25]

Insofar as the features of the testimonial encounter that an audience responds to are 'processed at an irretrievably sub-personal level', what

---

[23] See Adler (2002), p. 142.

[24] Adler calls his view a *reconciliationist* position. He observes that 'On the view I am defending, our normal situation is both Humean and Reidian. We both have enormous grounding for accepting a piece of testimony and do not first investigate its credulity.' Adler (2002), p. 157. I think that this latter claim is correct, but it leaves it open what explains our possession of testimonial knowledge. Is it the audience's own proprietary justification? Or the extended body of warrant? I am not sure what answer Adler gives to this question.

[25] Fricker (1994), p. 150.

could be 'fished into consciousness' might be little more articulate than 'I didn't like the look of him' or 'Well, she seemed perfectly normal'.[26] However, to say that an audience monitors a speaker for trustworthiness is just to say,

It is true throughout of the hearer that if there were signs of untrustworthiness, she would register them, and respond to them.[27]

And since the trustworthiness of a speaker entails the truth of what she says on Fricker's account, what Fricker is proposing, in other words, is that we have a *reliable testimonial faculty*.[28]

The hypothesis that we have a reliable testimonial faculty offers a simple solution to the observational problem. Even if our reasons for believing what we are told are limited—and are often little more than 'I liked the look of her'—this need not matter epistemically if our uptake of testimony is reliable. For then it can be proposed that our warrant for our testimonial beliefs is determined by the fact that our uptake is reliable, rather than by the goodness of the reasons we have for belief.

There are a couple of minor problems with this position as it is presented by Fricker. First, as she defines it an audience who monitors registers *any* sign of untrustworthiness and since a speaker's being trustworthy *entails* that her testimony is true, an audience who monitors will not form any false testimonial beliefs. But, of course, we do not have such an acute sensitivity. After all, the trustworthy can exhibit signs of untrustworthiness: speakers can be nervous and possess epistemically misleading manners. The trustworthy might seem to exhibit signs of untrustworthiness: audiences can be paranoid and deluded. The untrustworthy can exhibit signs of trustworthiness: speakers can be beguiling and persuasive. And the untrustworthy can seem to exhibit signs of trustworthiness: audiences can be gullible and naïve. However, whilst a faculty that never errs is entirely implausible, one that is merely reliable is not so, and monitoring can be understood in this way.

---

[26] Fricker (1994), p. 151.

[27] Fricker (1994), p. 150.

[28] 'A speaker S is trustworthy with respect to an assertoric utterance by her U, which is made on an occasion O, and by which she asserts that P if and only if (i) U is sincere, and (ii) S is competent with respect to "P" on O, where this notion is defined as follows: If S were sincerely to assert that P on O, then it would be the case that P.' Fricker (1994), p. 147.

The second problem is that it is not clear that this plausible hypothesis is true. Certainly, there will be evidence that indicates a lie. Lying requires extra mental effort, which will leave clues such as vagueness and hesitation.[29] In fabricating an event one cannot move around it with the ease of memory.[30] And lying tends to be associated with emotions that are revealed in the presence or absence of various signs and micro-expressions; for instance, the Duchenne marker—crow's feet around the eyes produced by genuine smiles—is impossible for most to fake.[31] However, despite all this evidence, there is no general and reliable sign of a lie; there is no 'Pinocchio Response'.[32] So we could never possess anything more than a reliable testimonial faculty, but there is much empirical evidence that do not even possess this. For despite the available evidence, we tend to be extremely poor at distinguishing liars from truth-tellers.[33]

However, for the sake of argument, suppose that the hypothesized testimonial faculty only operates at a 'sub-personal level'. In this case, our demonstrable inability to accurately say who is lying and who is not need not imply that at some sub-personal level we do make just this discrimination and do so successfully. Maybe the faculty goes wrong when we put it to the test rather than merely rely on it.

A more philosophical worry is the coherence of this theoretical position. Suppose that the argument from cooperation is taken to be persuasive—as I think it should be. Then what is instituted is the requirement that an audience have reasons for accepting a piece of testimony. On the present proposal, 'I didn't like the look of him', 'she seemed perfectly normal' and other such statements of intuition articulate our reasons for acceptance. Such statements might perfectly explain why an audience accepts a piece of testimony, but where acceptance is uptake what is required is an epistemic reason or a reason for belief. This is something that could be cited in an argument for the truth of what is accepted. And these statements of intuition are not epistemic reasons in this sense. Or at least they are not so unless the argument also has the premise that these statements of intuition manifest the operation of a reliable testimonial

[29] DePaulo et al. (2003), cited by Frank (2009), p. 60.
[30] Porter and Yuille (1995) and Undeutsch (1989), cited by Frank (2009), p. 61.
[31] Ekman (1985).
[32] Frank (2009), p. 70.
[33] Bond and DePaulo (2006), cited by O'Sullivan (2009), p. 74. And see Ekman (2009) which questions the significance of this review whilst agreeing with its conclusion.

faculty. But it is not part of the theory that we believe we possess this faculty, only that we in fact do so. And if it were part of the theory that we have this belief, then the problem posed by the empirical evidence just cited would become more significant.

The obvious solution is to regard the hypothesis that we possess a reliable testimonial faculty as undermining this requirement that an audience possess a reason for accepting a piece of testimony. Hence, the worry about theoretical coherence is that the hypothesis that we have a reliable testimonial faculty seems to motivate, and better fit with, a non-reductive theory of testimony, according to which we are warranted in the uptake of testimony *without* supporting reasons (other things being equal). We have this warrant just because we possess a reliable ability to filter out false testimony. A non-reductive theory of this form is advocated by Sandford Goldberg; and it is something I will consider in 4.1.

However, any theory of testimony must address two key epistemological questions: what warrants an audience's uptake of a bit of testimony? And what warrants an audience's testimonial belief? And, irrespective of whether the hypothesis that we have a reliable testimonial faculty fits best with a reductive or non-reductive answer to the question of the warrant of uptake, this hypothesis clearly lends itself to a reductive answer to the question of the warrant of belief. It is this answer that resolves the observational problem: what explains an audience's possession of testimonial knowledge and warranted testimonial belief is the fact that the audience's uptake of testimony is reliable. The big problem with any reductive answer to this question, I will then argue in the next chapter, is a failure to recognize how testimony makes us epistemically dependent on a speaker for knowledge and warrant. And in this respect Jennifer Lackey's incorporation of reliability considerations is a distinct improvement. The reliability that matters, she suggests, is not that of an audience's uptake of testimony so much as the reliability of the speaker's testimony.

Testimonial knowledge and warrant, Lackey proposes, are collaborative products. She labels this view *dualism* and it resolves the observation problem as follows. The reductive theory, as it has been presented so far, has an audience's proprietary justification determine the audience's possession of testimonial knowledge and warranted testimonial belief. Of course, for knowledge the bit of testimony accepted has to be true, and there must be no Gettier-type accidents, but provided these conditions are satisfied, it is an audience's own proprietary justification that determines that the audience possesses knowledge. And since this proprietary justification, so the criticism runs, needs to be grounded on an audience's observations of the truth of testimony, a limitation in this observational base implies a limit in what can be known on the basis of testimony. However, on Lackey's dualist theory, an audience's own proprietary justification gives only part of the warrant an audience has for a testimonial belief. The other part comes from the reliability of the bit of testimony whose uptake resulted in this belief. Moreover, it is the reliability of bits of testimony that accounts for the truth connection needed for warrant, so that all an audience's own proprietary justification need do is 'render it, at the very least, *not irrational for [the audience] to accept the testimony in question*'.[34] 'This', she rightly notes, 'is a substantially weaker condition than that required by reductionists.'[35] And to play this role it is not necessary that an audience's own proprietary justification be grounded on observations of the truth of testimony.

This is a satisfying resolution to the observational problem, but is it a reductive solution? Lackey argues that dualism is not a reductive theory. It endorses the reductive demand that the uptake of testimony be reasonable in the light of an audience's other attitudes; and so it denies the non-reductive claim that we have a general entitlement to accept testimony. The uptake of testimony 'in the complete absence of positive reasons can be just as epistemically irrational' as belief in the face of counter-evidence.[36] But it denies the reductive thesis under its internalist interpretation: testimonial warrant is not given solely by an audience's own proprietary justification. Rather, the dualist account of testimonial warrant takes the internalist reductive demand for reasons and supplements it with a reliability requirement: testimonial warrant is the product of an audience satisfying an 'audience condition' and having reasons for belief, and the speaker satisfying a 'speaker condition' that the speaker's statement, or act of communication, be reliable. In this sense, testimonial knowledge is a collaborative product. And since reliability 'is not something that can be reduced', 'there *is* justification, and hence knowledge, that is distinctly testimonial in nature'.[37]

Thus dualism purports to endorse the characteristic non-reductive claim that testimony is an epistemically distinctive source of knowledge and

---

[34] Lackey (2008), p. 181.   [35] Lackey (2008), p. 181.
[36] Lackey (2008), p. 170.   [37] Lackey (2008), p. 193.

warrant. It is so because testimonial warrant is irreducibly dependent on testimony being reliable. Now this pair—the non-reductive claim that testimony is an epistemically distinctive source and the reductive claim that an audience's uptake of testimony must be reasonable in the light of the audience's other attitudes—together defines the 'dualist' position that is the *trust* theory this monograph argues for.[38] Lackey acknowledges this structural similarity, observing 'While Faulkner endorses a view that is in some ways similar to the dualist view . . . he espouses [transmission], which I rejected.'[39] Here Lackey is correct: on my view what makes testimony epistemically distinctive as a source is not merely that it is reliable but that it transmits knowledge and warrant. Now Lackey's rejection of the idea that testimony transmits knowledge and warrant is something I will consider in 3.6. However, what I would like to argue here is that Lackey's view is straightforwardly reductive.

Lackey gives the following argument against the (internalist) reductive theory. It is an argument by counter-example. The case is 'nested speaker'.[40] Helen tells Fred that Pauline is reliable on birds, and Fred knows Helen can be trusted. So Fred believes what Pauline tells him about the albatross. But Pauline does not know what she is talking about, and is quite unreliable when it comes to birds. Letting 'p' refer to Pauline's statement, what this case shows is that one can fail to have knowledge despite having inductive reasons which are good on any internalist account of warrant. This is not, Lackey argues, because this is a Gettier case but because 'the possession of positive reasons . . . *does not necessarily put one in contact with testimony that is reliable*'.[41] So Lackey proposes a 'speaker condition' that specifies reliability. And since reliability is 'not something that can be reduced' but is a necessary condition on warrant, 'there is justification, and hence knowledge, that is distinctly testimonial in nature'.[42]

This argument against the reductive theory is rather uncharitable. It is true that reliability cannot 'be reduced to perceptual, memorial and inferential justification': facts about objective probability are true independently of what we think; and the Humean problem of induction

---

[38] I first introduced this combination as the hybrid view here: Faulkner (2000).
[39] Lackey (2008), p. 142, n.1.
[40] Lackey (2008), p. 149.
[41] Lackey (2008), p. 150.
[42] Lackey (2008), p. 193. (It should be clear Lackey is using 'justification' here in the general sense I am using 'warrant'.)

establishes that our reasons for thinking that these facts lie one way rather than another can never guarantee them to be that way. However, whilst I argued that a reductive account of testimonial uptake is best conceived in internalist terms, it is not essential to the *reductive thesis* that it be given an internalist interpretation. What is essential to the reductive thesis, what this thesis actually proposes, is simply the reduction of testimonial knowledge to inductive knowledge, and the consequent denial that testimonial knowledge constitutes a distinctive epistemological type.

What the observational problem could then be taken as establishing is that the reductive theory cannot work with a solely internalist notion of warrant. In this case, 'nested speaker' would simply show that a sophisticated reductive account must distinguish a strong or justificatory, and a weak or explanatory sense of warrant. Fred has reasons: his acceptance of what Pauline tells him is *reasonable*. But Fred's reasons are not objectively good: his reasons do not put him into 'contact with testimony that is reliable'. On this sophisticated reductive account, a complete account of testimonial warrant is specified by two conditions. Acceptance of testimony must be 'rationally acceptable', which is just Lackey's 'audience condition', and these reasons must connect up with reliable testimony, which is just Lackey's 'speaker condition'.[43] These conditions then specify how it is that we can gain inductive knowledge from testimony: we can reasonably and truly believe that testimony is a reliable sign. The knowledge thus acquired is, in a sense, a collaborative product. But if the *only thing* that a speaker contributes is being a vehicle for reliable testimony, the speaker's contribution is nominal; it is comparable to that made by a thermometer in telling the temperature.

2.2 The type identity problem

We rely on testimony because our experience is limited and this limitation implies that our observations cannot provide sufficient reason for testimonial uptake. The reductive theory, I have just argued, can respond to this objection in a number of ways. The first two responses preserved the internalism of the reductive theory effectively claiming that the acknowledged limit of our experience does not have this implication: our

---

[43] Lackey (2008), p. 181.

observations can supply more reasons for belief than this objection would recognize. However, this invites a rejoinder: whilst our observations might allow us to explain our acceptance of testimony, their poverty nevertheless ensures that our reasons for belief cannot explain the extent of the knowledge we acquire from testimony. Even if we have 'reasons' for the uptake of testimony, these do no more than explain our pattern of belief. Thus the poverty of our observational basis implies that our reasons for the uptake of testimony might be explanatory but they are not justificatory. If this rejoinder holds good, the only recourse for the reductive theory would be externalism.

This development of the observational problem could be presented as Coady's *problem of type identity*. Since we infer the probable truth of a piece of testimony by direct inference from the observed frequency of truth of its type it would therefore seem paramount that we get testimonial types correct. And here Coady objects,

> some sort of decision would presumably be required as to whether or not the report 'There is a sick lion in Taronga Park Zoo' belonged to the kind, medical report or geographical report or empirical report or existence report. . . . For instance, if the report were treated as belonging to the kind 'existence report' then it might be that Jones had personally established quite a large number of conjunctions between existence reports and the relevant existence situations . . . On the other hand, if it were treated as a medical report then Jones may have had very little personal experience of correlations between medical reports and medical facts.[44]

Coady's objection seems to be as follows. Any bit of testimony could be classified as more than one type. However, to begin with, the purpose of classifying testimony into types is to establish the relative frequency of truth for each type and any decision as to which type a bit of testimony belongs will therefore alter the relative frequency of truth for this type of testimony. And, having established generalizations about the truth of testimonial types, if any piece of testimony could be classified as more than one type, then it could be that classified as one type the piece of testimony is probably true whilst classified as another type it is probably false. So it seems that the process by means of which we come to possess a reason for the uptake of testimony is afflicted by a degree of arbitrariness.

---

[44] Coady (1992), p. 84.

And to this extent any warrant for belief these reasons provide would fail to be knowledge supporting.

On this interpretation of the problem of type identity, all that the reductive theory need do in order to respond is to outline some *principle* for typing testimony. Of course, there is such a principle available: a testimony should always be classified as belonging to the *narrowest type possible*.[45] This principle applies to both the generation of inductive generalizations and the direct inference from a generalization to an instance. True, there are complexities: reference classes can be artificially narrowed. To use Coady's example of the testimony 'there is a sick lion in Taronga Park zoo', the testimonial type *health reports* is less narrow than the type *health reports which contain the word 'sick'* but this narrowing should be ignored.[46] And, as the observation problem makes clear, the narrowest type possible will be determined by the observations an audience can make. However, all this suggests is that acquiring knowledge from testimony is subject to various complexities, it does not imply any insurmountable problem. Indeed, if this type identity problem were a genuine barrier to the acquisition of (inductive) knowledge from testimony, it would be a barrier to the acquisition of inductive knowledge in general. Again, this is to agree with Lyons: if Coady's argument shows that 'induction is insufficient for justifying testimonial beliefs, it shows that induction is insufficient for justifying *any* beliefs'.[47] And this, surely, cannot be claimed.

However, the problem Coady presents is deeper than the general difficulty of arriving at inductive knowledge just outlined. The deeper problem rests on two claims that the reductive theory must accept: (1) our generalizations about the credibility of testimonial types must be ultimately grounded on personal observations of the truth of testimony. And (2) the subjective probabilities we assign to a piece of testimony being true by direct inference from these generalizations must largely track its objective probability of truth *if* the warranted provided by this inference is to be knowledge supporting.

---

[45] Reichenbach (1949), p. 374 states: 'An individual thing or event may be incorporated in many reference classes . . . we then proceed by considering the narrowest reference class for which suitable statistics can be compiled.'

[46] That reference classes should not be artificially narrowed is formalized by Pollock as a *rule of domination defeat*. Pollock (1990), p. 283.

[47] Lyons (1997), p. 168.

Any reductive theory must accept (1): it simply states the idea that we draw distinctions among testimony, which constitute our reasons for the uptake of testimony. This is just the idea that the uptake of testimony must be reasonable; it is not an entitlement. And an *internalist* reductive theory must accept (2): it is just an internalist construal of the reductive thesis. In effect it is the claim that the justification we get from our observations of the truth of testimony can explain our acquisition of knowledge from testimony. However, the conjunction of (1) and (2) with the problem of type identity shows that this problem is really a version of *the generality problem*.[48]

The generality problem for reliabilism starts by observing that any given belief could be regarded as being formed by belief forming processes at different levels of generality. For instance, the belief that it is a chamois one is watching could be regarded as output by the processes, 'vision', 'vision of a medium sized object', 'vision of a medium sized object in the middle distance', 'vision of a medium sized object in the middle distance in good lighting conditions' and so on; schematically, the starting observation is that any belief that p could be regarded as being formed by processes A, B, or C, which differ in their generality. Now according to reliabilism a belief is justified to the degree that it is output by a reliable process.[49] However, processes A, B, and C can differ in their reliability. So, as a theory of justification, reliabilism must supply some account of how to identify belief forming processes. The generality problem is then the contention that there is no way of doing this that is consistent with the reductive aspirations of reliabilism.

Similarly, any testimony could be regarded as instantiating more than one testimonial type; 'There is a sick lion in Taronga Park zoo' could, as Coady observed, be regarded as belonging to the type 'empirical report', 'medical report', or 'existence report'. Now this need not be a problem if these types are related as determination to determinable as, for instance, 'veterinary reports on sick animals' is related to 'the Taronga Park vet's report on the sick lion'. However, and as Coady's example illustrates, it is possible for an utterance to fall under quite disjoint types. Schematically, the problem of type identity starts from the observation that any testimony to p could be regarded as instantiating testimonial types A, B, or C, *where these types do not merely differ in specificity but are disjoint*. Now according to

---

[48] See Connee and Feldman (1998).   [49] See, for instance, Goldman (1979).

the reductive theory, every testimony has some objective probability of truth and we acquire knowledge from testimony because we infer this probability, where this is claim (2). However, we might assign different probabilities to testimonies of types A, B, and C. So it is fundamental to the reductive theory, as a theory of testimonial knowledge, that it supplies some account of how to identify the *right type* and so get the *right objective probability*. The type identity problem is then the contention that there is no way of doing this that is consistent with the reductive aspirations of reductive theory. This is because whilst there is a principle for identifying the right type—roughly, the right type is the narrowest—the reductive aspirations of reductive theory require that our ability to type testimony be determined by *our experience* of the reliability of testimonial types. But then the limits of our experience ensure that we can only work with a restricted range of testimonial types. Consequently, we are often in no position to work with the narrowest type and so cannot follow this principle.

Reductive theories have a response to the type identity problem, which mirrors the first response made to the observational problem. The problem of type identity presumes that when a piece of testimony can be subsumed under more than one disjoint type there will be a difference in the objective probability of truth for these types. Schematically, when testimony to *p* could instantiate disjoint testimonial types A, B, or C there will be a different objective probability of truth for types A, B, and C. So, given that an internalist reductive theory cannot deny claims (1) or (2), what must be denied is this presumption. That is, what must be assumed is that *when a piece of testimony can be subsumed under more than one type, these types will be uniform with respect to their objective probability of truth.* Call this *the presumption of the uniformity of testimonial evidence*, or just the *presumption of uniformity* for short. Given this presumption, an audience need not use the narrowest reference class to get to the objective probability of truth of a piece of testimony but can instead use whatever reference class the audience's observations have made available.

2.3 Conclusion

Reductive theories of testimony claim that our warrant for the uptake of testimony is the warrant that supports our testimonial beliefs, and that this warrant is inductive. Given an internalist interpretation, ultimately we are warranted because we have observed that testimony is true. Any reductive theory must then be compatible with the problematic fact that our observations of the truth of testimony are quite limited. In different ways, this fact underlies both the observational problem and the problem of type identity; that is, it underlies the problems of explaining how our limited observations can supply sufficient reasons to justify our uptake of testimony, and can explain our acquisition of knowledge from testimony. Reductive theories, I've argued, can provide these explanations either by presuming that testimony is uniform in certain respects or by adopting a more externalist account of testimonial knowledge.

The importance of the presumption of uniformity to an internalist reductive theory can additionally be shown by a simple *reductio*. Suppose that testimony is not uniform and, more precisely, that whenever a piece of testimony can be construed as two types, the objective probability of truth of each of these types will be different. Insofar as a piece of testimony has some objective probability of truth, the observations of the truth of testimony of this type should reveal what this is. However, if any testimony could be construed as more than one type *and* these types differ in their objective probability, then without already knowing these objective probabilities, it would be impossible to judge which type one's observations are representative of. So given the starting supposition that the presumption of uniformity is false, we have no justification for generalizing observed frequency of truth. Thus, the objective probability of testimonial types becomes unknowable and the internalist reductive project impossible. But this project cannot be regarded as a priori impossible without induction being equally so regarded. Thus the presumption of uniformity cannot be false, or it cannot be false in the main.

Moreover, this same presumption of uniformity is also central to *any* reductive theory, be it internalist or externalist, since it is just the assumption that certain bits of testimony are evidence for their truth because testimonial type is a broadly reliable indicator of truth. That is, it amounts to the presumption that testimony is reliable in various broad ways, and so might equally be referred to as *the presumption of testimonial reliability*.

The claim that any reductive theory is then ultimately founded on this presumption is not a criticism of the reductive theory. It is merely to give expression to the idea that testimony is the kind of thing one could give a reductive theory of. The internalist project is to generate a 'science' of testimony—to establish a body of generalizations about which testimonial types are probably true—in the same way that we have empirically established generalizations about correlations existing between natural phenomena. Given that testimonial types identify specific sources of testimony, specific domains of testimony or specific combinations thereof, the presumption of uniformity then simply amounts to a series of presumptions about uniformities existing in the reliability of sources and domains, which need to be made in the course of gathering empirical evidence for existing uniformities. Whilst empirically establishing generalizations of probable truth may necessitate making certain presumptions about the uniformity of testimony, any given presumption can be abandoned if the experience shows it to be false. Or given an externalist slant, the presumption is no more than that testimony can reliably indicate its truth. And there can be no objection to this: testimony surely is reliable and is reliable in uniform ways that we could, in principle, be sensitive to.

Nevertheless, it might be said that the necessity of presuming uniformities in testimony as part of the project of establishing such uniformities shows the limits of an internalist reductive theory's explanation of testimonial knowledge. And parallel limits are revealed by the externalist reductive theory taking reliability as its basic epistemological datum. What is really required for a genuinely philosophical theory of testimony is some explanation as to *why* testimony can be presumed to be reliable and reliable in the way that it is. What is really required is some philosophical justification of this presumption of uniformity or reliability. From the perspective of the reductive theory, this would be a philosophical account of why it is that testimony is a source of knowledge.

I will return to this question of the foundations of a reductive theory in 7.1. But first I want to argue that the reductive theory provides the wrong account of testimony as a source of knowledge. The problem, I will start to argue in the next chapter, is that the reductive theory misconceives the nature of testimonial knowledge and warrant.

3

Trust and the Transmission of Knowledge

The reductive theory of testimony is commonly criticized for entailing scepticism. Our experience, it is claimed, is simply too impoverished to justify everything we believe through testimony. This is the criticism made by Reid and it has been echoed as the main criticism of reductive theories ever since. However, the last chapter argued that reductive theories can be defended in this matter. In this chapter I will argue that the reductive theory nevertheless fails in two respects.

First, the uptake principle the reductive theory proposes is wrong. That is, it gives a wrong account of when an audience is warranted in acquiring a belief on the basis of accepting a piece of testimony. The reductive theory correctly proposes that an audience is warranted in the uptake of testimony only if this is (subjectively or individually) reasonable for the audience. But then the reductive theory offers an overly restrictive account of what can make the uptake of testimony reasonable. In particular, the reductive theory fails to recognize how trust, or belief in a speaker, can warrant the uptake of testimony.

Second, the reductive theory is wrong to regard all transmission principles as false. That is, it is wrong to explain an audience's acquisition of knowledge and warranted belief from testimony solely in terms of the audience's own proprietary justification and further non-epistemic facts to do with truth and reliability. Testimony is epistemically distinctive as a source of knowledge and warranted belief, and what makes it so is that it is the extended body of warrant that explains an audience's acquisition of knowledge or warranted belief through testimony.

Both of these failures are exposed when the reductive theory is applied to the restricted domain that is a conversation whose ostensible purpose is the giving and receiving of information. It is with respect to such a conversation that the Testimony Game, which generated the problem of cooperation, was defined. And the first failure of the reductive theory can then be presented as the failure to adequately resolve this problem.

3.1 The reductive solution to the problem of cooperation

The Testimony Game, recall, involves a speaker and an audience engaged in a conversation whose ostensible purpose is the giving and receiving of information. The speaker tells the audience p, and the audience must decide whether to trust or not, where trusting implies the uptake of the speaker's testimony. Given certain plausible assumptions, the pay-offs in this game, I argued, are parallel to those in the Trust Game. The standard view of this game is that it is rational for the investor to trust his interaction partner if and only if he believes he will receive a return. The issue is then what grounds there are for this belief. The argument from cooperation draws the same conclusion: it is rational for the audience to trust the speaker if and only if trust is reasonable in the light of the audience's other attitudes. And the reductive theory finesses this as: an audience is warranted in the uptake of testimony to p if and only if the audience has some reason to believe that p is true.

The substance of the reductive theory then shows how an audience can have such reasons, be rational in trusting that testimony to p is true, and so be warranted in forming the belief that p on the basis of this testimony. These reasons could concern the testimony considered as a type. Or the reasoning could be explanatory and focus on the kinds of motivations at work in this testimonial situation. The audience could judge when a speaker is motivated to tell the truth, where such motives could include fear of sanctions, particular self-interest, a positive evaluation of truth-telling, and a positive evaluation of good relations with the audience. These motives need not occur only individually. The audience might judge that the speaker is moved by a norm of truth-telling and by the consequent opprobrium that would follow a failure to do so. The audience might equally judge that the speaker is moved by a desire for good relations and a desire to avoid losing the audience as a source of information (if the audience judges his disposition to play tit-for-tat is recognized). Thus the resources available for predicting the truth of testimony are manifold. Just as are the resources for predicting the trustee will make a back-transfer in the Trust Game.

This is all well and good as far as it goes. The problem is that the reductive theory nevertheless misses a central reason, arguably *the* central reason, why we trust testimony in such testimonial situations as that of the Testimony Game. In these situations, an audience's reason for the uptake of a speaker's testimony can be no more than that the audience *believes the speaker*, or *trusts the speaker for the truth*. Moreover, believing a speaker is different from merely predicting the truth of what the speaker says. One can predict that what a speaker says is true *without* believing them; and one can make one's lack of confidence in a speaker clear by making it clear that one accepts what the speaker says only because one has independent reasons for doing so. This is illustrated by case 15 (the hypnotized patient), which is presented by David Owens as the case of 'someone who asserts, as a result of post-hypnotic suggestion, that a certain woman was murdered. Perhaps this woman was indeed murdered, the hypnotist knew this fact and installed this belief in his patient as a way of bringing the murder to light without showing his hand.'[1] The audience, one may suppose, has enough background information—a good enough proprietary justification—to predict that what the patient says is true. But the content of this justification will also ensure that the audience *does not believe the patient*. Believing a speaker is something like a vote of confidence or expression of faith. Following Elizabeth Anscombe, I suggest that 'we can see that believing someone (in the particular case) as *trusting him for the truth*—in the particular case'.[2]

The reductive theory misses this distinction: it would draw no contrast between believing a speaker (or trusting a speaker for the truth) and believing what a speaker says (or trusting a bit of testimony to be true). According to the reductive theory, to trust is just to depend on someone doing something or something happening because one predicts that things will work out a certain way. So to trust a speaker for the truth is just to predict that what the speaker says is true, which is just to trust that the speaker's testimony is true. In the Testimony Game, trust is the uptake of testimony on the basis of the prediction that it is true. What the reductive theory shows is that we have ample resources to make this prediction.

---

[1] Owens (2000), p. 166. As referenced, Coady's comparable case is: Coady (1992), p. 45.
[2] Anscombe (1979), p. 151. My emphasis.

This is, I think, epistemically correct, but as a piece of moral psychology it simply misses the important point that belief in a speaker can be our reason for uptake. Consider the following couple of cases.

Case 3. The audience would like to purchase the used car he is presently looking at, but, more importantly he does not want to purchase a wreck. The salesman assures him, 'the car is as good as it looks: it has only had one previous lady owner'.

Case 17. A reformer decides to pick a new employee from a list of recently discharged prisoners the local prison circulates, and knowingly picks someone convicted for theft. Nevertheless, the reformer trusts her new employee with the till and at the end of the first day he reassures her, 'don't worry, the till balances'.

In these two cases, I hope the following is clear. First, the evidence the audience could marshal for predicting the truth of what is told is mixed. There is some basis for predicting truth and some predicting falsehood. Car salesmen have their reputation to care about, but they have their reputation. The ex-convict has a chance for change, but a record that suggests he will not. So, second, the audience cannot support the uptake of the speaker's testimony to p with the prediction that p is true. However, third, in both cases the audience could decide to trust the speaker for the truth. In doing so, the buyer would choose to believe the salesman when told the car's history, and the reformer would choose to believe her new employee when he tells her the till balances. The trust that the audience hereby places in the speaker is not a prediction of outcome; rather, the audience trusts in the affective sense I introduced in 1.3.7 and will define in 6.2. However, hopefully enough of a contrast has been made to make this point: these cases show that our reason for the uptake of testimony need not be any prediction of truth, but can be simply that we believe the speaker, or trust the speaker for the truth.

Of course, it is not so much that the reductive theory misses the explanatory role this thicker, more normative attitude of trust can play in the uptake of testimony, rather it is that the reductive theory regards this as merely a matter of moral psychology.[3] An audience's uptake of testimony to p is warranted if and only if the audience has an *epistemic reason* for believing that p. And while the attitude of affective trust might give an audience a practical reason for belief, it does not, the objection runs, give an epistemic reason for belief. At this juncture I can only issue

---

[3] See for instance Lackey (2008), ch. 8, which I discuss in 6.5.

a promissory note: the attitude of affective trust does provide an epistemic reason for belief. And it does so even though its motivations are at root practical. I will argue this in 6.3, after giving an analysis of trust.

If this promissory note is accepted and it is allowed that affective trust, which is a non-evidence-based attitude, can nevertheless provide epistemic reasons for belief, then the implication for the reductive theory is that there are more ways in which the uptake of testimony can be justified than it would allow. And a consequence of this, I think, is that the reductive solution to the problem of cooperation should be regarded as a sceptical solution. This point can be made by analogy with the Trust Game. Ordinarily, an investor has many reasons for judging that an interaction partner will make a back-transfer. But suppose the game is played as a one-off interaction under conditions of ignorance. These are the conditions the game is played under in the laboratory, and under these conditions the rational thing for the investor to do is not make any transfers and simply keep his starting sum.[4] However, the experimental result is that investors do trust. This gives something of a sceptical problem for practical rationality: why it is that investors trust under conditions that seem to make it rational not to do so? (Here is another promissory note: I think that the answer to this question is that the judgement of irrationality misses the normative structure of the trust-situation, where I will argue this in 7.3.)

The analogy to be made, then, is that the reductive theory generates the same sceptical problem. Suppose that the Testimony Game is similarly a one-off interaction set against a background of ignorance. To the extent that these suppositions take away an audience's ability to predict the truth of a bit of testimony, they ensure that the uptake of testimony would be similarly unjustified. However, just as the audiences could trust in cases 3 and 17, we can and do trust under such conditions. We can put our faith in others and choose to believe them, or trust them for the truth. Moreover, just as the interaction parties in the Trust Game did make back-transfers under these conditions, so speakers can tell us what they know under these conditions. The reductive theory would then be committed to the claim that any true belief formed in such a situation would not be warranted. It would not be warranted because the audience does not have the necessary

---

[4] See Fehr, Fischbacher, and Gachter (2002).

proprietary justification to warrant it. In excluding trust-based reasons for uptake what is then excluded is *the possibility that testimonial knowledge can be got on trust.*

Take case 3: irrespective of what the audience believes, the car sales-man might have decided to tell the audience the truth on this occasion. The salesman might know the car has only had one previous lady owner. In this case, if only the audience could psychologically bring himself to trust, if he could believe the salesman, then it seems that the audience could know what the salesman tells him. But if this is the case, it is the car salesman's knowing that p that is relevant to the audience's getting to know that p; it is the extended body of warrant that matters, not the audience's own proprietary justification. Thus the reductive solution to the problem of cooperation is a *sceptical* solution because the limits it imposes on when the uptake of testimony is justified wrongly limit possibilities of acquiring testimonial knowledge. Given that the reduc-tive theory is able to explain most, if not all, of the knowledge we *actually* acquire from testimony—or so I argued in defending the reductive theory in the last chapter—what is excluded are certain *possibilities* of knowledge acquisition.

3.2 The transmission of knowledge and warrant

In the last section I argued that the uptake principle proposed by the reductive theory is too restrictive. In the remains of this chapter I want to focus on the second failing of the reductive theory: its denying that testimonial knowledge is the epistemically distinctive type transmitted knowledge. However, before starting this argument I want to get a little clearer on what is being argued for. How should the claim that testimony transmits knowledge and warrant be characterized? What is a transmission principle for testimony?

The idea that testimony transmits knowledge and warrant, Jennifer Lackey suggests, can be broken down into a necessity thesis and a sufficiency thesis.

TEP-N. For every speaker, S, and hearer, A, A knows (believes with justification/warrant) that p on the basis of S's testimony that p only if S knows (believes with justification/warrant) that p.

TEP-S. For every speaker, S, and hearer, A, if (1) S knows (believes with justification/warrant) that p, (2) A comes to believe that p on the basis of the content of S's testimony that p, and (3) A has no undefeated defeaters for believing that p, then A knows (believes with justification/warrant) that p.[5]

For the moment let me focus on knowledge and the sufficiency thesis, TEP-S. With this focus this thesis could be rewritten thus:

(1) Where A believes that p through uptake of S testimony to p, if (i) S knows that p and (ii) A has no undefeated defeaters for believing that p, then A knows that p.

As it stands (1) is false. The audience A would not know that p unless A's uptake of S's testimony to p were warranted. It is not enough that A has no undefeated defeaters for believing that p, A also needs to be warranted in acquiring this belief. Adding this condition to the sufficiency thesis gives:

(2) Where A believes that p through uptake of S testimony to p, if (i) S knows p, (ii) A is warranted in the uptake of S's testimony to p and (iii) A has no undefeated defeaters for believing that p, then A knows that p.[6]

The problem with claim (2) as a transmission principle is that it is consistent with both reductive and non-reductive theories of testimony. These theories simply give different accounts of how the uptake of testimony is warranted; that is, different accounts of (ii). And so different accounts of why (2) is true, that is of why it is that A knows that p. For the reductive theory, warrant for the uptake of testimony comes by way of A's proprietary justification for p. For the non-reductive theory it comes by way of a general entitlement to p. And for the trust theory warrant is equally conferred by A's proprietary justification but trust can provide this; all that is needed is that uptake be reasonable in the light of A's other attitudes. Then for the reductive theory A knows that p because (ii) and (iii) hold: A has an undefeated proprietary justification. For non-reductive theories A knows that p because (i) holds: it is the extended body of warrant—the fact that S knows that p—that underwrites A's knowing.

---

[5] Lackey (2008), pp. 39–40. (I've changed the names of the speaker and hearer to 'S' and 'A' for consistency.)

[6] Lackey cites a number of authors who endorse (1), however, it is (2) that these authors endorse. This is very clear for authors cited like Adler (1996), Burge (1993), McDowell (1994a), and Williamson (2000) who take the warrant for uptake to come from a general entitlement.

And for the trust theory it is this latter explanation that characterizes *testimonial* knowledge.

That (2) is consistent with both reductive and non-reductive theories, however, is to be expected. If knowledge is assumed to be undefeated warranted true belief, conditions (ii) and (iii) in (2) imply that A knows that p provided that p is true. This is guaranteed by condition (i). And since A knows that p on the basis of S's testimony to p, statement (2) seems to be a minor variant of:

(3) Where A believes that p through uptake of S's testimony to p, if A knows that S knows that p, then A knows that p.

And (3) is a general truth about knowledge since it is the application to testimony of the principle:

(4) If A knows that S knows that p, then A knows that p.

In developing his logic of knowledge and belief Jaakko Hintikka demonstrates that (4) is valid ('self-sustaining' in his terms).[7] Its truth is shown by our finding its negation—A knows that S knows that p but A does not know that p himself—to be inconsistent. Moreover, Hintikka claims, (4) defines what it is for knowledge to be 'transmissible'. However, this sense of 'transmissible' is not the one I am trying to capture here as can be shown by the fact that both (3) and (4) are consistent with the reductive theory, which would merely emphasize that it is A's *knowing* that S knows that p— A's own proprietary justification—that explains A's knowing that p.

What would make (3) and (2) into transmission principles, as opposed to general truths about knowledge applied to the testimonial process, would be their conjunction with a certain explanation as to why they hold true, namely that, in each case, it is S's *knowing that p* that explains A's knowing that p. In each case, it is the extended body of warrant that is relevant to explaining A's knowing that p. This explanation is brought to the surface by the necessity thesis. Focusing again on knowledge, this thesis, Lackey's TEP-N, could be initially formulated thus:

(5) Where A believes that p through uptake of S's testimony to p, A knows that p only if S knows that p.

---

[7] See Hintikka (1989), §4.1 for his proof.

The problem with this initial formulation is that even the advocate of transmission must allow that we can gain inductive knowledge from testimony. Consider case 15 where the audience believes what the speaker says because he believes that the speaker's utterance is post-hypnotically induced. If the speaker said that p, then the audience could get to know that p through uptake of this testimony even though the speaker does not know that p but has just blurted it out unthinkingly. The problem is that (5) is not consistent with the reductive explanation of our acquisition of knowledge from testimony and the advocate of transmission must allow that this explanation can be good on occasion. Thus the necessity thesis needs to be rewritten thus:

(6) Where A believes that p through uptake of S's testimony to p, A *testimonially* knows that p only if S knows that p.

Statement (6) is not compatible with the reductive theory since the reductive theory draws no distinction between testimonial knowledge and knowledge acquired from testimony. And in not recognizing that testimonial knowledge is a distinctive epistemic type, the reductive theory would take counter-examples to (5), such as case 15, to be equally counter-examples to (6). The advocate of transmission meanwhile would regard these cases as merely illustrating the falsity of (5) not the falsity of (6).

Statement (6) is still false as it stands, however, because testimonial knowledge can skip a link. Consider case 18: a speaker S tells a gossip T that p knowing that p; the gossip T doesn't believe S but knowing that p will upset audience A maliciously tells A that p. What matters in this case is that the non-immediate speaker S knows that p and in telling T that p did intend to inform T of this fact. A related case where the chain of transmission skips the speaker is case 19: a creationist teacher's testimony puts a student in a position to know some true statement implied by evolutionary theory even though the teacher, as a creationist, does not believe what she says and tells what she does out of duty rather than to inform.[8] Thus (6) should be modified to:

(7) Where A believes that p through uptake of S's testimony to p, A *testimonially* knows that p only if S knows that p or S's testimony to p is the end of a testimonial chain and some speaker prior to S in this testimonial chain knew that p.

---

[8] See Lackey (1999), p. 477, Graham (2000a), p. 377, and Faulkner (2000), p. 595.

Since (7) is rather cumbersome, I will abbreviate it thus:

(8) Where A believes that p through uptake of testimony to p, A *testimonially* knows that p only if a prior speaker knew that p.

A parallel statement then holds for warrant:

(9) Where A believes that p through uptake of S's testimony to p, A is *testimonially* warranted in believing that p only if S is warranted in believing that p or S's testimony to p is the end of a testimonial chain and some speaker prior to S in this testimonial chain is warranted in believing that p.

Where (9) can be similarly abbreviated to:

(10) Where A believes that p through uptake of testimony to p, A is *testimonially* warranted in believing that p only if a prior speaker was warranted in believing that p.

Statements (7) and (9) are transmission principles for testimonial knowledge and warrant respectively. Call (7) the *transmission principle for testimonial knowledge*; and call (9) the *transmission principle for testimonial warrant*.[9] And for ease of exposition let me henceforth work with the abbreviation of these principles (8) and (10), which I shall refer to by the acronyms (TK) and (TW) respectively.

Thus the idea that testimony transmits knowledge is the idea that there is a way of knowing through testimony that necessitates that a prior speaker in the chain of testimony knew; and the idea that testimony transmits warrant is the idea that there is a way of being warranted in belief through testimony that necessitates that a prior speaker in the chain of testimony was warranted in belief. The second criticism I now want to make of the reductive theory is that it is wrong to deny this necessity claim; it is wrong to regard transmission principles (TK) and (TW) as false.

3.3 The problem of intentionality

It must be acknowledged that we can acquire inductive knowledge from testimony. It is possible for our experience to support judgements of a speaker's reliability that allow us to conclude that something is true from

---

[9] Advocates of (7) and (9) include Ross (1986), Plantinga (1988), Burge (1993), Webb (1993), Welbourne (1993), McDowell (1994a), Audi (1997), Williamson (2000), Adler (2002), Reynolds (2002), Weiner (2003), and Moran (2006).

the fact that the speaker said it. The problem with the reductive view comes with the claim that *this is all there is* to acquiring knowledge from testimony. The problem is that this claim misses the distinction between *acquiring knowledge from testimony* and its subset *acquiring testimonial knowledge*. Of course, the reductive theory misses this distinction because it denies that there is a distinctive epistemic type 'testimonial knowledge'; it takes all transmission principles to be false. Testimonial knowledge is just knowledge acquired from testimony, where acquiring knowledge from testimony is just a matter of having an inductive argument—a proprietary justification—which, when added to the premise that one has received testimony to p, suffices for knowledge that p.

For example, consider the following case, already encountered at the beginning of Chapter 2.

Case 20. The audience is told that the American President is at such-and-such location. The audience has an excellent proprietary justification for believing this: he has observed, due to his line of work, that this speaker has been entirely reliable in this matter.

It does not matter, according to the reductive theory, whether the reliability of the speaker is due to his being part of the special services responsible for the President's welfare or whether it is due to his possession of a clairvoyant power. What matters for the audience's acquisition of knowledge from testimony is the audience's proprietary justification. The difference in the extended body of warrant in these sub-cases is immaterial.

Given this understanding of what the acquisition of knowledge from testimony involves, the reductive theorist should equally draw no distinction between acquiring knowledge from *how* a speaker says what she says and acquiring knowledge from *what* a speaker says. Thus consider the following pair of cases.

Case 21. Having just discovered clear evidence of his wife's long-suspected infidelity, the anxious husband confronts her. She confesses to the affair.
Case 22. Having just discovered clear evidence of his wife's long-suspected infidelity, the anxious husband confronts her. She denies the affair but he observes reliable indicators that her denial is a lie.[10]

---

[10] The kinds of micro-expression that reveal lies are present in abundance and the husband, one may suppose, has trained himself to observe them. See Ekman (1985).

There might be an emotional contrast between these cases in that case 22 would allow the husband the possibility of self-deception. But, for the reductive theorist, there is no essential epistemic difference. All that matters is that testimony, in some way, is a sign of the truth. Since the knowledge we acquire from testimony is merely inductive knowledge, cases 21 and 22 are epistemically on a par; the only difference is the causal difference flagged by the fact that a premise in the husband's proprietary justification refers either to what his wife said or how she said what she did. However, I suggest, we would epistemically distinguish cases 21 and 22, and we would distinguish them on the same basis that we would distinguish the variations of case 20: only one case is a case of acquiring testimonial knowledge. Moreover, the distinction between acquiring knowledge of what people say versus acquiring knowledge from how people say what they do is arguably a distinction that the reductive theory should acknowledge even in its own terms.

The issue for the reductive theory starts with the recognition that we control what we say in a way that we do not control other aspects of our behaviour. Suppose, then, that in case 22 the husband infers that his wife is lying on the basis of a certain cluster of signs. And it then comes to light that his wife was acting and the subtle set of expressions and behaviours he took to be cues of her deceit was in fact faked for his benefit.[11] This supposition radically changes things. The husband would now rightly wonder about his wife's reasons for this behaviour. Was she trying to end the marriage but trying to get him to make the decisive move with his accusation of deceit? Was this an attempt to gain ground that would be lost with a confession? And following on her affair, how far did her deception go? A host of questions would be raised, but one thing would be clear: the husband would no longer think that how his wife gave her testimony was evidence for its truth, or at least not straightforwardly so. The fact that the husband's 'evidence'—the nature of how his wife's testimony was delivered—turned out to be an intentional product undermines its evidential value. However, if this is correct, the same is true of what people say.

---

[11] Unlikely, of course, since in most part we have neither the sophistication to recognize the cues of deceit nor the sophistication to ape them. However, there is no sign of deceit that could not in principle be aped; as observed, there is no 'Pinocchio Response' that unfailingly identifies liars and only liars. See Frank (2009).

Ordinarily, *how we say things* is *not* put on, but *what we say* is very much an intentional product. This fact then devalues testimony *as evidence*.

This *problem of intentionality*, as it could be called, is well presented by Richard Moran who observes the following:

> [I]f we are considering speech as evidence, we will have eventually to face the question of how recognition of its intentional character could ever *enhance* rather than detract from its epistemic value for an audience. Ordinarily, if I confront something as evidence (the telltale footprint, the cigarette butt left in the ashtray), and then learn that it was left there deliberately, and even with the intention of bringing me to a particular belief, this will only discredit it as evidence in my eyes. It won't seem *better* evidence, or even just as good, but instead like something fraudulent, or tainted evidence.[12]

Thus, the reductive theory should draw a distinction between acquiring knowledge from what people say and acquiring knowledge from how people say what they do because the latter *is a better source of evidence*. Of course in many cases there is no other way of learning what people believe than through what they say. But the point is that insofar as what we say, our testimony, is a voluntary expression, it is to this extent of lesser value as evidence.

The problem for the reductive theory is that commitment to giving the same inductive explanation of acquiring knowledge from what people say (or knowledge from testimony) as acquiring knowledge from how people say what they do (or knowledge from behaviour more generally) carries the implication that the straight uptake of testimony is always the worse route to knowledge of the two. For any case where an audience is in receipt of a speaker S's testimony to p, it would be better, according to the reductive theory, for the audience to have a less intentionally mediated access to S's beliefs, such as that ordinarily provided by an inference from behaviour. Ideally, Moran quips, the reductive theory should prefer 'those ways, real or imaginary, of learning someone's beliefs directly and without the mediation of voluntary expression or behaviour at all (i.e. whatever is imagined in imagining the effects of truth-serum, hypnotism, or brain scans)'.[13] This is a problem because sometimes we think that someone's telling us something can put us *in a better epistemic position* that any inference

---

[12] Moran (2006), p. 277.   [13] Moran (2006), p. 277.

from their behaviour.[14] It is not merely that the husband's position is emotionally clearer in case 21, where his wife confesses, he is in a better epistemic position in this case (no matter how good his evidence in case 22). Or so, I suggest, we think. And if this is taken as an epistemic datum, it is a fact that is well explained by the idea that testimony transmits knowledge since this idea makes testimonial knowledge epistemically disjoint from any inductively acquired knowledge from testimony. As such there is no trouble with the idea that someone's choosing to tell us something can put us in the best epistemic position that we could be in.

3.4 Telling and knowing

The receipt of testimony could put us in the best possible epistemic position we could be in with respect to some fact because there is no better way of knowing some facts than being told of them. Hence we can be willing to answer a question as to how we know something to be the case with the simple reply, 'I was told it'. Austin makes this observation:

Among the cases where we give our reasons for knowing things, a special and important class is formed by those where we cite authorities. If asked 'How do you know the election is today?', I am apt to reply 'I read it in *The Times*', and if asked 'How do you know the Persians were defeated at Marathon?' I am apt to reply 'Herodotus expressly states that they were'. In these cases 'know' is correctly used: we know 'at second hand' when we can cite an authority who was in a position to know (possibly himself also only at second hand). The statement of an authority makes me aware of something, enables me to know something, which I shouldn't otherwise have known. It is a source of knowledge.[15]

Contrast this with how we respond when we are interrogated about something we know on the basis of induction. In response to 'How do you know the gem will be green?' or 'How do you know that cry is an owl?' we respond by citing a generalization, a bit of theory; we say 'It is an

---

[14] Lackey misses this point. She mistakenly argues that Moran's point is that the intentional character of testimony '*destroys*' the epistemic value of testimony, before correctly observing that: 'A proponent of the Evidential View could obviously grant that the intentional nature of testimony *detracts* from the epistemic value of testimony (compared, say, to straight perception), while also holding (i) that testimony is still an adequate source of knowledge and (ii) that testimony provides knowledge that we couldn't get any other way.' Lackey (2008), p. 224, n.5. This is correct, but the point is that intentional character of testimony can actually *add to* its epistemic value.
[15] Austin (1946), pp. 49–50.

emerald and emeralds are green' or 'owls make that sound'. However, the generalization '*The Times* is a reliable paper' would constitute *a further response*. It is the response if doubts were raised by the initial citation of *The Times* as one's knowledge source.

Moreover, our general practice of asking questions also lends evidence to the claim that we think about what we know through testimony in transmissive terms. Consider what we do when we are ignorant as to whether something is so; suppose we want to know whether or not the election is today, and so whether to schedule a visit to the polling station. How do we resolve our ignorance? We ask someone. Asking someone can achieve this because if the person asked knows what we desire to know, they can tell us. And this is brought out by the fact that question forms can introduce the verb object for both 'know' and 'tell'. For example, consider these questions, which might be asked in the course of a police investigation. Who robbed the bank? Why did they rob this bank and not the other one? How did they get away? Where did they hide the money? A member of the gang who robbed the bank will be able to answer these questions. He will be able to do so just because he knows who robbed the bank; he knows why the gang robbed this bank; he knows how they got away; and he knows where the money is hidden. In possessing this knowledge and so being able to answer these questions this gang member can tell the police office who robbed the bank; he can tell the police office why they robbed this bank, and so on. Thus, Welbourne makes this observation:

In standard cases, when you ask someone a question it is because you want to know something.... You ask me where the cat is. Why? Because, for whatever more particular motive, you want to know where it is.... It seems as if the idea that knowledge is transmissible by say-so dominates the practice of enquiry from other people, and we may learn from the existence of the practice that we have such a notion.[16]

That is, consideration of our ordinary practices of enquiry shows that there are basic connections between questioning, knowing, and telling.

These connections, Vendler argues, have a startling consequence. Since being able to take the question form as a verb object is 'the most reliable grammatical mark of factivity', 'know' and 'tell' are *factive verbs*.[17] 'He knows who robbed the bank' entails that someone did indeed rob the bank and he

---

[16] Welbourne (1986), p. 8.   [17] Vendler (1979), p. 225.

knows whom this person is; and 'He told me who robbed the bank' equally entails that someone robbed the bank and he knows who this person is. And 'He told me' has this implication. Zeno Vendler argues that it has another implication as well: I now know who robbed the bank as well as him. Vendler states:

If you say 'He told me who she was', you *imply* that both he and you know who she was. You came to know as a result of his telling you what he knew. . . . 'I told him that it was his wife' may report an attempt at persuading (causing belief); 'I told him who she was' does not. . . . 'I told him who she was, but he still does not know it.' This is inconsistent.[18]

This conclusion is too strong since a speaker can know something and tell it but not be believed by an audience. Accordingly, we can remove the factive implication: 'He told me who robbed the bank' we might report, and then add, 'but he was lying' or 'but he was only guessing'. Moreover, Vendler goes on to acknowledge that telling is only '*half-factive*': 'telling *that* can be false, telling *what* cannot. "Tell," therefore, is factive in front of a *wh*-clause, but not necessarily in front of a *that*-clause.'[19] One cannot know falsehoods but one can tell falsehoods; one can lie and honestly get things wrong.

What, then, is needed to acquire knowledge that p from a speaker who knows that p and tells one that p? Not an inductive argument which has the telling as premise but, Welbourne claims, the only required 'uptake condition' for the successful communication or transmission of knowledge is belief in the speaker.

The mechanism by which knowledge is transmitted is *belief*. More precisely, in the simplest kind of case where you address me directly, it is sufficient and necessary for the transmission of your knowledge that p to me that I *believe you* when, speaking (or writing) from knowledge, you tell me that p.[20]

Since one can tell a falsehood, the police officer who is told where the money is need not accept what he is told. But suppose that the police officer does believe the gang member's confession and yet still reports 'He told me where the money is and I believe him, but I do not know where the money is.' Now Vendler's suggestion of inconsistency seems pressing. If he did tell the officer where the money was and the officer *did believe*

[18] Vendler (1979), p. 231.   [19] Vendler (1979), p. 228.
[20] Welbourne (1979), p. 3.

him, then both now know where the money is. That we read this sentence as 'inconsistent' then affirms that our intuitions about telling and knowing very much support the idea that we think of the knowledge we acquire from testimony as a unique epistemic kind: *knowledge got by believing a knowledgeable speaker.*

3.5 Lying and epistemic defeat

So far I have considered the epistemic supports relation that distinguishes testimonial knowledge, which is that it is transmitted knowledge. As transmitted knowledge, testimonial knowledge is also subject to a distinctive kind of defeat. Crucially, it is subject to defeat in a way that inductively acquired knowledge from testimony is not. That a speaker *lied* or was *incompetent* can both defeat the transmission of knowledge. Case 15 (the hypnotism case) illustrates the latter. Suppose that I know nothing of the hypnotism and accept what the patient tells me. If the hypnotism then comes to light, this is a reason to not believe the patient; it is a reason not to take what she says on her authority, or on trust, because it is a reason to think that she does not know what she says and, in this way, is an incompetent speaker. However, it need not be a reason to think her testimony is unreliable. Indeed, it could be a reason to think that her testimony is a reliable indicator and so could ground an inductive argument to the truth of what she said. In this way the acquisition of inductive knowledge from her testimony need not be undermined.

This illustrates defeat in the acquisition of testimonial knowledge. However, there are complexities to this process that need to be observed. First, a speaker's lying is the central instance of a broader category of defeater: a speaker's not engaging in communication with informative intent. We do not acquire testimonial knowledge if we acquire a belief through mistakenly accepting an ironically made utterance or a tall story. Lies are thus the principal subset of what could be called 'artful' utterances, or utterances presenting a proposition that the speaker does not believe.[21] However, second, it is not always the attitudes of the *immediate* speaker that matter because a chain of knowledge transmission can skip a speaker. Hence transmission principles must concern either the immediate speaker

---

[21] See Faulkner (2000), p. 586.

or some prior speaker in the testimonial chain. Third, since testimony can function to pass on both knowledge and warranted belief, a speaker can be incompetent either by not being warranted in believing or not knowing what was said. So I can pass on the warranted belief that Goldbach's conjecture is probably true on the basis of knowing that it has been shown to hold up to very high numbers, but I would be incompetent if I claimed to know this conjecture and attempted to pass this on as knowledge because Goldbach's conjecture is exactly that: a conjecture.[22] However, fourth, a speaker might be incompetent, in the sense that she does not know what she tells an audience, and yet might still put an audience in a position to know what is told through the audience's possession of additional information. Such a case would be one where a speaker says that she saw a red barn on the hill at such and such location but does not know there are many barn façades, or indeed anything about the local practices, whereas the audience does know this and knows that barn façades are not painted red.[23] Finally, fifth, just as audiences can overcome defeaters that prevent speakers knowing so too can new knowledge be generated through testimony. This is illustrated by Plantinga's example, case 23, where 'you and I and many others together map the coast of Australia: then I know by nontestimonial means that *this* bit has *this* shape; you know similarly *that* bit has *that* shape, and so on'.[24] However, the cartographer that puts the map together only knows by testimony that the coast of Australia has such and such shape, even if he is the first to know this.[25]

The idea that testimonial knowledge and testimonially warranted belief are distinctive epistemic kinds is consistent with these complexities. Moreover, these complexities can be taken into consideration in formulating a general defeater of the testimonial process. *The uptake of testimony can transmit knowledge or warrant only if it originates from a source who is in a position to inform, or support (i.e. who knows or is warranted in belief) and intends to*

---

[22] Goldbach's conjecture is that every even number is the sum of two primes. At January 2010, Goldbach's conjecture had been verified for numbers up 20×10^{17} by distributed computer search. See http://www.ieeta.pt/~tos/goldbach.html for details.

[23] The barn-façade case is from Goldman (1976) and the red barn twist from Kripke (from an unpublished paper given at an APA session in the 1980s). Compare Lackey's Farmer Brown case, Lackey (1999), p. 487.

[24] Plantinga (1988), p. 87.

[25] Elaborate but actual cases are detailed in Hardwig (1985) and Hardwig (1991).

do so.[26] What needs to be noted is: this source need not be the immediate speaker; her audience need not be the audience; and what the source is in a position to tell need not equate with what the testimony puts the audience in a position to know. However, what is important is that there is a general defeater for the acquisition of testimonial knowledge and warrant but there is no such general defeater for the acquisition of inductive knowledge or warranted belief from testimony. Of course that a speaker lied or was incompetent *could* defeat an inductive argument for the truth of what the speaker said. But whether it does so would be entirely contingent on the nature of the argument. So, even given the complexities that can bedevil both the testimonial process and the arguments we can mount for the truth of testimony, the important contrast remains. And to recognize that testimony thereby constitutes a way of acquiring knowledge and warranted belief that is associated with distinctive defeat relations is to recognize that testimonial knowledge and warrant are epistemically distinctive kinds.

3.6 Lackey's argument against transmission

Jennifer Lackey's monograph *Learning from Words* argues for two principal claims. The first is that testimonial knowledge is a collaborative product. She labels this view *dualism*, and I considered it above in 2.1.3. Lackey's second principal claim is the rejection of what she terms the *belief view of testimony* and the endorsement of the *statement view of testimony* in its place. We should focus on testimony as a statement, and not as an expression of belief. Lackey favours this statement view because we can supposedly imagine cases where reliability in belief and reliability of testimony come apart. And it is the reliability of testimony that matters. So we should reject the view that 'testimony involves a speaker transmitting her belief to a hearer, along with the epistemic properties it possesses'.[27]

The belief view Lackey then characterizes in terms of TEP-S and TEP-N—respectively the sufficiency thesis and necessity thesis quoted in 3.2. For convenience I quote again.

---

[26] The complexity 'or support' is needed because the audience might already believe what is told. So just as the uptake of testimony is defined as acceptance that results in the acquisition of belief or that causally sustains belief, so the intention here is to inform or to support.

[27] Lackey (2008), p. 38.

TEP-N. For every speaker, S, and hearer, A, A knows (believes with justification/warrant) that p on the basis of S's testimony that p only if S knows (believes with justification/warrant) that p.

TEP-S. For every speaker, S, and hearer, A, if (1) S knows (believes with justification/warrant) that p, (2) A comes to believe that p on the basis of the content of S's testimony that p, and (3) A has no undefeated defeaters for believing that p, then A knows (believes with justification/warrant) that p.[28]

In 3.2 I argued that the transmission principle should not be formulated as TEP-S and that TEP-S is false. So I have no disagreement with Lackey's claim that TEP-S is false. And I think it is false for the same reason as Lackey: A's uptake of S's testimony that p needs to be warranted if A is to know that p on this basis; and this requirement translates into an 'audience condition' on the acquisition of testimonial knowledge. The uptake of testimony must be rationally supported by an audience's other attitudes if it is to be warranted. Like Lackey I think that the uptake of testimony 'in the complete absence of positive reasons can be just as epistemically irrational' as belief in the face of counter-evidence.[29] However, the claim that TEP-S is false, and false for this reason, is entirely consistent with the idea that testimony transmits knowledge and warrant. Moreover, this consistent pair—transmission plus an audience condition—constitutes the trust theory I argue for.

Thus what matters is Lackey's argument for the falsity of TEP-N. If this thesis is meant to capture the idea that testimony transmits knowledge and warrant, then, I argued in 3.2, it is better expressed as the transmission principles (TK) and (TW):

(TK) Where A believes that p through uptake of testimony to p, A *testimonially* knows that p only if a prior speaker knew that p.

(TW) Where A believes that p through uptake of testimony to p, A is *testimonially* warranted in believing that p only if a prior speaker was warranted in believing that p.

So what matters is Lackey's argument that these transmission principles are false. Lackey's argument is a series of counter-examples. We can supposedly imagine cases which show (TK) and (TW) to be false. This argumentative strategy is a risky one. The problem with arguing by counter-example is that the counter-examples cannot be theoretically contentious; they must be

---

[28] Lackey (2008), pp. 39–40. (I've changed the names of the speaker and hearer to 'S' and 'A' for consistency.)

[29] Lackey (2008), p. 170.

plausible. Lackey's cases, which follow, do not come near satisfying this desideratum.

Case number one is that of the 'creationist teacher'.[30] A devout Christian but law-abiding teacher, Stella teaches evolutionary theory but does not believe what she teaches. Letting 'p' refer to some statement Stella makes about evolution, Stella does not believe that p and so does not know that p but her testimony puts her pupils in a position to know that p. So Lackey concludes that TEP-N is false.

This case does show this. But all this shows is that TEP-N is a poor formulation of the moot transmission principle. It shows that speakers can pass on what others know, and that all that matters is that someone in the testimonial chain possesses knowledge that can be passed on. This fact is accommodated by (TK). Lackey thinks that this response is problematic because it denies that Stella is 'the source of the children's knowledge'.[31] But the response is not so unsubtle. Stella is the source of the children's testimonial belief that p, and it is true that this belief amounts to knowledge, but Stella is not the source of this knowledge that p. What explains the children's possession of knowledge is that Stella's testimony connects the children's belief to someone else who knows that p. This is the crux of the necessity claim: it is a view about the nature of testimonial knowledge, to wit that to possess testimonially based knowledge is to have the epistemic standing of another explain one's possession of knowledge. Lackey does not pick up on this equivocation in 'source' because she rejects the idea that testimony transmits knowledge, and so rejects the idea that testimony can be a source of knowledge *in this sense*.

Case number two is the 'consistent liar'.[32] This case is a little puzzling, but it runs as follows. Bertha has a brain lesion so that for some ordered set of animals $\{a_1, a_2, \ldots, a_n\}$ when Bertha sees animal a_j she believes it is animal a_{j+1}. Bertha then has this lesion surgically modified so that when she decides to make a statement about animal a_{j+1} she makes it about animal a_j. Letting 'p' refer to some statement Bertha makes about animal a_j, Bertha's belief concerns animal a_{j+1} so she does not believe that p and nor, therefore, know that p. But given that her testimony reliably reports what she sees to be the case it puts her audience in a position to know that p. So Lackey concludes the necessity claim is false.

---

[30] Lackey (2008), p. 48. [31] Lackey (2008), p. 53. [32] Lackey (2008), p. 53.

Certainly it is true that one could acquire knowledge from Bertha's testimony. One could treat Bertha as a thermometer and justify believing what she says on the basis of the reliability of her saying. This is the reductive model of testimonial knowledge and the view that testimony transmits knowledge and warrant is consistent with this model in that it is consistent with our being able to learn inductively from testimony. The issue is what gives the best explanation of the central cases. For the consistent liar to be a counter-example it has to be such a central case: one needs to think that the knowledge acquired from Bertha *is testimonial*. Thus (TK) and (TW) refer to the audience *testimonially* knowing or being *testimonially* warranted in belief. Now Lackey does think that the knowledge we acquire from Bertha is testimonial, but only because she draws no distinction between such knowledge and inductive knowledge acquired from testimony. However for the counter-example to work the advocate of transmission—someone who endorses (TK) and (TW)—must see knowledge acquired from Bertha as testimonial. As things are described it could never be so: Bertha knows nothing about animals (in the set $\{a_1, a_2, \ldots, a_n\}$) and her testimony is a lie.

Lackey might push the idea that this case is nevertheless central, saying 'learning from Bertha's words falls under the general category picked out by paradigmatic instances of testimony', but surely it is at least part of our conception of central cases that they involve others telling us what they know to be the case?[33] (Recall the connections between knowing and telling outlined in 3.3.) Yet this is something that Bertha is not in a position to do. However, if any knowledge gained from Bertha's testimony is not testimonial, then what this case does establish is that the acquisition of testimonial knowledge is responsive to defeaters that need not undercut the acquisition of inductive knowledge from testimony. Again: to recognize that testimonial knowledge is associated with distinctive defeat relations is to recognize that it is an epistemically distinctive kind.

Cases three and four are structurally the same, where case four is 'serious student'.[34] Bartholomew is persuaded by scepticism, Audrey asks him directions to the nearest café and he tells her what he would know to be the case were he not in the grip of sceptical doubt. Letting 'p' refer to Bartholomew's statement of the whereabouts of the café, Bartholomew is

[33] Lackey (2008), p. 56.   [34] Lackey (2008), p. 61.

not justified in believing that p given that he believes that he is a brain-in-a-vat, so does not know that p. Nevertheless, Bartholomew's testimony puts Audrey in a position to know that p. So Lackey concludes the necessity claim is false.

It is possible, like in the previous case, to explain Audrey's coming to know that p on the basis of her possessing evidence for Bartholomew's reliability. However, if this is to be a counter-example, this cannot be the nature of Audrey's knowledge. Rather, we must think both that Audrey's knowledge that p is testimonial, in the sense intended by those who advocate transmission, and that Bartholomew does *not* know that p. However, there is space to argue that this conjunction is only delivered by a failure to recognize the nature of testimonial knowledge. For suppose that Audrey's knowledge is testimonial in the required sense; if we suppose this, we are supposing that Bartholomew tells Audrey something he knows to be case, and so we are supposing that he *really knows* that p. This is not implausible; after all, since Hume, it has been observed that sceptical doubts tend to evaporate outside the study (or classroom). However, if we suppose that Bartholomew is *genuinely troubled*, and genuinely believes he is a brain-in-a-vat, then we must recognize that he tells Audrey that p despite thinking that p is false, or despite thinking that for all he knows, that p is false; from his perspective, what he says is just a stab in the dark. But then it seems that the only way Audrey could get to know that p is if she has independently good reasons for believing that p, such as that supplied by her belief that Bartholomew's word is reliable. Whilst Audrey acquires knowledge from testimony, on this understanding, her knowledge is not distinctively testimonial, so the case is not a counter-example to transmission.

3.7 Conclusion

The reductive theory of testimony, I have argued, fails in two respects. First, its account of when an audience is warranted in the uptake of testimony is wrong. This failure is *not* one of sufficiency: it is certainly true that if an audience has an inductive argument to the conclusion that a piece of testimony is true, then the audience is warranted in the uptake of that bit of testimony. The failure is one of necessity: there are more ways of being warranted in the uptake of testimony than the reductive theory would allow. In particular, the attitude of trust can warrant the uptake of testimony. In not recognizing that our warrant for the uptake of testimony can come from trust, the reductive theory over-intellectualizes our relationship to testimony. We do not always base uptake on the belief that what is told is true, sometimes we merely trust a speaker for the truth. It is a characteristic of testimony that a speaker can tell an audience what she knows and the audience can believe her and not merely what she says. In acquiring belief on this basis, what explains the knowledge the audience acquires is not the audience's own proprietary justification but the fact that speaker knows what she tells him. Through testimony we can, as speakers, tell what we know and we can, as audiences, get to know what speakers know. Thus the second failing of the reductive theory is that it is wrong to regard all transmission principles as false.

These two failings of the reductive theory are connected. The reason why the reductive theory has a restrictive conception of what warrants uptake is that it assumes it to be this body of warrant—the audience's own proprietary justification—that also explains the audience's acquisition of knowledge from testimony. Correlatively, part of the explanation of why trust can warrant uptake will be that in trusting others for the truth we put ourselves in a position of depending on them for knowledge. This dependence is epistemic and not merely informational: we depend on their knowing or being warranted in believing what they tell us. Hence the transmission principles (TK) and (TW) state that an audience's acquisition of testimonial knowledge and testimonially warranted belief necessitate that a prior speaker in the chain of testimony knows or is warranted in belief. One explanation of why these principles hold could then be as follows. Suppose, with the reductive theory, that evidence can warrant a belief if and only if the belief is based on the evidence. Given this supposition, (TK) and (TW) would be true if the warranted uptake of testimony were a mechanism for basing belief on the speaker's evidence. Call this the *evidential explanation of transmission*. It explains transmission because insofar as it is the extended body of warrant that thereby determines the audience's epistemic standing, the speaker's knowledge or warrant, in effect, gets passed on or transmitted through testimony.

To illustrate this explanation of transmission consider cases 1 and 2; respectively, the cases where the husband is told that the flight he is taking with his wife is not boarding yet, and where the newspaper reader reads that the distance from the Earth to the Sun is some 150 million kilometres.

Consider case 2 first, and call the evidence that grounds the knowledge presented in the newspaper report E1. This evidence is the extended body of warrant. Since the uptake of this report is a paradigm case of knowledge acquisition, it must be possible to explain this in reductive terms. So the newspaper reader must have sufficiently good reasons to justify believing what he reads, and these reasons must be capable of explaining the reader's acquisition of knowledge. Call the evidence that explains the newspaper reader's uptake of this bit of testimony E2. This is the reader's own proprietary body of justification. In this case, it will be an inductive argument to the conclusion that what the newspaper reports is true. And call the reported fact p. What principles (TK) and (TW) propose is that the evidence that determines the warrant for the audience's belief that p is E1. Contrastingly, the reductive theory regards evidence E1 as essentially irrelevant to the newspaper reader's possession of knowledge; it is evidence E2 that determines both the newspaper reader's warrant for the uptake of this bit of testimony to p and the newspaper reader's warrant for believing that p.

The evidential explanation of transmission could be similarly applied to case 1. This case is differentiated in two ways. The extended body of evidence will be perceptual rather than scientific or theoretical. And what warrants the husband's uptake of testimony will be an attitude of trust. No doubt he has ample good reason to believe what his wife tells him, and could give an inductive argument to the truth of what she says. But it distorts, and over-intellectualizes, his reasons to claim that such an argument is his reason for uptake, which is rather that he simply trusts her in this matter.

4

The Non-Reductive Theory

According to the non-reductive theory, testimony is epistemically similar to perception and memory. It is similar, as a source of knowledge and warrant, in this respect: when an audience receives a bit of testimony to p, the audience has the kind of warrant for believing that p that does not presuppose or rest on the audience's warrant for anything that could be cited in an argument for p. There are, I suggested, two claims being made here.

First, the receipt of testimony to p can give an audience a unique warrant for believing that p. That is, testimony is *an epistemically distinctive source of knowledge and warrant*. Testimonial knowledge and warrant are not merely inductive: the warrant that supports an audience's testimonial belief does not reduce to the audience's own proprietary justification; rather, testimony transmits a speaker's knowledge and warrant. In the previous chapter, I argued for this claim.

Second, the receipt of testimony to p gives an audience a warrant for believing that p that does not presuppose or rest on anything the audience could cite in an argument for p. That is, we possess, as audiences, a *general entitlement to believe testimony, other things being equal*. What renders an audience warranted in the uptake of a piece of testimony is *not* the audience's own proprietary justification; rather, just as we do not need to justify our acceptance of perceptual appearances or what we appear to recollect, so we do not need to justify our uptake of testimony. We possess a general entitlement to believe the deliverances of these sources. In this chapter, I want to consider this claim, and the arguments that have been made for it.

The idea that we have a general entitlement to believe testimony can be presented as the claim that we are warranted in adopting a credulous attitude towards testimony. Moreover, that we have a psychological tendency towards such an attitude is often presented as a descriptive truth. Thomas Reid asserts:

> It is evident that, in the matter of testimony, the balance of human judgement is by nature inclined to the side of belief; and turns to that side of itself, when there is nothing put into the opposite scale.[1]

Thus Reid agrees with David Hume: we are credulous by nature. They disagree in that for Reid this *principle of credulity* is at once a descriptive and a normative epistemological claim: we are credulous *and* we are entitled to be so. Similarly, Michael Dummett makes the observation quoted that

> If someone tells me the way to the railway station, or asks me whether I've heard that the Foreign Secretary has just resigned, or informs me that the museum is closed today, I go through no process of reasoning, however swift, to arrive at the conclusion that he has spoken aright: my understanding of his utterance and my acceptance of his assertion are one.[2]

Dummett then adds that this feature of our receipt of testimony is not 'mere psychological phenomenon' but is also an 'epistemological principle'. However, what is important to a non-reductive theory of testimony is *not* this psychological claim. Maybe we are credulous, or maybe we are not. Maybe some of us are more credulous than others. These claims are interesting in themselves—and they bear on the claim I will make later that testimony is governed by a norm of trust—but a non-reductive theory of testimony is not defined by any commitment here. What defines the non-reductive theory is the normative claim that an audience's *warrant* for the uptake of testimony does not presuppose that the audience can cite an argument for the truth of testimony. On occasion, the uptake of a bit of testimony might be warranted only if such an argument is available to an audience. But this would be an occasion where the general entitlement to believe testimony was defeated and the audience needed an argument to defeat this defeat. Other things being equal, an audience need not argue for the truth of a piece of testimony to be warranted in its uptake, therefore our reasoning about the truth of testimony plays no *essential* justificatory role. *In this sense* one could say that the non-reductive theory proposes something like Reid's principle of credulity.

---

[1] Reid (1764), p. 197.   [2] Dummett (1993), p. 419.

What I now want to consider is what arguments can be presented for this general entitlement. In the next section I consider Sandford Goldberg's claim that it rests on reliability considerations. In the section after I consider one of Tony Coady's arguments for this entitlement that grounds it on Davidsonian considerations. Neither of these arguments, I contend, is successful. In the following two sections I consider the arguments put forward by Tyler Burge and John McDowell, which I take to be good. How the non-reductive theory of testimony fails is then the subject of the next chapter.

4.1 Goldberg's reliability-based entitlement

In his monograph on testimony, *Anti-Individualism: Mind and Language, Knowledge and Justification*, Sanford Goldberg defines the non-reductive theory of testimony in terms of the following thesis.

AR A hearer is justified in accepting (has the epistemic right to accept; is epistemically entitled to accept) another's testimony so long as there are no undefeated good reasons *not* to accept the testimony.[3]

Goldberg labels this thesis 'AR' for the 'anti-reductive' rather than non-reductive theory. The non-reductive theory can be defined *solely* in terms of the general entitlement stated in AR because *any* theory of testimony should accept the following two *anti-individualistic* theses.

AI-K When S's belief that p is formed through testimony whether S counts as knowing (as opposed to merely truly believing) p depends on facts regarding one (or more) of S's social peers.

AI-W When S's belief that p is formed through testimony the warrant (= total truth-conducive support) enjoyed by S's belief depends on facts regarding one (or more) of S's social peers.[4]

The transmission principles TK and TW, defined in 3.2, are 'anti-individualistic' in this sense in that they make the possession of testimonial knowledge and warrant depend on facts concerning someone else. More precisely, TK and TW respectively make an audience's possession of testimonial knowledge or testimonially warranted belief depend on some prior speaker *possessing knowledge or warrant*. In rejecting any

---

[3] Goldberg (2007), p. 144.   [4] Goldberg (2007), p. 141.

transmission principles, a reductive theory of testimony would equally reject Goldberg's anti-individualistic theses AI-K and AI-W *assuming* the 'facts regarding one (or more) of S's social peers' are *epistemic facts*; that is, facts about how things stand epistemically with S's social peers. All that matters epistemically, for the reductive theory, is an audience's own proprietary justification.

Goldberg thinks the reductive theory of testimony should accept the anti-individualistic theses AI-K and AI-W (ostensibly) because these theses are established by the following two comparative cases.

Case 24. Fred and Wilma have been married for three decades. Wilma knows Fred to be a highly reliable reporter. Fred tells Wilma that Professor Swinegarten was in attendance at the conference.

Case 25. Fred* and Wilma* are the same as Fred and Wilma (case 24) in every respect except Fred* wrongly suspects Wilma* of having an undue interest in Professor Swinegarten. So when Fred* tells Wilma* that Professor Swinegarten was in attendance at the conference he is lying. Wilma* notices nothing untoward, and it turns out that Fred*'s lie is true.[5]

There are two natural things to say about these cases, Goldberg contends. 'First, Wilma but not Wilma* counts as acquiring knowledge through the testimony she accepts. Second, . . . Wilma's and Wilma*'s beliefs differ along the warrant dimension as well.'[6] I agree because I think testimonial knowledge and warrant are governed by transmission principles TK and TW. But a reductive theorist would disagree. Wilma and Wilma* do *not* differ with respect to the warrant they possess, since both possess the same proprietary justification. And if Wilma and Wilma* differ with respect to the knowledge they possess, this is merely because case 25 is a Gettier case. These cases alone, therefore, do not suffice to establish Goldberg's anti-individualistic theses.

Goldberg finds a difference between Wilma and Wilma* with respect to warrant because he presupposes 'a reliabilist account of knowledge and justification'.[7] And, following this presupposition, he defines 'warrant' as 'the total truth-conducive (knowledge-relevant) support enjoyed by a belief, where this includes . . . *any* . . . *factors bearing on the likelihood that the belief is true*'.[8] Since the testimony of Fred* is unreliable when it comes to Professor Swinegarten, given his suspicions of Wilma*, the factors that

---

[5] Goldberg (2007), p. 138. My wording.   [6] Goldberg (2007), p. 139.
[7] Goldberg (2007), p. 133.   [8] Goldberg (2007), p. 139. My italics.

bear on the truth of Wilma★'s belief will be different to those that bear on the truth of Wilma's. So the two will enjoy different warrant for their beliefs that Professor Swinegarten was at the conference, on Goldberg's understanding of warrant. However, this conclusion—the anti-individu-alistic thesis about warrant or AI-W—is thereby established by Goldberg's definition of warrant rather than by comparative cases 24 and 25. If the reductive theorist understands warrant differently, he can reject this thesis.

It is Goldberg's view that reductive and non-reductive theories are differentiated solely in terms of the answer each gives to the question of our warrant for testimonial uptake. Non-reductive theory proposes an entitlement to testimony, which in Goldberg's view takes the form of AR, and reductive theory rejects this entitlement. This makes sense given the presumption that any theory should accept the anti-individualistic theses AI-K and AI-W since—by claiming that testimonial knowledge and warrant are determined not by how things are with an audience but by how things are with a prior speaker—these theses, in effect, fix an answer to the question of the warrant of belief.

From this starting point Goldberg's argument for an entitlement to accept testimony runs: AR is motivated by the fact that this hypothesis preserves the following theoretical claim.

JES One who is justified in accepting a piece of understood testimony *ipso facto* acquires the sort of belief that enjoys the expanded (distinctly testimonial) episte-mic support characteristic of testimonial belief and knowledge.[9]

The hypothesis of an entitlement to testimony, stated by AR, preserves JES provided: (i) a reliabilist account is given of epistemic warrant and (ii) the 'no defeaters' clause allows factual defeat, where a factual defeater is a true proposition that would render the subject unwarranted if believed. Thus, referring to case 25, Wilma★ is *not entitled* to Fred★'s testimony about Professor Swinegarten because there is a fact about her situation—Fred★'s unreliability on this matter—that defeats this entitlement.[10] Given these

---

[9] Goldberg (2007), p. 146.

[10] Moreover, Goldberg claims that were the entitlement not to be defeated by factual defeaters it would be 'obviously false'. Goldberg (2007), p. 159. He then cites Burge's Acceptance Principle (see 4.3 below) in support, noting that it contains 'no "awareness" restriction'. Goldberg (2007), p. 160. This is unfortunate since Burge notes that '[t]he force of "unless there are stronger reasons not to do so" is to indicate that the person's entitlement is prima facie. The principle says that the entitlement holds unless there are stronger reasons (*available to the person*) that override it.' Burge (1997), p. 22, n.4, my italics.

two provisos 'in any case where a hearer is AR-justified in accepting a piece of testimony, the testimony-itself will be based on some non-negligible degree of distinctly epistemic support'.[11] Thus AR entails JES.

By contrast, the reductive view implies the falsity of JES. In my opinion it does so trivially because it denies that there is such a thing as 'distinctly testimonial support', where this is understood by Goldberg as 'the support provided by the testimony itself (as opposed to the hearer's reasons for accepting the testimony)'.[12] For the reductive theory all warrant comes by way of an audience's own proprietary justification, which states the audience's reasons for the uptake of a piece of testimony. However, suppose it is granted that cases 24 and 25 have established the anti-individualistic theses AI-K and AI-W, and with them the idea that there is distinctly testimonial support, so that the 'reductive view' is defined, as Goldberg defines it, solely by its denial of AR.[13] The problem with *this view*, Goldberg argues, is that it (non-trivially) implies the falsity of JES through allowing *double dissociation*. That is, it allows that 'there can be cases of justified testimonial belief without any further distinctly testimonial support; and there can be cases of unjustified testimonial belief with distinctly testimonial support that would have been sufficient for the acquisition of testimonial knowledge'.[14]

This may be illustrated. Consider case 25. Wilma★ has a good proprietary justification for believing that Professor Swinegarten was at the conference, but there is no warrant transmitted by Fred★'s testimony: there is no body of extended warrant. And consider the mirror of this: case 26, which combines Goldberg's cases 24 and 25.

Case 26. Fred★★ is exactly like Fred in every respect. He innocently tells Wilma★★ that Professor Swinegarten was at the conference and in doing so he both knows this fact and intends to inform Wilma★★ of it. Wilma★★, however, is anxious and mistakenly believes that Fred★★ is like Fred★ and suspects her feelings towards Swinegarten. So when Fred★★ tells her the truth about Swingarten she presumes an agenda and takes his telling to be a lie.

---

[11]   Goldberg (2007), p. 149.
[12]   Goldberg (2007), p. 145.
[13]   This 'reductive view' occupies the theoretical space of the trust view I argue for. And Goldberg cites me as a 'defender' of the reductive view. Goldberg (2007), p.144. I think this mischaracterizes things.
[14]   Goldberg (2007), p. 145.

Wilma★★ lacks a supporting proprietary justification for believing Fred★★'s testimony, but Fred★★'s testimony is supported by an extended body of warrant. If it is allowed that there is distinctly testimonial warrant and yet AR is rejected, the consequence is double dissociation. This entails the falsity of JES. But a desideratum is that JES be preserved. So once it is allowed that there is distinctly testimonial support, AR must be hypothesized: we have an entitlement to testimony, other things being equal.

The obvious problem with this argument is that JES is false, and it cannot be a desideratum on a theory that it preserves a falsehood. It is false precisely because of the phenomenon of double dissociation. Cases like 25 illustrate that an audience can be justified in the uptake of a piece of testimony and yet end up believing a lie (which in this case happens to be true but such good fortune is extraordinary). Moreover, it is a virtue not a failing of a theory of testimony that it allows for double dissociation. Our epistemic situation involves such complexities. It is not uncommon for us to have good reasons for believing a lie, or for us to have good reasons to be suspicious of an honestly told truth. It might make theory simpler to preserve JES but that is no virtue if our reality is complex. These complexities cannot be plausibly ignored. Thus consider case 26. Wilma★★ has a doxastic defeater for her entitlement to Fred★★'s testimony. This entails that she would be unwarranted in believing Fred★★'s testimony and would be so 'even though there is plenty of evidence "upstream in the chain of informants"'.[15] But this is a case of double dissociation as Goldberg defines it.

The only way this double dissociation could be avoided by Goldberg is by making the entitlement stated by AR conditional on an audience *monitoring* for defeaters. This he does, amending AR to AR+:

AR+ A hearer H is epistemically justified in accepting (has the epistemic right to accept; is epistemically entitled to accept) another's testimony on occasion O so long as (i) there are no undefeated good (doxastic, factual or normative) reasons *not* to accept the testimony, and (ii) on O H's acceptance was the outcome of a process that exhibited a 'counterfactual sensitivity' to the presence of defeaters (which, given (i), turns up no defeaters on O).[16]

And then hypothesizing that case 26 could never happen: Wilma★★'s monitoring would ensure that she would pick up on the factual defeater

---

[15] Goldberg (2007), p. 145.   [16] Goldberg (2007), p. 168.

of her doxastic defeater, namely that she would be responsive to the fact that Fred✸✸ was actually innocently and honestly telling her the truth. However, irrespective of whether we possess the capacity to monitor, it is surely implausible to hypothesize that we have such a finely tuned capacity. For what this hypothesis implies is that an audience could never reject testimony on the basis of mistaken beliefs. But if an audience could reject testimony on the basis of mistaken beliefs, as in case 26, Goldberg must allow double dissociation.

Once JES is dropped as a desideratum on theory choice, Goldberg's argument for an entitlement to testimony, which in his view takes the form of AR (or AR+), fails.[17] However, Goldberg's view of testimony allows a simple argument for such an entitlement: an argument that is driven by a natural empirical conception of testimony rather than claims about the correct shape of epistemological theory. The hypothesis that we possess an entitlement to testimony, Goldberg claims, is advanced against 'the backdrop of two particular empirical assumptions'.[18] First, the uptake of testimony involves *monitoring* the speaker and testimonial situation. Monitoring is not a matter of reasoning but, as just quoted, a matter of demonstrating 'a "counterfactual sensitivity" to the presence of defeaters'.[19] Second, the process of testimonial uptake, which has monitoring as a sub-process, is reliable. The simple argument for our possession of an entitlement to testimony then runs: suppose that these two empirical assumptions are true. And suppose that epistemic warrant is merely a matter of reliability. If the process of testimonial uptake is reliable, then the beliefs that are output by this process are warranted. So the uptake of testimony is epistemically warranted. So, otherwise put, we are entitled to our uptake of testimony, as AR states.

The problem with this argument is that is rests on the two stated empirical assumptions.[20] And both of these assumptions are arguably

---

[17] Moreover, JES is also the major premise in Goldberg's argument for implausible anti-individualistic theses concerning justification and rationality, AI-J and AI-R. See Goldberg (2007), p. 150 and p. 194 respectively.

[18] Goldberg (2007), p. 148.

[19] Goldberg offers no further definition. But he provides an analogy: monitoring is analogous to having a built-in buzzer that goes off whenever one confronts unreliable testimony. See Goldberg (2007), pp. 166–8. Thus, if Wilma✸✸ both possessed and knew she possessed such a buzzer, she could know her doxastic defeater was factually defeated because her buzzer hadn't gone off.

[20] And an implausible view of epistemic warrant, but let that go.

false. First, it is far from clear whether we actually do monitor speakers and the testimonial situation. Recall that many non-reductive theorists take our response to testimony to be essentially credulous. Moreover, I will argue later that our uptake of testimony is often based on trust, and trust demonstrates a wilful insensitivity to defeaters. It is, if you like, an *anti-monitoring* attitude. And, I will argue, there are social norms prescribing that we take this attitude towards testimony. These claims are advanced as at least partly empirical.[21] Second, even if, or when, we do monitor testimony, it is far from clear that actual processes of monitoring are reliable. A factual defeater of AR would be that a bit of testimony was a lie. So Goldberg's empirical assumption entails that we demonstrate a reliable ability to discern lies. However, all the empirical evidence suggests that we are poor at distinguishing liars from truth-tellers. (I cited some of this evidence when first considering the hypothesis that we have a faculty for monitoring testimony in 2.1.3.) This is not to say that testimony is unreliable as a source of belief. Rather, it is to say that its reliability is not established by any faculty we have for monitoring. So the hypothesis that we possess such a faculty cannot ground a reliability-based entitlement to accept testimony.

4.2 Coady's justification of our reliance on testimony

In chapter 9 of his ground-breaking monograph *Testimony: A Philosophical Study*, C. A. J. Coady sets out to provide 'some justification or philosophical rational for what is in fact our very extensive trust in testimony'.[22] This justification amounts to an argument for our possessing a general entitlement to believe testimony. The exact form of this justification is debatable; I give what I think is its best reconstruction.[23]

The major premise in Coady's justification of our trust in testimony is Davidson's idea that interpretation is guided by the principle of charity and so proceeds by an interpreter optimizing agreement between himself and a speaker. This could be illustrated. Suppose that a radical interpreter sees a

---

[21] The psychological literature supports the idea that we are disposed to be credulous. See Gilbert, Krull, and Malone (1990) and Gilbert, Tafarodi, and Malone (1993).

[22] Coady (1992), p. 152.

[23] For alternative reconstructions and criticisms see Graham (2000b) and Fricker (1995).

rabbit scurry and a speaker respond by uttering 'Gavagai'. The interpreter will judge the cause of the utterance to be the scurrying rabbit and so assign the utterance the truth conditions of his sentence 'Rabbit'. In this way interpreter and speaker are put in agreement. Suppose, on another occasion, the speaker utters 'Gavagai' in response to a trotting wart-hog. This disagreement generates a dilemma for the radical interpreter: either he is wrong in his judgement that the speaker held true what she uttered; or the speaker has an obviously false belief; or he doesn't understand this, and therefore previous, utterances of 'Gavagai'. In resolving such difficulties a radical interpreter is guided by 'hunches about the effects of social conditioning, and of course common-sense, or scientific knowledge of explicable error'.[24] So if a radical interpreter succeeds in producing a theory that makes a speaker's utterances intelligible, this theory will have optimized agreement between the interpreter and speaker. A condition on understanding the utterances of a speaker, therefore, is that by and large what the speaker holds true an interpreter must equally hold true.

The first part of Coady's argument, I think, then runs: (1) Interpretation puts a speaker and an interpreter mostly in agreement as to what is held true; (2) when a speaker makes a report, this will, by and large, be a report of something that the speaker holds true; therefore (3) most of what speakers report, an interpreter will accept as true.

The second part of Coady's justification then argues that most of what the interpreter accepts as true will be true. The move here is again familiar from Davidson. Premise (1) states the principle of charity. This governing principle of radical interpretation follows from radical interpretation's methodologically basic evidence being those cases where a speaker's utterance seems to be an obvious response to something salient in the environment. These cases produce agreement because an interpreter assigns truth conditions on the basis of what is judged to be the salient cause of utterance. In this way, radical interpretation makes the salient objects and events that cause a speaker's utterance of sentences held true 'constitute the truth conditions, and hence the meanings, of [these] sentences'.[25] From this Davidson concludes that belief is by its nature veridical

---

[24] Davidson (1975), p. 175. Sometimes a radical interpreter will be forced to attribute a false belief rather than alter the axioms of his theory and so 'the methodology of interpretation is, in this respect, nothing but epistemology seen in the mirror of meaning'. Davidson (1975), p. 169.

[25] Davidson (1996), p. 275.

because the content of a belief, in the methodologically most basic cases, is largely determined by the circumstantial causes of that belief.

To illustrate this Davidson supposes an omniscient interpreter, who proceeds, despite his omniscience, in the manner of the ordinary interpreter, optimizing agreement between his beliefs and those he interprets.[26] Since the omniscient interpreter's beliefs are objectively true, a fallible speaker's beliefs are seen to be objectively true by and large.

Using this notion of an omniscient interpreter, Coady's argument could be extended with the premise (4) if what a speaker says is intelligible, then the omniscient interpreter will likewise accept most of the speaker's reports as true. Thus (5) since what the omniscient interpreter accepts as true is true, most of the speaker's reports will thereby be true. So the intelligibility of testimony is thereby a priori evidence that testimony is largely true. And we are, Coady has previously argued, very limited in our ability to empirically justify our acceptance of testimony—this is the 'observational problem' discussed in 2.1. So this a priori reason must suffice, other things being equal, to warrant our uptake of testimony without supporting empirical reasons. We must be entitled to the uptake of testimony, other things being equal.

Now it should be noted that Coady does not extend his justification of testimony this far because of worries about the notion of an omniscient interpreter.[27] However, if the argument stops at its intermediate conclusion (3), then it is questionable whether it is of any use to a non-reductive theorist. All that is established with (3) is that the mere intelligibility of testimony implies that we by and large believe it. However, that we have such a disposition to be credulous is a claim that is compatible with reductive theories of testimony; indeed, it is Hume's view that we are inclined to credulously believe what we understand. So it is compatible with the view that we do not have any entitlement to believe testimony. However, putting this infelicity aside, Coady's argument fails in three crucial ways even in its first part.

---

[26] See Davidson (1983 and 1977b).

[27] See Coady (1992), pp. 174–5. I take Davidson's use of the omniscient interpreter to be merely a heuristic: omniscience, as Coady points out, is too problematic a notion for it to be otherwise. Compare Foley and Fumerton (1985) and Vermazen (1983) for different interpretations and criticisms.

First, what is the epistemic status of premise (2) that most of a speaker's reports will be sincere? Presumably this is not intended to be an empirical claim. However, if it is not an empirical claim, then it is not clear what justification Coady would have for making it. It certainly does not follow from Davidson's claims about what is necessary for interpretation. All that is required for radical interpretation to succeed is that an interpreter can fathom what a speaker would report to be true, *if sincere*. It follows that 'a speaker who wishes to be understood cannot systematically deceive his would be interpreters about when he assents to sentences—that is, holds them true'.[28] But this is not to say that most of a speaker's utterances will be sincere reports. 'Lies, commands, stories, irony, if they are detected as attitudes, can reveal whether a speaker holds his sentence to be true.'[29]

One possible argument for premise (2) suggests itself, which is that the sincerity of reports follows from their being testimony. That is, Coady, at this point in the argument, could appeal to his definition of the speech act of testifying.

A speaker S testifies by making some statement p if and only if

1. His stating that p is evidence that p and is offered as evidence that p
2. S has the relevant competence, authority, or credentials to state truly that p.
3. S's statement that p is relevant to some disputed or unresolved question (which may, or may not be, p?) and is directed to those who are in need of evidence on the matter.[30]

Moreover, if this were the argument for (2), there would be no need for the second part of the argument that invoked the omniscient interpreter. As Coady understand it, the evidence condition on a statement being testimony requires an objective connection between it and what it is evidence for.[31] So it follows that by and large most instances of testimony will be both sincere and true. Of course, the problem with this argument is that it merely shifts the epistemic issue. This observation was made by Elizabeth Fricker in her review of Coady's book.

If the authority of the testifier were built into the definition of testimony, it might seem plausible that there is a general epistemic right to believe what is 'testified' to

---

[28] Davidson (1983), p. 315.   [29] Davidson (1973), p. 135.
[30] Coady (1992), p. 42.   [31] See Coady (1992), p. 44.

one; but this would simply pass the epistemic buck, from the hearer's point of view, to the question: is what I have just received a piece of 'testimony' or not?[32]

Moreover, it follows that speakers could not testify about 'UFO sightings, alien encounters, spontaneous human combustion, and the like'.[33] They could not do so because such statements cannot be evidence for their truth in the sense Coady requires. But we clearly think that speakers can testify to such things, and it is the fact that speakers can do this—that testimony can be such a poor guide to the truth—that presses the epistemic question of what warrant we have for the uptake of testimony.[34]

Second, premises (1) and (2) do not suffice for the intermediate conclusion (3). That an interpreter A will believe most of a speaker S's reports does not follow from A and S being mostly in agreement in what they believe and most of what S says being reports. It does not follow because S might be particularly taciturn and the few reports S does make might be made in jest; S could be Davidson's perennial kidder. This would not damage the intelligibility of what S says, provided only that A is not conned.[35] What follows from (1) and (2) is merely that most of S's reports will be held true by A *insofar as most of S's reports are sincere or held true by S*. This follows given that S's reports are testimony in Coady's sense. But, as just observed, understanding testimony in this way simply obscures the epistemological issues, which in this case centre on the question of whether a speaker does indeed hold true what is reported.

However, third, even if speakers could be presumed to be sincere there remains a problem with inferring (3) from (1) and (2). The problem is Davidson's observation that 'What is shared does not in general call for comment; it is too dull, trite or familiar to stand notice.'[36] However, on

---

[32] Fricker (1995), p. 397.

[33] Lackey (2008), p. 17.

[34] Coady offers an a priori argument against the reductive view in Coady (1992) ch. 4, which duplicates material from Coady (1973). Roughly, the argument runs: the reductive theory requires it to be possible for reports to be largely false; but on this supposition there would be no institution of reporting; and clearly we have such an institution. Now I don't think the reductive theory does require this. All it requires is explicable falsehood. But this suggests another argument for premise (2): since we have an institution of reporting, reports must be largely true. Of course, the problem with this argument is parallel. It merely generates the epistemological question, is this seeming report actually a report? Do we really have the institution of reporting? See Graham (2000b).

[35] Davidson (1974a), p. 145.

[36] Davidson (1977a), p. 199. This sentence is from a passage quoted by Coady (1992), p. 156.

Coady's definition, testimony is not the presentation of the dull and familiar, it is statements 'relevant to some disputed and unresolved question'.[37] So even if speaker and interpreter may agree in most of what they believe, it does not follow that they will agree on what the speaker reports. Certainly, it could be conceded that there will be some reports—what Williams calls 'plain truths'—whose truth is visible for all to agree on, but the epistemological issues start with reports whose truth is not so plain.[38] Moreover, the problem here is not simply a function of Coady's particular definition of testimony. The problem is that the epistemologically relevant case is when a speaker S reports something that an interpreter A does *not* already believe, so that agreement marks the *acquisition of a testimonial belief*. In this case some argument is required as to why A's prior agreement with S itself gives A reason for believing what S reports in this case. After all, disputants no doubt share much background belief in common. This is just to say that (1) and (2) alone do not suffice for (3).

What is at issue here is the bigger problem of extracting epistemological conclusions from Davidson's use of the principle of charity. This problem could be presented in Gricean terms. Ordinary conversation, Grice claims, is guided by a maxim of quantity dictating that a speaker should make his conversational contribution as informative as required but not more so.[39] So in conversation if a speaker presents something as true, then the speaker should presume that what is presented is *not* 'dull, trite or familiar' because to state something obvious is to implicate that it is not obvious.[40] In intelligibly presenting that p as true—in giving testimony to p—a speaker should presume to be informative.[41] Coady is sensitive to this thought when defining testimony, which, again, must be 'relevant to some disputed or unresolved question'. So whilst it may be that the intelligibility of

---

[37]   Coady (1992), p. 42.

[38]   See Williams (2002), pp. 45ff.

[39]   Grice (1967), p. 26.

[40]   Catherine Elgin, in discussing Coady's argument, gives the nice example of two captions at an art museum where the first says '*Madonna and Child*, Giotto' and the second says '*Madonna and Child*, attributed to Giotto'. The first caption attributes the work and the second in stating that it does this implicates that there is something suspect about the attribution. See Elgin (2002).

[41]   Obviously there are exceptions and speakers can and do state the obvious—as when a speaker draws attention to something salient in the mutual environment in order to strike up a conversation. But then Grice brackets the maxim of quantity: 'Make your contribution as informative as required (for the current purposes of the exchange).' Grice (1967), p. 27.

testimony to p implies that its speaker and interpreter must largely believe the same things, insofar as there is the presumption that testimony be informative, there is the presumption that speaker and audience *do not both believe that p.* The truth of this presumption is then the epistemological starting point for asking what warrants an audience's uptake of testimony. Moreover, this epistemic question remains open even if it is true that intelligibility implies a speaker cannot systematically deceive an interpreter about what she holds true, where this is implied by Davidson's use of the principle of charity. It remains open because this inability to deceive a successful interpreter is compatible with the interpreter's not knowing whether the speaker holds true what she presents as such on any given occasion. Further appeal to Davidson at this juncture draws a blank because he offers no account of how particular beliefs are warranted. As quoted, how an interpreter resolves such interpretative difficulties as those generated by undetected insincerity or error is simply left to the interpreter's 'common sense'.[42]

4.3 Burge's Acceptance Principle

Ordinarily, communication is not radical interpretation; we do not ordinarily need to work out what a speaker is saying. Rather, Tyler Burge claims, understanding 'seems, in normal cases, to be epistemically immediate, once the capacity for understanding is in place'.[43] And *given that* a capacity for understanding is in place, *we are entitled to presume that we understand what we seem to understand.* With this entitlement Burge draws an epistemic consequence from the principle of charity that Davidson does not. To show this consider the example of radical interpretation given in 4.2, where a radical interpreter has assigned the utterance 'Gavagai' the truth conditions of his sentence 'Rabbit' and then a speaker responds to a perceptually salient wart-hog by uttering 'Gavagai'. If the radical interpreter were advanced in the process of constructing a theory of interpretation, changing the postulated interpretation of 'Gavagai' would be costly: though it would achieve agreement in this instance it would

---

[42] And in general Davidson is not interested in giving an account of our sources of knowledge; our beliefs just happen to be caused in the way that they are caused and warrant is a matter of relations between beliefs. See Davidson (1991).

[43] Burge (1997), p. 30.

produce disagreement where there was previously none. So given certain advancement in theory construction, if the process of optimizing agreement in accordance with the principle of charity is to succeed, a radical interpreter must be entitled to presume the correctness of postulated axioms. If the interpreter were not entitled to this presumption, interpretation would become impossible. However, Burge claims that given this entitlement to presume that one understands what one seems to, others' utterances become *a source of information rather than an object of interpretation*. Thus, the capacity for understanding changes the *epistemology* of communication: it ceases to be grounded on the principle of charity and is rather grounded on, what Burge calls, the *Acceptance Principle*.

Burge's Acceptance Principle is a non-reductive uptake principle stating a general entitlement to believe testimony.

A person is entitled to accept as true something that is presented as true and that is intelligible to him, unless there are stronger reasons not to do so.[44]

By 'to accept as true' Burge just means 'to believe' (he does not draw the distinction between accepting and believing that I do). What the Acceptance Principle states is an audience is entitled to form belief on the basis of accepting the content of a piece of testimony; that is, the uptake of testimony is entitled, other things being equal. To see how Burge argues for this principle, it is important to get clear on Burge's notion of entitlement, which is key to his epistemology.

For Burge entitlement is one type of epistemic warrant with justification being the other. Justification is warrant by reasons that are available to the believer. A central characteristic of entitlement, by contrast, is that it 'is warrant that need not be fully conceptually accessible, even on reflection, to the warranted individual'.[45]

The distinction between justification and entitlement is this: Although both have positive force in rationally supporting a propositional attitude or cognitive practice, and in constituting an epistemic right to it, entitlements are epistemic rights or warrants that need not be understood by or even accessible to the subject.[46]

---

[44] Burge (1993), p. 467. Burge states that this should be read '*A person is [a priori] entitled to accept a proposition that is [taken to be] presented as true and that is [seemingly] intelligible to him, unless there are stronger reasons not to do so.*' Where this 'entitlement holds unless there are stronger reasons (available to the person) that override it'. Burge (1997), p. 22, n.4.

[45] Burge (2003), p. 504.

[46] Burge (1993), p. 458.

Paul Boghossian suggests that the distinction Burge is making here is one of intellectual sophistication.

> Philosophers are often in a position of articulating a warrant for an ordinary belief that the man in the street would not understand. If we insist that a person counts as justified only if they are aware of the reason that warrants their belief, then we will simply have to find another term for the kind of warrant that ordinary folk often have and that philosophers seek to articulate. Tyler Burge has called it an 'entitlement'.[47]

Certainly, epistemology needs a notion of entitlement, on Burge's view, at least in part because '[c]hildren and higher non-human animals do not have *reasons* for their perceptual beliefs'.[48] However, the distinction between justification and entitlement is not a matter of intellectual sophistication. Rather, it is a distinction between two different ways in which a belief may be warranted.

A belief can be warranted because a believer has access to a set of premises that make it (subjectively) probably true. And a belief can be warranted because a believer acquired it in a way that can be justified irrespective of whether the believer had such reasons. Epistemic warrant may be 'an entitlement that consists in the status of operating in an appropriate way in accord with the norms of reason'.[49] As Boghossian is right to point out, it is philosophers who articulate justifying descriptions of a belief forming process that show that it 'accords with the norms of reason' to form beliefs this way. However, what matters is not the fact that this is what philosophers, as opposed to men in the street, do but what philosophers do by doing this. And that is to identify special sources of knowledge and warrant. Crucially, in proposing the entitlement stated by the Acceptance Principle Burge is proposing that testimony is a faculty of knowledge comparable to perception and memory.

To say that one is *entitled* to accept testimony is to say that this way of acquiring belief—the uptake of testimony—can be justified. The justification Burge offers is highly abstract. It consists of a series of stacked entitlements. The entitlement, encountered above, to presume that if a message seems intelligible, then it is intelligible. An entitlement to presume that if a message is intelligible, then it has a rational source. An entitlement to

[47] Boghossian (1996), p. 387.   [48] Burge (2003), p. 528.
[49] Burge (1996), p. 93.

presume that if a message seems to be presented as true, then it is presented as true. And an entitlement to presume that if something is presented as true by a rational source then it is true. All of these entitlements are defeasible—they all hold unless they are defeated by stronger reasons *available* to the entitled person. But when these entitlements are not defeated they carry to give the Acceptance Principle: the entitlement to the uptake of what is seemingly intelligibly presented as true.

This argument for the Acceptance Principle rests on the crucial entitlement to presume that *if something is presented as true by a rational source, then it is true*. Thus Burge observes 'A *presupposition* [*not* a consequence] of the Acceptance Principle is that one is entitled not to bring one's source's sincerity or justification into question, in the absence of reasons to the contrary.'[50] However, any worry about a non-reductive entitlement will focus precisely on the fact that speakers can be insincere and sincerely get things wrong. So unless this crucial entitlement can be supported, Burge's justification of the Acceptance Principle will not persuade anyone who worries about whether the correct answer to the question of our warrant for the uptake of testimony is given by a general entitlement like the Acceptance Principle.

Burge acknowledges this problem of lies in his own inimitable way.

The straight-line route from the prima facie intelligibility of a presentation-as-true to prima facie rational characteristics of the source to prima facie acceptability (truth) of the presentation, is threatened by the fact that certain aspects of *rationality* (rational lying) may go *counter* to true presentations. So why should rationality, especially in another person, be a sign of truth?[51]

Now the general strategy for justifying the Acceptance Principle is to suppose that we must be entitled to rely on memory and then extend this assumption: 'rational sources' are equally a 'resource for reason'.[52] The fact that it can be rational to lie then suggests that testimony is fundamentally

---

[50] Burge (1993), p. 468. My emphasis.   [51] Burge (1993), p. 474.

[52] The justification of the Acceptance Principle, Burge claims, takes the following form. '*A person is entitled to accept a proposition that is presented as true and that is intelligible to him, unless there are stronger reasons not to do so, because it is prima facie preserved (received) from a rational source, or resource for reason; reliance on rational sources—or resources for reason—is, other things equal, necessary to the function of reason.*' Burge (1993), p. 469. Thus, we are entitled to rely on memory, a 'resource for reason' and 'The Acceptance Principle is an extension of this assumption: we are rationally entitled to rely on interlocution because we may presume that it has a rational source.' Burge (1993), p. 470.

different to memory; it threatens this argumentative strategy by implying that we are not entitled to presume something is true *merely* from the fact that it is presented as true *by testimony*.

Burge's response to this problem is effectively an assertion of his idea of epistemic entitlement.

One of reason's primary functions is that of presenting truth, independently of special personal interests. Lying is sometimes rational in the sense that it is in the liar's best interests. But lying occasions a disunity among the functions of reason. It conflicts with one's reason's transpersonal function of presenting the truth, independently of special personal interests. . . . Reason has a function in providing guidance to truth, in presenting and promoting truth without regard to individual interest. . . . Unless there is a reason to think that a rational source is rationally disunified—in the sense that individual interest is occasioning conflict with the transpersonal function of reason—one is rationally entitled to abstract from individual interest in receiving something presented as true by such a source.[53]

Elizabeth Fricker argues that this defence of the crux entitlement 'involves an equivocation in the notion of rationality'.[54] The intelligibility of testimony secures the entitlement to presume its source is rational in the sense of being a 'subject of propositional attitudes'.[55] Whilst this defence requires the source be rational in the sense of being 'wholly impartial and disinterested'.[56] Now it is true that there are different notions of rationality involved here, but there is no equivocation. Rather, there is the change of perspective that comes with considering our epistemic entitlements.

To see the point Burge is making recall case 3, where a nervous buyer receives a vendor's testimony that the used car he is considering 'only had one previous lady owner'. Suppose that this is the lie it appears to be. This lie might be perfectly rational. It would be so if the vendor's overall desire in this situation was to make a sale, and if the vendor both believed that the nervous buyer needed persuasion and that telling him this would persuade him. Given this background of belief and desire, the (practically) rational thing to do would be to tell this lie. And, in general, to understand a lie as rational one needs to consider the liar's perspective because the rationality of lying depends on the liar's particular background propositional attitudes. By contrast, Burge's claim, in the passage just quoted, is that to understand the presentation of a truth as rational *no such relativization is needed*. It is not

[53] Burge (1993), p. 475.   [54] Fricker (2006), p. 78.
[55] Fricker (2006), p. 77.   [56] Fricker (2006), p. 78.

needed because from a certain perspective—what Burge calls 'God's eye' view—the presentation of truth is a primary function of reason.[57] And this is the perspective that the philosopher takes when articulating a justification of a certain way of forming belief, which constitutes our entitlement to beliefs formed this way. So when considering our *entitlement* to rely on rational sources, the deliverances of a rational source can be equated with the deliverance of reason, other things being equal. Given this equation, the crux entitlement follows. Unless there is a reason to think that a rational source is 'rationally disunified', one is entitled to presume that what is presented as true is true.[58]

The Acceptance Principle provides an account of our warrant for the uptake of testimony. It does not yet explain our acquisition of knowledge from testimony. Burge makes this point by analogy with memory. We are similarly entitled to believe a proposition that we seem to remember but the truth of this proposition would not be enough for present knowledge. What is required for present knowledge is that we previously knew what we presently seem to remember. Memory is not a source of knowledge but a way of *preserving* knowledge, and the same is true of testimony.

If the recipient depends on interlocution for knowledge, the recipient's knowledge depends on the source's having knowledge as well. . . . The recipient's own proprietary entitlement to rely on interlocution is insufficient by itself to underwrite knowledge.[59]

The Acceptance Principle states an audience's 'proprietary' entitlement, and this entitlement is insufficient for knowledge because testimonial knowledge is supported by the extended body of warrant. The definition I gave of the extended body of warrant in 1.3.5 essentially copied Burge, who states,

in interlocution we distinguish two bodies of epistemic warrant: (i) the recipient's *proprietary warrant* for a belief—that is, the reasons available to him together with his epistemic entitlements for holding the belief; and (ii) the *extended body of warrant* for a belief—which includes not only the recipient's proprietary warrant, but those warrants for the belief that are possessed or indicated by interlocutors on whom the recipient depends for his knowledge (though not for his proprietary warrant).[60]

---

[57] Burge (1998), p. 28.
[58] Otherwise put, we are entitled to presume that if the source is rational, it is fully rational, or rational in both of Fricker's senses, and so to presume that what is presented as true is true.
[59] Burge (1993), p. 486.   [60] Burge (1998), pp. 5–6.

Testimonial knowledge is knowledge because it is supported by an extended body of warrant. Just as memory preserves knowledge through time, testimony transmits it across persons. So whilst we might be entitled to the uptake of testimony, we acquire testimonial knowledge only when it is knowledge that we accept.[61]

Thus Burge's theory of testimony is non-reductive in that it combines the idea that testimonial uptake is entitled with the idea that testimony functions to transmit knowledge and warrant. It is the former idea—the non-reductive answer to the question of our warrant for uptake—that I want to take issue with. The problem, I will argue, is that Burge's justification of the Acceptance Principle does not pay due attention to the fact that telling is a practical activity. Its being so establishes the problem of cooperation outlined in 1.1. And this problem causes trouble for the claim that we can presume a source is sincere merely because the source is rational. However, I will not develop this problem until the next chapter because I think the problem confronts any argument for an entitlement to testimony, and first I want to consider another sophisticated argument for our having such an entitlement.

4.4 McDowell's entitlement 'to take things at face value'

According to McDowell, any account of our sources of knowledge should distinguish between those cases where a source yields knowledge from those cases where it does not. Thus in the case of perception 'an appearance that [p] can be *either* a mere appearance *or* the fact that [p] making itself perceptually manifest to someone'.[62] On this disjunctive account, perception can put a subject in a position to know something because it makes facts 'perceptually manifest'. Of course, the situation where the fact that p is made 'perceptually manifest' can be subjectively indistinguishable from a situation where that p is a mere perceptual appearance, but these

---

[61] And if there is no extended body of warrant but an audience has no defeaters for the entitlement articulated by the Acceptance Principle and the testimonial belief is by chance true, then we have a Gettier case. 'The recipient's dependence for having knowledge on the interlocutor's having knowledge is itself an instance of the Gettier point. The recipient could have true justified belief, but lack knowledge because the interlocutor lacked knowledge.' Burge (1993), p. 486, n. 24.

[62] McDowell (1982), pp. 386–7. I've replaced McDowell's 'such-and-such is the case' by '*p*'.

two situations do not have anything more in common than that a subject can fail to tell them apart: we can quite blamelessly take ourselves to perceive that *p* when we do not. As a source of knowledge, perception puts us in a position to know things; it is just that we can sometimes unknowingly fail to perceive things as they are.

McDowell then offers a parallel disjunctive theory of testimony. Like seeing that *p*, hearing from another that *p* is a way of acquiring knowledge that *p*.[63] McDowell illustrates this with the following case, case 27.

Consider a tourist in a strange city, looking for a cathedral. He asks a passer-by, who is in fact a resident and knows where the cathedral is, for directions, hears and understands what the passer-by says . . . Intuitively, this counts as a case of acquiring knowledge by being told; what makes it so is that the informant knows where the cathedral is, and passes on his knowledge in the linguistic exchange.[64]

As with perceptual appearances, receipt of testimony to *p* will *either* be a case of hearing from another that *p or* merely be a case of hearing another say that *p*. The passer-by could be another tourist 'equally ignorant of the city's layout' and his testimony a mere 'practical joke'.[65] But to get to know where the cathedral is, the tourist does not need to exclude such possibilities. To get to know where the cathedral is, the tourist need merely hear from the passer-by where it is and *not be doxastically irresponsible* in the uptake of this testimony; that is, have no reason not to believe the passer-by. Thus, McDowell considers story of the boy who cried 'Wolf': the boy's first cry did not offer anyone the opportunity of knowledge because it was not itself an expression of knowledge; but his third cry did not offer those who knew him the opportunity of knowledge because it would have been doxastically irresponsible to believe his testimony.[66]

Being doxastically responsible is a matter of being sensitive to those considerations that could be advanced in favour of the truth or falsity of a piece of testimony. The epistemic role this sensitivity plays is to ensure that

---

[63] Or, more, generally, learning from another that *p* is. See McDowell (1994a), p. 433, n.29.

[64] McDowell (1994a), p. 417.

[65] McDowell (1994a), p. 419.

[66] 'After a long series of frivolous cries, those who knew the boy were rendered unable to derive knowledge of the presence of a wolf from him, even on an occasion when his cry really was an expression of knowledge; it would have been doxastically irresponsible for them to take his word for it.' McDowell (1994a), p. 436. Doxastic irresponsibility is an epistemic concept: it might still be prudent to accept the boy's testimony; for instance, if one were an impoverished shepherd who could not suffer such an economic loss.

there is no doxastic irresponsibility in the uptake of a piece of testimony, and so to ensure that entitled uptake is not defeated.

The idea of knowledge by testimony is that if a knower gives intelligible expression to his knowledge, he puts it into the public domain, where it can be picked up by those who can understand the expression, as long as the opportunity is not closed to them because it would be doxastically irresponsible to believe the speaker.[67]

Whether or not an audience acquires testimonial knowledge is then down to whether the accepted testimony is an expression of knowledge. It is down to whether the case is one of hearing from the speaker that p or one of merely hearing the speaker say that p.[68]

On the basis of this disjunction, McDowell offers an argument for our possessing an entitlement *to believe testimony when there is no doxastic irresponsibility in doing so*. This argument is an application of a quite general argument for an entitlement to take at face value the deliverances of a source of knowledge.[69] It starts from McDowell's presumption that knowledge requires that a subject have reason for belief; borrowing Sellars's expression, knowledge, McDowell claims, is a certain standing in the logical space of reasons.[70] The argument could be presented as a *reductio*.

Suppose that we are *not entitled* to the uptake of testimony, which must then be supported by an argument to the conclusion that the testimony is true. Now consider the case where an audience acquires the belief that p by accepting testimony to p. Given the starting supposition, the audience is not entitled to take the testimony to p as a hearing from another that p—as an expression of knowledge. Since knowledge requires an audience have reasons for belief, it follows that these reasons must consist of an argument to the conclusion that p from the major premise that the speaker gave testimony to p and further premises about this situation. That is, an audience's reasons for belief must be the kinds of inductive reasons the

---

[67] McDowell (1994a), p. 438.

[68] 'One cannot count as having heard from someone that things are thus and so, in the relevant sense, unless, by virtue of understanding what the person says, one is in a position to know that things are indeed thus and so.' McDowell (1994a), p. 434.

[69] The phrasing comes from: 'Only if the veil is supposed to be in place can it seem that one would need to establish, or equip oneself with good reason to suppose, that one is not dreaming *before* one can be entitled to take one's apparent perception at face value.' McDowell (1995), p. 408, n.19.

[70] Thus McDowell (1995), p. 395, begins 'I am going to work with an idea from Wilfrid Sellars, that knowledge—at least as enjoyed by rational animals—is a certain sort of standing in the space of reasons.'

reductive theory is at pains to articulate. Such an argument is neutral between the situation where a speaker knows that *p* and that where the speaker is merely saying that *p*—it is neutral between the cases of hearing that *p* from a speaker and merely hearing the speaker say that *p*. The case is considered merely as one of the uptake of testimony to *p*. However, knowledge is factive and so McDowell argues the following conditional principle must be accepted:

> If we want to be able to suppose the title of a belief to count as knowledge is constituted by the believer's possession of an argument to its truth, then it had better not be the case that the best argument he has at his disposal leaves it open that things are not as he believes them to be.[71]

The problem is that the premises needed to infer that *p* from a speaker's giving testimony to *p* are never going to be available. The belief that a speaker knows what she is saying is not sufficient as a premise: since one's beliefs might be false, the most that this could support is the inference that *p* is *probably true*. Knowledge that the speaker knows what she is saying would be sufficient as a premise, but this knowledge is not inductively available given that 'it is always possible for a human being to act capriciously ... however favourable the case'.[72] So the problem with forgoing the entitlement to presume that testimony is an expression of knowledge is that no account can be given of our acquisition of testimonial *knowledge*. The problem is that without this entitlement scepticism ensues.

The solution is to reject the starting supposition: we must be entitled to the uptake of testimony other things being equal, where this is just the entitlement to take things at face value and presume that a given piece of testimony is an expression of knowledge—or a case of *hearing from a speaker* that something is the case—when it appears to be this.[73]

---

[71] McDowell (1994a), p. 421. McDowell claims, 'this principle strikes me as obviously correct'. Similar principles can be found at: McDowell (1982), p. 372, McDowell (1995), p. 399, and McDowell (1981), p. 335.

[72] McDowell (1994a), p. 420.

[73] It should be noted that McDowell observes, 'I do not want to defend the idea that ... there is a general presumption of sincerity and competence (as if gullibility were an epistemic right, or even an obligation). In the case I am considering, I think the tourist is entitled to his belief about where the cathedral is, without taking care to rule out the possibility of a practical joke; but I do not think that is because he is exercising a general presumption of sincerity and competence. That is the sort of thing it is natural to appeal to in a version of the conception I am attacking, one that keeps the idea that mediated standings consist in the cogency of arguments, but is less optimistic than [the reductive theorist] about how cogent the available

This argument for a non-reductive entitlement is an instance of a general argumentative strategy going back to Thomas Reid, which is to hypothesize such an entitlement on the basis of the claim that it is needed to stop scepticism of testimony. Reid argues that our reasons for accepting testimony are so impoverished that the reductive demand that our testimonial beliefs be justified by these reasons implies scepticism. On this basis he concludes that our psychological tendency to credulity must be warranted.

> It is evident that, in the matter of testimony, the balance of human judgement is by nature inclined to the side of belief; and turns to that side of itself, when there is nothing put into the opposite scale. If it was not so, no proposition that is uttered in discourse would be believed, until it was examined and tried by reason; and most men would be unable to find reasons for believing the thousandth part of what is told them.[74]

Similarly, what I termed in 2.1 the observational problem for the reductive theory of testimony is often presented as a premise in an argument for a non-reductive entitlement.[75]

However, in McDowell's hands this argument is much more than this: it is also an application of a general argument against fallibilist conceptions of knowledge; that is, against any epistemology that allows a belief to be justified and false, and so requires a further truth condition on knowledge.[76] Many non-reductive theories of testimony will be fallibilist in this sense; for instance, Burge's epistemology makes warrant both highly

---

arguments are, unless they are beefed up with general presumptions of this sort. I want a more radical departure from the governing conception.' McDowell (1994a), p. 419, n.11. In denying that there is an epistemic right to presume sincerity and competence McDowell seems to deny that we have any non-reductive entitlement. He seems to deny this on the basis of supposing the non-reductive theorist agrees with the reductive theorist: an audience's warrant for the uptake of testimony comes from the audience's proprietary justification, but it is just that this justification is supplemented, 'beefed up', by the right to presume sincerity and competence. But this gets the non-reductive theory wrong; this is not the role these general presumptions play in this theory. For the non-reductive theorist, an audience's warrant for the uptake of testimony is specified by a general entitlement, and the presumption of sincerity and competence is merely an implication of this entitlement. It is not the right to make certain justificatory moves, but the claim that warrant does not depend on these moves being made. McDowell's account of the nature of knowledge may involve a departure from 'the governing conception', and more on this shortly, but the account he gives of our warrant for the uptake of testimony is non-reductive (all be it with a McDowellian gloss).

[74] Reid (1764), §24, p. 197.

[75] Specifically see Coady (1992), ch. 3 and Dummett (1993).

[76] In McDowell's terms the target is justified true belief analyses of knowledge wherein 'a satisfactory standing in the space of reasons is only one part of what knowledge is; truth is an

defeasible and fallible, and even allows that one could be a priori entitled to false beliefs.[77] Given that McDowell's argument for an entitlement to take things at face value has this scope, its premise conditional principle is not merely an innocent statement of the factiveness of knowledge but an assertion of the requirement that a knower possesses truth-entailing reasons for belief. This raises the question of why knowledge requires this. What is wrong with the kinds of reason for belief that reductive theories of testimony are at pains to outline?

Why is a fallible inductive argument to the truth of *p* from the premise that a speaker gave testimony to *p* insufficient for knowledge *when* its conclusion happens to be true? McDowell's view is that we are forced to accept his conditional principle because fallible reasons for belief allow for the unacceptable possibility that there could be two situations where such a reason is possessed in both, but where the fact that is believed to hold only holds in one situation. This is unacceptable for McDowell because it raises the question:

> How can a difference in respect of something conceived as cognitively inaccessible to both subjects, so far as the relevant mode of cognition goes, make it the case that one of them knows how things are in that inaccessible region while the other does not—rather than leaving them both, strictly speaking, ignorant on the matter?[78]

A fact that *p* is cognitively *inaccessible* to a subject if a subject's reasons for believing that *p* are consistent with not-*p*. This is true of an audience whose testimonial belief that *p* is based on an argument which starts from a speaker's giving testimony to *p*. It is not true of an audience who hears from a speaker that *p*. Through being in this epistemic position, such an audience is in a position to know that *p* and, thereby, to satisfy McDowell's conditional principle because 'hearing from someone that things are thus and so is . . . a "guaranteeing" informational state'.[79]

To clarify why hearing from another that *p* is a 'guaranteeing state' that makes 'the fact that *p* manifest' and so 'cognitively accessible', it is helpful to step back and consider Gareth Evans's notion of the informational

extra requirement'. McDowell (1995), p. 403. It is this bigger epistemic agenda that comes out in the quote given in note 73.

[77] Burge (1993), p. 473.

[78] McDowell (1982), p. 374. This rhetorical question is also posed at McDowell (1995), p. 403.

[79] McDowell (1994a), p. 434, n.30.

system. Our thoughts, Evans suggests, are based on information about the world and this information grounds our thinking about the world.

People are, in short and among other things, gatherers, transmitters and storers of information. These platitudes locate perception, communication, and memory in a system—the informational system—which constitutes the sub-stratum of our cognitive lives.[80]

When we perceive something we receive or gather information about the world. In communication we can pass this information on. This information gives content to our thoughts: in perceptually receiving information from and about a particular object or event we are put in a mental state that is a causal consequence of our engagement with this particular object or event, and it is this information that allows us to think about that object or event. For Evans, the idea of being in a particular informational state with such and such content is thereby primitive, and it explains how our experience can ground knowledge of the world.

Now McDowell rejects this view that perceptual experience is a non-conceptual informational state. If the content of experience is non-conceptual, it cannot provide any *reason* for belief and so cannot explain how experience can ground knowledge, which as a certain 'standing in the space of reasons' requires a believer have reasons. What McDowell takes from Evans is the idea that knowledge is grounded by experiences that have their *content determined* by those particular objects and events the experiences are of. However, for McDowell this determination is rational:

In a particular experience in which one is not misled, what one takes in is *that things are thus and so. That things are thus and so* is the content of the experience . . . But *that things are thus and so* is also, if one is not misled, an aspect of the layout of the world: it is how things are. . . . Experience enables the layout of reality itself to exert a rational influence on what a subject thinks.[81]

Perceptual experience can put a subject in a position to know things just because experience is 'openness to the layout of reality': in perceiving that *p*, this perceptible fact is made manifest and the perceptual experience had is thereby not consistent with not-*p*.[82] Since the experience had in perceiving that *p* is not consistent with not-*p*, it provides a percipient with a conclusive reason for believing that *p*. This is something that a

[80] Evans (1982) p. 122.   [81] McDowell (1994b) p. 26.
[82] McDowell (1994b) p. 26.

subject does not have in the situation where appearances are misleading. One could borrow Evans's term 'information'—provided one understands that for McDowell 'informational states' are fully conceptual—and say that *seeing that p and hearing from someone that p* both function to produce a *state of informedness* with regard to *p*. If one is in a state of informedness with regard to *p*, that fact that *p* is cognitively accessible: one has a conclusive reason for believing that *p*. One is in a 'guaranteeing' informational state, and thereby in a position to know that *p* provided only there is no doxastic irresponsibility involved in accepting appearances.

Thus McDowell's theory of testimony is non-reductive in that it combines the idea that testimonial uptake is entitled with the idea that testimony functions to 'put knowledge into the public domain' for others to pick up. The former entitlement states that the uptake of a piece of testimony to *p* is entitled, unless doxastically irresponsible, because an audience 'can take at face value' that in receiving this testimony the audience is learning from a speaker that *p*.

McDowell's argument for this entitlement, to my mind, exhibits the same failing as Burge's: it does not properly recognize that giving testimony is something that speakers do. Telling is a practical activity. McDowell certainly recognizes that we can be epistemically blameless in the uptake of testimony and still end up with a false belief. But, in his view, this is just to say, 'our powers of acquiring and retaining knowledge . . . are at the mercy of factors that cannot be made subject to our rational control'.[83] It is to say that there is an ineliminable element of epistemic luck in our acquisition of knowledge. However, I will argue, this is not a plausible treatment of error when our 'luck' as audiences is determined by the good-will or communicative intentions of speakers. Again it is the problem of cooperation, outlined in 1.1, that will prove pressing.

However, before developing these arguments, and thereby describing why I think that there cannot be any entitlement to testimony, I want to examine the non-reductive theories of Burge and McDowell a little further. In particular, the explanations of knowledge transmission each offers are interestingly different, and these differences bear on the manner in which testimonial knowledge is social, or 'anti-individual' in Goldberg's sense. This matter is important because whilst the trust theory I am

---

[83] McDowell (1994a), pp. 442–3.

developing rejects the idea that our uptake of testimony is entitled it sides with the non-reductive theory in taking testimonial knowledge and warrant to be the unique epistemic kind transmitted knowledge and warrant.

4.5 Conclusion: the transmission of knowledge and warrant

Testimony is an epistemically distinctive source of knowledge and warrant. It is distinctive in that the following two transmission principles hold:

(TK) Where A believes that p through uptake of testimony to p, A *testimonially* knows that p only if a prior speaker knew that p.

(TW) Where A believes that p through uptake of testimony to p, A is *testimonially* warranted in believing that p only if a prior speaker was warranted in believing that p.[84]

Non-reductive theories of testimony are defined by their endorsement of one or both of these principles. Thus, and for instance, Burge observes that 'there must be knowledge in the chain if the recipient is to have knowledge based on interlocution'.[85] Similarly, McDowell claims that 'if . . . the person from whom one took oneself to have heard it did not know it, one cannot persist in the claim that one heard from him that things are thus and so'.[86] A question for any theory that makes such positive claims is then: what is it that explains the transmission of knowledge and warrant? That is, in virtue of what do principles (TK) and (TW) hold true? The non-reductive theories of Burge and McDowell suggest different answers to this question.

Burge's explanation of transmission has already been encountered; it is what I called in 3.7 the *evidential explanation*. According to this explanation, what makes the transmission principles true is the fact that the warranted uptake of testimony is a mechanism for basing belief on a speaker's evidence. Thus, it is the extended body of warrant that determines the epistemic status of an audience's testimonial belief. For example, take case 27: the case of the tourist asking a passer-by for directions to the cathedral. The passer-by knows where the cathedral is through perception. He is acquainted with it. Call this epistemic ground E. The tourist is warranted

[84] Recall that these principles respectively abbreviate (7) and (9) in 3.2.
[85] Burge (1993), p. 486, n.24.   [86] McDowell (1995), p. 434.

in the uptake of the passer-by's testimony—for Burge this warrant takes the form of the entitlement stated by the Acceptance Principle—so the tourist's belief as to the whereabouts of the cathedral equally gets to be grounded on E. The tourist thereby inherits the passer-by's warrant for belief, which, in this case, is knowledge-supporting.

McDowell's explanation of transmission is different. He draws a sharp distinction between hearing from a speaker that p and hearing a speaker merely say that p; or between the case where receipt of testimony to p puts an audience in a position to know that p and the case where its receipt would not do so even if acceptance were doxastically responsible. McDowell draws this sharp distinction because only in the former case would understanding the testimony engender a *state of informedness* with regard to p, where an audience's being in this state is dependent on the particular objects and events that make it true that p. This disjunction then specifies the following explanation of transmission: the uptake of testimony can function to transmit knowledge, and trivially warrant, because it can create in an audience the same state of informedness with regard to the facts that the speaker enjoys. Call this the *same-state explanation*. On this explanation warrant is both trivial and truth-guaranteeing: if a subject is in a state of informedness with respect to p, the subject's reason for belief is just this state, and this reason is trivially truth entailing having the form 'p therefore p'. For example, consider again the case of the tourist, which is case 27. Given that the passer-by knows where the cathedral is, in understanding the passer-by's testimony, the tourist is put in a state that he could not be in unless the passer-by knew, namely a state of informedness with respect to where the cathedral is. Provided there is no doxastic irresponsibility associated with the uptake of the tourist testimony, this state is one of knowledge and gives a conclusive reason for belief.

Despite the differences in these explanations of transmission, there are certain commitments that follow from the endorsement of (TK) and (TW). Any theory that endorses these principles will be anti-individualistic in Goldberg's sense that it will make an audience's possession of testimonial knowledge or warranted testimonial belief depend 'on facts regarding one or more of [the audience's] social peers'.[87] Anti-individualism, Goldberg claims, is an *externalist* view because it denies that epistemic status is

---

[87] Goldberg (2007), p. 141.

determined by facts that 'are discernible through the subject's searching reflection alone'.[88] On this understanding, the evidential explanation of the truth of (TK) and (TW) implies an externalist account of testimonial knowledge and warrant: whether or not an audience's testimonial belief is grounded by evidence possessed by some prior speaker is not a fact that the audience can determine by 'searching reflection alone'. And the same-state explanation of the truth of (TK) and (TW) equally implies an externalist account of testimonial knowledge and warrant: whether or not a speaker's testimony is an expression of knowledge or merely appears to be such is equally not a fact that an audience can determine by 'searching reflection alone'.[89]

However, (TK) and (TW) do not imply commitment to externalism understood as the claim that a belief's epistemic status supervenes on its non-epistemic properties. Reliabilism is externalist in this sense because warrant is taken to supervene on reliability, which is a matter of objective probability.[90] And Goldberg's anti-individualism is based on a reliabilist account of knowledge and warrant: the epistemic status of an audience's testimonial belief 'depends on facts regarding [the audience's] social peers' because these facts are relevant to the reliability of the audience's testimonial belief. That the evidential and same-state explanations of transmission do not imply this commitment can then be seen by the fact that neither Burge's nor McDowell's theory of testimony is externalist in this sense. For Burge a testimonial belief is warranted if its acquisition was entitled and it is supported by an extended body of warrant. Whilst for McDowell a testimonial belief is warranted if the receipt of testimony provides an audience with a conclusive reason for belief that the audience can endorse without doxastic irresponsibility.

Nevertheless, there is a significant contrast to be drawn here. The contrast is that on McDowell's view the relevant epistemic properties are properties of the audience's mental states. It is an audience's reasons for belief that determine the epistemic status of the audience's testimonial belief; it is just that testimony can supply these reasons. Whereas on

---

[88] Goldberg (2007), p. 135.

[89] McDowell would object. He observes, 'When someone has a fact made manifest to him, the obtaining of the fact contributes to his epistemic standing on the question. But the obtaining of the fact is precisely not blankly external to his subjectivity.' McDowell (1982), p. 391. I discuss this objection further in 5.4.

[90] See Goldman (1979).

Burge's account the epistemic properties are socially distributed. Whether or not a piece of testimony comes with the support of an extended body of warrant is a social fact. So this contrast could be marked by saying that the evidential explanation of transmission gives a *socially externalist* account of testimonial knowledge and warrant.

The question, then, is which one of these explanations of transmission is correct? Does testimony imply a more social account of the nature of warrant and knowledge? Or can we keep hold of the idea that testimonial knowledge, like knowledge more generally, is just a certain 'standing in the space of reasons'?

The following two cases, I think, suggest that the same-state explanation of transmission is limited.

Case 28. A mathematician who has proved theorem p tells a lay audience this theorem.

First, suppose for the sake of argument that mathematical knowledge is identified in terms of proof. If the lay audience's *only* reason for believing that p is hearing from the mathematician that p, then the audience does not possess a proof of the known proposition. So if knowledge requires support by proof, the lay audience does not know this proposition. Maybe one could separate knowing that p and knowing that p is true, where testimony only allows the latter knowledge.[91] But the problem with this separation is that it threatens to generalize to the conclusion that one fails to know every proposition that is supported by reasons of which one is ignorant. However, this is to say that testimony could only ever yield knowledge that p is true and never yield simply knowledge that p. But surely we think that testimony is a source of knowledge and not merely a source of knowledge of what things are true? It can be admitted that the lay audience's believing the proved proposition is not consistent with the falsity of this proposition, but in this case this inconsistency cannot define the audience's state as one of informedness since it is equally true of any cognitive state the audience is in that this state is not consistent with the falsity of the proved proposition. Thus for the case of mathematical knowledge, a better explanation of transmission seems to be the evidential explanation: testimony to the mathematical proposition allows the lay audience to form a belief that is warranted on the basis of evidence the

---

[91] See Williams (1972), p. 9.

audience does not possess, *viz.* the extended body of warrant that is the mathematician's proof.[92]

Now consider testimony to some complex experimental result, such as that cited by John Hardwig to calculate the cross-section of charm particles.[93]

Case 29. A complex physics experiment (involving 99 collaborators and taking approximately 280 man/years to execute) yields the result that *p*. A lay reader encounters the article in *Physical Review Letters* stating this experimental result.

The scientific justification of this result requires the support of the experimentally made observations and calculations documented in the *Physical Review Letters*. In this case, neither the lay reader of this article nor its first author will have the conclusive reason provided by a state of informedness: the beliefs of both are consistent with the falsity of what is believed.[94] However, the experimental result is well supported, and it is this external body of warrant—the experiment described in the paper and all the calculations and theory that went into it—that surely determines the warrant that both the first author and the reader have for belief. This follows from the evidential explanation of transmission: in accepting the testimony of the *Physical Review Letters*, the lay reader forms a testimonial belief that inherits the evidential support of the experiment documented in this article.

Cases 28 and 29, I think, provide a good reason for preferring the evidential explanation of transmission over the same-state explanation. The evidential explanation is broader, and able to accommodate the transmission of non-conclusive warrant. However, I do not think that

---

[92] Indeed the principal conclusion of Burge (1993) is advertised as: 'Sometimes, the epistemic status of beliefs acquired from others *is not empirical*. In particular, it is not empirical just by virtue of the fact that the beliefs are acquired from others.' Burge (1993), p. 466. This conclusion follows from (i) the apriority of the Acceptance Principle; (ii) the evidential explanation of transmission; and (iii) Burge's view that perception of utterance can merely play the role of 'triggering' understanding. In my opinion, (iii) is problematic. For a similar view see Bezuidenhout (1998).

[93] See Hardwig (1985). The article Hardwig cites is 'Charm Photoproduction Cross Section at 20 GeV', *Physical Review Letters*, 51 (5) (1983): 156–9. Knorr-Cetina observes that the trend in high-energy physics experiments at least is towards ever greater collaboration; she cites the ATLAS experiment at CERN with approximately 2,000 collaborators. See Knorr-Cetina (1999), p. 20.

[94] Indeed Hardwig noted in Hardwig (1985) the expectation that the result would be superseded and in Hardwig (1991) that this expectation had been fulfilled.

these cases conclude the argument. The evidential explanation of these cases focuses on the transmission of warrant. So it is an advantage of the evidential explanation that it explains these cases *only if* we can understand the transmission of warrant independently of understanding how testimony functions to transmit knowledge. And there is some reason for thinking that we cannot. For instance consider the grammatical connections between 'knowing' and 'telling' described in 3.4; and the fact that knowledge seems more 'transmissible': one cannot truly believe a speaker knows without being in a position to know oneself but one can truly believe a speaker is warranted in belief without being warranted in belief oneself. However, if the transmission of knowledge is basic, then it might then be arguable that the same-state explanation gives a better explanation of the fundamental cases, like case 27.

Something like this, I think, is true. But making this claim requires much more subtlety, which I will try to show when I return to these issues in 7.4. For the moment let me leave the matter unresolved, and simply conclude that there are different, competing, but not obviously inconsistent explanations of how testimony functions to transmit knowledge and warrant.

This chapter has largely considered what arguments can be given for an entitlement to form the belief that p on the basis of testimony to p. In conjunction with the previous chapter, which presented arguments for the transmission principles (TK) and (TW), and this section which considered how to interpret these principles, this completes the positive case for the non-reductive theory of testimony. In the next chapter I want to argue that we do not have any entitlement to believe testimony, and must support the uptake of testimony with reasons.

5

Trust and the Uptake of Testimony

Testimony is an epistemically distinctive source of knowledge and warrant. In this respect it can be compared to perception and memory. And this comparison, according to the non-reductive theory, suggests another: just as we do not need to justify our acceptance of perceptual appearances or what we appear to recollect, so we do not need to justify our uptake of testimony. Thus, the non-reductive theory proposes the following uptake principle: receipt of testimony to p entitles an audience to believe that p, other things being equal. This uptake principle, I will argue in this chapter, is wrong in two respects.

First, this uptake principle gets things wrong *descriptively*; that is, it gives a wrong account of *when* an audience is warranted in acquiring a belief on the basis of accepting a bit of testimony. The problem is that any formulation of this general entitlement suffers either one of two descriptive failings. Either it allows plain gullibility to be warranted when it is not. Or it fails to allow for cases where credulity is warranted. That is, if the entitlement is formulated in such a way as to ensure that it does not sanction gullibility, it implies that trust is unwarranted. But, I will argue, we can be warranted in acquiring a testimonial belief on trust. However, if the entitlement allows for this, its formulation is so liberal that gullibility is also sanctioned.

Second, this uptake principle gets things wrong *normatively*; that is, it gives a wrong account of *why* an audience is warranted in acquiring a belief on the basis of accepting a bit of testimony. The idea that we have certain general entitlements is the idea there are ways of being warranted in belief other than by argument, and being in receipt of a piece of testimony is one such way. Others are having things perceptually appear a certain way or recollecting something. When it perceptually seems to a subject that p, or when a subject recollects that p, the subject has a warrant for believing that p that does not presuppose their being able to argue for p; and, the non-reductive theory argues, the same goes for testimony: an audience's warrant for believing that p, given receipt of a piece of testimony to p, does not presuppose the audience could cite an argument for p. And this is the problem: it does presuppose precisely this. The idea that we are entitled to believe testimony simply fails to recognize how giving and accepting testimony is a practical activity governed by considerations of practical rationality. These considerations determine that it is not reasonable for an audience to accept testimony to p *without* being able to cite something in support of doing so. And when acceptance is uptake this means being able to cite an argument for p. The epistemology of testimonial uptake is framed by the problem of cooperation, described in 1.1, and this problem has no analogue for perception or memory.

It is the normative failing that is worse for the non-reductive theory, of course. So this will occupy all of this chapter except the next section.

5.1 Gullibility and trust

In this section, I will argue that the non-reductive uptake principle gets the epistemology of testimony descriptively wrong. This principle faces a dilemma: either it implies that gullibility is warranted, or it implies that beliefs formed on the basis of trust are unwarranted.

For the sake of argument let me formulate the non-reductive entitlement as a named principle thus:

(PC) Confronted by (intelligible) testimony to p, an audience A is entitled to believe that p, *other things being equal*.[1]

The question is: how should we interpret the 'other things being equal' clause? Suppose, first and following Burge, that the entitlement stated by (PC) holds 'unless there are stronger reasons (*available to the person*) that override it'.[2] With respect to the entitlement stated by (PC), call a proposition that is entertained by A as a reason to believe not-p, a *doxastic*

---

[1] 'PC' for a *principle of credulity* in homage to Reid, the first non-reductive theorist.
[2] Burge (1997), p. 22, n.4, my italics.

defeater. On this first interpretation, the entitlement stated by (PC) holds provided *A* has no undefeated doxastic defeater.

The problem with this interpretation is that it is a sanction of gullibility. Elizabeth Fricker makes this argument.[3] And it can be made by the following the case.

Case 30. *Caravaggio's 'The Fortune-Teller'*: in the sway of the pleasurable thoughts evoked by the fortune-teller's vision of his future wife as being both beautiful and rich, the young man fails to notice the fortune-teller pick his pocket.

In this case nothing the young man entertains gives him a reason to reject the fortune-teller's testimony. The young man is gullible. But since he entertains nothing that gives him a reason to reject the fortune-teller's testimony, he is entitled to accept it. He is gullible but entitled to his belief that his wife will be beautiful and rich; and he is entitled to this belief *merely because* he is gullible. This is wrong. In this case, it is more plausible to say that the young man's testimonial belief is unwarranted.

The source of this problem is that the entitlement stated by (PC) is *only* subject to doxastic defeat. Other defeaters could be identified. With respect to the entitlement stated by (PC), call a proposition that is not entertained by *A*, but which should be entertained by *A* given what else *A* believes, and which gives a reason to believe that not-*p*, a *normative defeater*. And call a *true* proposition that, if entertained by *A*, would give *A* reason to believe not-*p*, a *factual defeater*.[4] It is Goldberg's opinion that (PC) is 'obviously false' unless the entitlement it states is subject to all three of these defeaters.[5] Let this be the second interpretation of (PC): the entitlement it states holds unless there are undefeated doxastic, normative, or factual defeaters.

On this interpretation, the young man in case 30 is not entitled to believe that his wife will be beautiful and rich. The case is one of plain gullibility; the young man is wilful in his naïvety in that he ignores his own good counsel merely because he enjoys entertaining what the fortune-teller tells him. As such, on this interpretation, the entitlement stated by

---

[3] Fricker (1994).

[4] See Lackey (2008), p. 45.

[5] Goldberg (2007), p. 159. This is made explicit in Goldberg's formulation of (PC) at p.168—his AR+. See 4.1.

(PC) is defeated; it is normatively defeated. So the young man is unwarranted in his testimonial belief.[6]

This second interpretation of (PC) ensures that it is not a sanction of gullibility. The problem now—the second horn of the dilemma—is that thus interpreted (PC) will not allow *any* credulous attitude to yield an entitled testimonial belief. However, there is a credulous attitude that can be the basis of warranted testimonial uptake, namely trust. So the problem is that on this interpretation we are not entitled to beliefs formed merely on trust. To illustrate this point let me return to case 17, the case of the good shopkeeper.

Case 17. *The good shopkeeper*: the shopkeeper knowingly employs someone convicted for theft. She trusts her new employee with the till and trusts him when, at the end of the first day, he reassures her that the till balances.

The shopkeeper is like the young man: she ignores her own good counsel. She knows that her new employee has a track-record of theft, and that he has recently been released from prison for this. These facts give her a reason to reject what he tells her, when he tells her that the till balances. And she has nothing to counter-balance these reasons with—or at least nothing more than the presumptions that accompany her trust. So the shopkeeper has an undefeated normative defeater of the entitlement stated by (PC). As such she is not entitled to believe that the till balances.

However, this gives the wrong judgement of the shopkeeper's epistemic position. To see this suppose that things are as the shopkeeper presumes in trust. The new employee recognizes his chance and tries to go straight; his testimony is honest. In this case, it is plausible to claim that the shopkeeper gets to know that the till balances. But if she gets to know this, her uptake of her employee's testimony must be warranted. It must be warranted even though, on this second interpretation, she has an undefeated normative defeater and so is not entitled. Hence, this interpretation gets this case wrong.

Both trust and gullibility are credulous attitudes; but, I contend, whilst we judge gullibility negatively, we judge trust positively. Only trust can be the basis of testimonial knowledge. This positive judgement of trust

---

[6] There is also factual defeat: there is a true proposition—the fortune-teller's purpose is to rob me—which if entertained by the young man gives him a reason to reject what the fortune-teller says.

follows from the first interpretation of (PC). In trusting her new employee, nothing the shopkeeper entertains gives her a reason to reject what he tells her. Her trust 'brackets' what she otherwise believes. So the first interpretation of (PC) gets it right that the shopkeeper is entitled to her testimonial belief, but gets it wrong that the young man is entitled to his. Whereas the second interpretation of (PC) gets it right that the young man is not entitled to his testimonial belief, but gets it wrong that the shopper is not entitled to hers. There is no way of resolving this dilemma because the mechanism of defeat has no way to discriminate these two cases of wilfully ignoring the evidence.

The shopkeeper is warranted in her testimonial belief. If this intuition is not fixed, the most I can do is issue the same promissory note I issued when claiming that the reductive theory's uptake principle is similarly wrong in not recognizing that trust can be a reason for testimonial uptake: I will theoretically substantiate this claim in 6.3 after giving an analysis of trust. Here, however, it must be recognized that when a theory implies a different judgement of cases—as the first and second interpretations of (PC) imply a different judgement of cases 30 and 17—it is always possible to revise intuitions. There is a cost to the plausibility of the theory in this; and this cost, I feel in this case, is already too high. The intuitions that the young man is not warranted but the shopkeeper is warranted are robust.

Nevertheless, it is possible to allow that gullibility is warranted, or conclude that believing on the basis of trust is not warranted. And, arguably, Burge and Goldberg respectively take these options. Thus Burge observes, 'one might wonder, with some hyperbole, whether it [(PC)—his Acceptance Principle] can ever be the last word in the epistemology of acceptance for anyone over the age of eleven'.[7] There is an assertion and implicit argument here: a theory of testimony must sanction gullibility if it is to get the epistemology right for under-elevens. Meanwhile, implicit in Goldberg's requirement that an audience monitor the testimonial situation for 'the presence of defeaters', is the rejection of the idea that a trust-based testimonial belief can be warranted since trust involves believing a speaker, or to use an old phrase, putting your faith in them. It does *not* involve '*being on the look out*' for reasons not to believe.[8]

---

[7] Burge (1993), p. 468.   [8] Goldberg (2007), p. 166.

In my opinion both these views go wrong descriptively. A testimonial belief formed gullibly is not warranted, so Burge's 'epistemology of acceptance' gives the wrong account of the epistemology of under-elevens. And trust can be the basis of warranted testimonial uptake, so there can be no monitoring requirement on warranted uptake. What I think is the right account of the epistemology of under-elevens I give in 8.0, and I argue for the claim that trust can warrant belief in 6.3.

The point to be made here is that whilst I think the foregoing dilemma establishes that the non-reductive uptake principle gets the epistemology of testimony descriptively wrong, it must be acknowledged, given the role of intuition in this dilemma, that this is no knock-down argument against the non-reductive theory. But then the real problem with this theory, I think, is with the very idea that we are entitled to accept testimony. The case for thinking we have no such entitlement I review now.

5.2 The problem of cooperation and the uptake of testimony

Telling is a practical activity; it is something we do, and something we do for reasons. In 1.1, I illustrated this with case 3: the case of purchasing a used car. In this case, the potential buyer would rather make no purchase than waste money on a jalopy, so acquiring a false belief about the quality of the car would leave the buyer in a worse position than ignorance. The salesman might tell the buyer that the car is a deal, but given that acceptance is uptake, and will see the buyer believing the car a deal and so purchasing it, what the buyer needs is a reason for thinking that this statement is true. A belief about the salesman's communicative intentions—that the salesman was being informative—would supply such a reason, as would the belief that there are sanctions on deceit and so on. This case is not meant to illustrate any problem in finding reasons for acceptance—though, with much financial at stake, this can be notoriously difficult in this case. Rather, what this case illustrates is how the testimonial situation is structured by interlocutors' practical interests.

The problem of cooperation, described in 1.1, is then the claim that this particular testimonial situation is not in any way peculiar. The testimonial situation, which is a conversation whose ostensible purpose is the giving and receiving of information, always involves a confluence of practical interests. So in general audiences need reasons for accepting testimony. This is because an audience's basic interest is learning the truth whereas a speaker's basic interest is being believed. That is, a speaker's basic interest, qua speaker, is not informing but exerting an influence. Of course, how and whether these basic interests determine the shape of a particular conversation is another matter; but the point is that these basic interests determine the nature of the testimonial situation. This problem therefore implies that the following principle of practical rationality holds for the testimonial situation: it is reasonable to accept a piece of testimony only given reasons for doing so; or, acceptance is something that is made reasonable by an audience's other attitudes. Acceptance here need not be belief; I might have reasons for accepting what you say, such as that you will be upset if I don't, which are not reasons for belief. However, this principle stating what makes acceptance reasonable implies a particular uptake principle, *viz.*: *confronted by testimony to p, an audience A is warranted in believing that p if and only if A's other attitudes make it reasonable for A to believe that p.*

Call this principle established by the argument from cooperation *the principle of reasonable uptake*, or just (R) for short. There are two things that need to be observed about (R). First, it is very similar to the reductive uptake principle, which similarly requires that uptake be subjectively reasonable. It differs in that it requires uptake be reasonable in the light of an audience's 'other attitudes', rather than in the light of 'other things the audience believes'. This difference is due to the fact that (R) is motivated by considerations of practical rationality whereas the reductive principle is part of a reductive explanation of how an audience acquires knowledge from testimony. Thus, whilst the reductive theory requires that audience A be able to cite an argument for p premised on other things believed, this principle merely requires that A be able to cite an argument for p. Crucially, this allows that this argument could be premised on what A accepts in a context of practical reasoning or presumes in adopting an attitude of trust. Again this is something I will come back to in 6.3. Nevertheless, second, (R) makes A's possession of warrant for testimonial uptake conditional on A possessing reasons that could be cited in the form of an argument for p. Since the very idea of a non-reductive entitlement to testimony is the idea that an audience's warrant for testimonial uptake is not so conditional, (R) is not consistent with any such entitlement. It is not possible for (R) and (PC), the formulation of the non-reductive uptake principle given in the previous section, to both be true.

Uptake principles (R) and (PC) are inconsistent. So the argument from cooperation that motivates (R) should undermine the case for any non-reductive entitlement. This is what I want to argue in the remains of this chapter. The focus will be how the positive arguments Burge and McDowell give for (PC), which were outlined in 4.3 and 4.4 respectively, determine the falsity of (R). The best that can be said is that these positive arguments can be directed against and successfully undermine one set of considerations favouring (R). These are the considerations that are marshalled by an *argument from error*.

The idea that a principle such as (R) holds for some source of knowledge has traditionally been argued by an argument from error. The argument is that the acceptance of a deliverance of a source of knowledge must be rationally supported insofar as this source is fallible or liable to error. Thus, and for instance, it has been argued that we are justified in believing perceptual appearances if and only if we have a reason to believe that things are as they appear *because* things can be otherwise than they appear and we can be in error in our appearance-based perceptual beliefs. As a source of knowledge, testimony seems particularly vulnerable to an argument from error. McDowell is surely right when he says,

The supposition that the informant is, perhaps uncharacteristically, misleading the hearer or, perhaps surprisingly, misinformed about the topic is not like the typical suppositions of general sceptical arguments (e.g. 'Maybe you are a brain in a vat'), where it is at least arguable that no real possibility is expressed. In Simon Blackburn's phrase, mistakes and deceptions by putative informants are 'kinds of thing that happen'.[9]

This is to say that the possibilities of mistake raised by an argument from error are quite ordinary in the case of testimony, so the demand that acceptance be supported seems, to this degree, more plausible.

Similarly, Lackey observes that testimony differs from other sources in its reliability.

For instance, the possible worlds in which most of my perceptual beliefs are indistinguishably false—for instance, worlds in which I am unknowingly a bran-in-a-vat or the victim of an evil demon—are quite distant from the actual world.

---

[9]   McDowell (1994a), p. 420. The reference is to Blackburn (1984), p. 185.

Indeed, even possible worlds in which *many* of my perceptual beliefs are indistinguishably false are rather far away—worlds, for instance, where my perceptual faculties frequently malfunction and yet I do not suspect that they do. In contrast, the possible worlds in which most of my testimonial beliefs are indistinguishably false—for instance, worlds in which I was raised by parents who belong to a cult, or worlds in which my government is highly corrupt, or worlds in which my society is highly superstitious—are much closer.[10]

On this basis Lackey concludes that an audience must have reasons for the uptake of testimony.

> Given this much greater chance of error in the case of testimony, the rational acceptance of the report of others requires positive reasons in a way that is not paralleled with other cognitive faculties.[11]

It is not true that there is no parallel with other cognitive faculties: this is just an argument from error, and this argument can be given for any fallible source. But Lackey is right to conclude both that this argument is forceful for testimony, and that it establishes the demand that an audience have 'positive reasons' for uptake.

In the next two sections, then, I examine how the positive arguments Burge and McDowell give for (PC) tell against (R). These positive arguments imply different strategies for resisting the argument from error. The problem for the non-reductive theory, I will argue, is that the considerations that inform the argument from cooperation are of a different kind to the considerations that inform the argument from error. What matters is not the mere fallibility of testimony as a source of knowledge but what explains this fallibility. Whilst the fact that testimony can be misleading does motivate (R), the deeper and testimony-specific reason for (R) concerns not the fact that testimony can be misleading, but why it can be so.

5.3 Burge and the nature of epistemic entitlement

The argument from error, as applied to testimony, concludes that the uptake of testimony must be supported by reasons, where this is uptake

---

[10] Lackey (2008), p. 190.

[11] Lackey (2008), p. 190. A conclusion, she goes on to add, which is further supported by the fact that testimony is 'heterogeneous' in that much of it is particularly unreliable, pp. 191–2.

principle (R). A premise in this argument is that knowledge requires reasons for belief. Hence, it is claimed, we need reasons for thinking of a present case that it is not a case of error. And this, Burge claims, presumes a restricted view of epistemic warrant because 'it ignores epistemic entitlement'.[12]

For Burge epistemic entitlements are contrasted to epistemic justifications. Where justification is warrant by reasons that are available to a believer, entitlement is warrant that comes from forming belief in a certain way. There exists an entitlement when it is possible to give a justification of a given way of forming belief. Entitlements need not be accessible to the entitled subject; and ordinarily they would not be so because most believers lack the reflective powers necessary to offer such a justifying description of a way of acquiring belief. However, being entitled to belief does not rest on being able to articulate such a justification. Rather, a subject can be warranted in belief even if the subject lacks reasons for belief because the subject can be entitled to belief. Consequently, the validity of any application of the argument from error to a fallible source of knowledge hinges on the assumption that one is *not entitled* to acquire beliefs by way of this source. Burge's Acceptance Principle then specifies the idea that we do possess such an entitlement when it comes to testimony. As such, we do not need *reasons for belief* to be warranted in the uptake of testimony because 'we are entitled to acquire information according to the principle [i.e. the Acceptance Principle]—without *using* it as justification—accepting the information instinctively'.[13]

What is wrong with the argument from error on this account is that it fails to recognize that there are more ways that a belief can be warranted than by reasons available to the believer. Some beliefs are warranted for a subject because the subject is entitled to them by virtue of facts about how the belief was acquired. This is true of beliefs acquired by way of testimony. As such the fallibility of testimony as a source of knowledge does not itself provide any reason for doubt. The mere fact that an audience has been mistaken in the past is not a counter-consideration that defeats the audience's entitlement. Equally, the mere possibility that the uptake of present testimony could be mistaken is not a counter-consideration that defeats an audience's entitlement. The fact of past mistakes and possibility

---

[12] Burge (2003), p. 526.   [13] Burge (1993), p. 467.

of a present error do not by themselves provide any reason to doubt testimony because they do not relate to the particular case of a piece of present testimony but raise a general issue. However, given that uptake can be justified as a rational policy, the general reason for doubt that fallibility provides can be put to one side. Where there is entitlement, doubt requires a specific ground but belief does not.

The problem with this reason for rejecting uptake principle (R) is that whilst the argument from error might presume a particular conception of epistemic warrant, the argument from cooperation presumes no more than a particular conception of practical rationality. The argument from cooperation starts with the fact that telling is a practical activity. And once it is conceived as such, it is far from obvious that the uptake of testimony without supporting reasons is a way of forming belief that can be justified, or shown to accord with the norms of reason. The justification Burge gives, as outlined in 4.3, consists of a series of stacked entitlements with the crux entitlement being one to presume that if something is presented as true by a rational source, then it is true. This entitlement holds because the testimony of rational sources—i.e. speakers—can be construed as the presentations of reason at that level of abstraction characteristic of entitlement. And then there is a basic conceptual connection between being backed by reason and being true. However, once telling is conceived as a practical activity, there is no implication from the practical rationality of sources—i.e. speakers—to the truth of testimony. Thus, the considerations that establish the argument from cooperation, and with it uptake principle (R), would seem to undermine the legitimacy of the perspective needed to justify the Acceptance Principle.

Nevertheless, the Acceptance Principle could be defended if the justification Burge offers for it were good *either* to establish that the credulous uptake of testimony is reliable, *or* to supply an audience with a reason to justify the uptake of a particular bit of testimony. To focus this issue, consider the Testimony Game described in 1.1. This is a conversation, whose ostensible purpose is the giving and receiving of information, between an audience A and a speaker S where A wants to know whether p. And following Burge, suppose that sceptical considerations are put to one side: either S knows that p and believes that she knows that p, or S does not know that p and believes that she does not know that p; that is, S does not have a false belief about whether she is in the epistemic position to tell A whether p. In the Testimony Game, what A wants is the cooperative outcome whereby S tells him that p if and only if p. Suppose that S does tell A that p, if this is a cooperative outcome, the case is informative. What principle (R) demands, if A's uptake of S's testimony to p is to be warranted, is that A have some reason for thinking this case is informative. The challenge can then be put thus: do the considerations Burge advances in justifying the Acceptance Principle *either* establish that in this Testimony Game the cooperative outcome predominates so that credulous uptake would be reliable? *Or* supply a reason to believe, in this particular outcome of the Testimony Game, that the case is informative? In the former case, if the cooperative outcome a priori predominates, then A only needs lack reasons for thinking the present case is not informative. Principle (R) is undermined. Whilst, in the latter case, if a priori considerations could be cited in any particular case as a reason for uptake, principle (R) is default satisfied. And either way Burge's Acceptance Principle—or principle (PC)—would seem to get the epistemology right.

Consider the issue of reliability. First, it is worth observing that reliability is arguably a necessary condition on epistemic warrant *if* it is to play an explanatory role in accounting for our acquisition of knowledge. This much at least can be concluded from Getter's cases: the subjects in these cases have reasons for belief but it is the unreliability of their routes to belief that explains their lack of knowledge.[14] That way of acquiring belief described by the Acceptance Principle—the credulous uptake of testimony—is meant to be a way of acquiring knowledge, so it ought to be reliable. And this is a condition on entitlement that Burge accepts when considering perception. When talking about perception, he states:

Reliability is necessary for epistemic entitlement because all epistemic warrant is fundamentally an epistemic good in as much as warrant is a good route to truth and knowledge.[15]

However, the justification of the Acceptance Principle operates at a very high level of abstraction taking a 'God's eye', or distinctively philosophical, view of the process of acquiring testimonial beliefs. It does so because its crucial premise involves equating the presentations of speakers qua rational sources with the presentations of reason. This equation is needed for the presumption that testimony is true; it is needed so that lies, which are

---

[14] This is to consider the cases found in Gettier (1963), and not 'Gettier cases' generally.
[15] Burge (2003), p. 532.

rational for a liar to make, can nevertheless be regarded as somehow non-rational. The intended effect of this equation is to remove testimony from the reasons people have for giving it; that is, to remove it from the sphere of practical activity. Giving testimony—telling people things—ceases to be something speakers do and becomes merely an expression of reason. Consideration of the Testimony Game then shows the problem with this. The problem is that whether or not S's testimony is reliable—whether or not it puts A in the informative situation—will all come down to whether or not S *chooses to tell A whether p*. So in operating at a level abstract from the reasons speakers have for communicating, the considerations that go into justifying the Acceptance Principle become detached from the facts that determine the reliability of testimony.

Burge recognizes this: the justification of the Acceptance Principle is consistent with the credulous uptake of testimony being an unreliable way of acquiring belief. As he observes, 'The Acceptance principle is not a statistical point about people's tending to tell the truth more often than not. Falsehoods might conceivably outnumber truths in a society.'[16] However, it ought not to be possible for falsehoods to outnumber truths in a society because were this the case, the credulous uptake of testimony would be an unreliable way of acquiring belief. Burge simply dodges this possibility, claiming that to raise it is to raise the 'sceptical question about how putative rationality or justification is associated with truth'.[17] How-ever, this dodge is unacceptable because the justification of the Acceptance Principle does more than set scepticism aside: *it abstracts from the facts that actually explain the reliability of testimony*. In the Testimony Game I've equally put scepticism aside and assumed that S has no false belief about her epistemic position. Given this assumption, what explains A's being in the informative situation is S's particular reasons for communicating. If S intends to inform A whether p, S's testimony will be reliable since worries about S knowing have been put aside. So the goodness of S's testimony as a source of knowledge all comes down to facts about S's communicative intentions, or reasons for utterance. It is these facts that determine reliabil-ity. And it is facts at this level that both establish uptake principle (R), and are ignored by the justification of the Acceptance Principle.

---

[16] Burge (1993), p. 468.   [17] Burge (1993), p. 470.

Consider now, second, whether the considerations Burge advances in justifying the Acceptance Principle could give A reason to believe this particular testimonial situation is informative, and so justify A's uptake of S's testimony to p. For the Testimony Game such a reason would paradigmatically be the proposition that S intended to tell A whether p, or intended to be informative in telling A that p. The crucial premise in Burge's justification of the Acceptance Principle is the entitlement to presume that if something is presented as true by a rational source, then it is true; otherwise put, the entitlement to presume that if a speaker tells something, then what the speaker tells is true. However, this crucial entitlement will not shed any light on S's reasons because the truth of this entitlement depends on abstracting from the particular reasons that speakers have. The a priori connection between testimony—conceived as a presentation-as-true—and truth is broken at the level of speakers' motivations because at this level lying can be rational. The idea that we possess an entitlement to presume that what is presented-as-true is true cannot supply us with reasons for thinking that a particular testimony is true because it is rather the idea that warrant need not hinge on our possessing such reasons.

However, if A cannot gain a reason for thinking that he is in the informative situation by reflecting on the considerations that go into justifying the Acceptance Principle, then just as these considerations do not establish the reliability of the credulous uptake of testimony, they equally do not give any reason to believe a particular bit of testimony. The reason that neither of these things can be done is that the justification of the Acceptance Principle does not engage with the communicative intentions of speakers. However, a consideration of the intentions that speakers can have in giving testimony also shows that audiences need reasons for the uptake of a piece of testimony, where such reasons are paradigmatically some view of speakers' communicative intentions or reasons for utterance. It is some such reason that principle (R) then requires for warranted uptake.

This raises a question: if the argument for the Acceptance Principle is valid, at a certain level of idealization, how should our entitlement to accept testimony be understood? One possibility is to pursue an analogy suggested by Burge. 'The Acceptance Principle', Burge states, 'is clearly similar to what is widely called a "Principle of Charity" for translating or interpreting others.'[18] The principle of charity is primarily a methodological rule for radical interpretation stating that an interpreter should optimize agreement (truth from the interpreter's point of view). According to Davidson, the principle of charity does not entitle an interpreter to believe of any sentence that is held true that it is true. In forming beliefs as to *which* sentences held true are true the interpreter is guided by 'hunches about the effects of social conditioning, and of course common-sense, or scientific, knowledge of explicable error'.[19] How these beliefs are warranted, Davidson claims, 'is no easier to specify than to say what constitutes a good reason for holding a particular belief'.[20] The suggestion then is that Acceptance Principle should be thought of similarly. It supports the belief that most intelligible presentations-as-true—most testimony—are backed by reason. However, there are different ways in which testimony can be backed by reason and, in particular, one way is that testimony can be backed by practical reasons—as the rationality of lying illustrates. Thus, the Acceptance Principle does not state the conditions that warrant the acquisition of *particular* testimonial beliefs.

5.4 McDowell and the disjunctive nature of knowledge

The argument from error, as applied to testimony, concludes that the uptake of testimony must be supported by reasons, where this is uptake principle (R). This requirement, John McDowell would allow, is entirely correct *provided* one gets clear about the nature of the reasons available. The problem with the argument from error lies in a mistaken conception of our reasons for belief; specifically, the problem is the assumption that our reasons for belief must be *non-question-begging* in the sense that they cannot be conditional on non-mental facts. This assumption, in McDowell's view, 'deforms' epistemology through making the argument from error into a sceptical argument.[21] But once it is abandoned the requirement that the uptake of testimony be supported by reasons can be seen to be entirely consistent with the claim that testimonial uptake is entitled.

---

[18] Burge (1993), p. 487.   [19] Davidson (1974b), p. 196.
[20] Davidson (1984), p. xvii.   [21] See, in particular, McDowell (1995).

The argument from error concludes that for any fallible source of knowledge, a deliverance of that source provides a subject with the opportunity to acquire knowledge only if epistemically things are favourable *and* the subject has a reason for believing that things are so favourable. Applied to the Testimony Game, described in 1.1, in order to know that *p* on the basis of *S*'s testimony to *p*, it is not enough that the case be informative, or instantiate the cooperative outcome; *A* must also possess a reason for believing that this is the case. This implies that *A* could fail to know that *p* either (case one) because the testimonial situation is not informative, or (case two) because *A lacks* a reason for believing that the testimonial situation is informative, even though it is. However, on the assumption that reasons for believing this *cannot* be conditional on non-mental facts, any reason *A* could have to believe that the testimonial situation is informative in case two is equally a reason that *A* could have in case one. On this assumption, the two cases are *the same with respect to the reasons available*. This conclusion, McDowell contends, is in effect a sceptical conclusion.

McDowell argues as follows. If these two cases are the same with respect to the reasons available, then it is not clear how *A*'s coming to possess this reason in case two, and so coming to satisfy (R), could subsequently explain *A*'s coming to know that *p*. This is because if available reasons *do not suffice* for case one being favourable, it is not clear how they make any difference to case two. If the reasons that are available are the same across these cases then, in McDowell's view, grounds for doubting whether the case is informative will persist even given the possession of these reasons. Consequently, if it is a condition on the warranted uptake of testimony, that an audience must have reasons for believing the case is informative, these reasons *cannot leave open the question of whether the case actually is informative*. This is to say that any condition imposed by an argument from error must be interpreted in the light of the following conditional principle:

If we want to be able to suppose the title of a belief to count as knowledge is constituted by the believer's possession of an argument to its truth, then it had better not be the case that the best argument he has at his disposal leaves it open that things are not as he believes them to be.[22]

---

[22] McDowell (1994a), p. 421. Quoted in 4.4.

Of course, if A's reasons for believing that the testimonial situation is informative are constant across cooperative and non-cooperative outcomes, this condition cannot be satisfied. This, McDowell concludes, has the consequence that the argument from error is a sceptical argument.

In order to avoid scepticism, it must be possible to discriminate between these cases in terms of the reasons available to audience A. That these cases are distinguished in this way follows if A's reason for belief is the state of informedness A is put in when A does learn from S whether p. In the case of perception, when a percipient believes that p because he can see that p, his reason for belief will be the cognitive state he is in, in seeing that p. Seeing is a way of getting to know because when a percipient sees that p, he is in a cognitive state which is not consistent with *not-p* and which thereby provides a conclusive reason for believing that p. This is a reason for belief that is not possessed by the subject who merely hallucinates that p. The same goes for testimony. When the testimonial situation is informative, when S knows that p and tells A that p, the receipt of this testimony puts A in a state of informedness such that A has a conclusive reason for believing that p. This reason would not be available were the outcome of the Testimony Game non-cooperative.[23]

So, McDowell claims, once one gets clear about what our reasons for belief are, one can see that the argument from error is not a sceptical argument. Moreover, once one gets this clear, one can equally see that the condition on warranted uptake implied by the argument from error— namely that an audience have a reason for believing the testimonial situation informative—can be trivially satisfied. If S knows that p and tells A that p, then the fact that A is thereby in a position to know that p itself provides A with a reason for believing that the testimonial situation is informative.

[I]f we stop looking for non-question-begging certifications of epistemic standing, we may be able to retrieve a possibility of crediting the [audience] with knowledge that his informant is competent and trustworthy, as something on a level with the knowledge he acquires in the transaction, not prior to it in the space of reasons.

---

[23] Since the state providing this reason is not common to deceptive and non-deceptive cases, McDowell argues that the related *argument from illusion* is invalid. See McDowell (1982).

In parentheses McDowell adds:

Compare the idea that knowledge that one is not dreaming is on a level with the knowledge of the environment that one's senses are yielding one.[24]

So for the Testimony Game being considered, McDowell's suggestion is that A's reason for believing that the testimonial situation is informative can be the following argument, where the state of informedness A is put in by hearing from S that p provides the first premise: 'that p; if that p, then this testimonial situation is informative, therefore this testimonial situation is informative'. Since this argument requires no further grounds than the non-deceptive operation of testimony, the condition placed by the argument from error on the warranted uptake of testimony can, on these occasions, be trivially satisfied. As such there is no inconsistency between uptake principle (R) and the non-reductive entitlement, stated in 5.1 as (PC). Rather, our entitlement to testimonial uptake is just our entitlement to these kinds of reasons for belief.

The claim is this: learning from a speaker that p puts an audience in a position to know that p *and in part it does so because it puts the audience in a position to know that the testimonial situation is informative*. However, I would now like to argue that uptake principle (R) cannot be so trivially satisfied. Rather, its satisfaction requires that an audience's other attitudes *make testimonial uptake reasonable for the audience*. The thought that a speaker has informative intentions or a reliable track-record would do this, but the simple affirmation of the content of the speaker's testimony would not. There are two arguments I want to give for this.

First, McDowell's claim that the subject in the informative case has a reason for belief—that just described—that is not possessed by the subject in the deceptive case is at odds with traditional internalist epistemological thinking. McDowell has a strategy for reconciling his claims with traditional internalism. But this reconciliation is not in any way plausible for the case of testimony. Thus consider the two cases that inform the argument from error. In the informative case, a subject sees that p or hears from a speaker that p. In the deceptive case, the subject suffers a visual hallucination or is told a falsehood but there is nothing from the subject's point of view that allows the subject to tell these cases apart. According to traditional internalist thinking r is A's reason for believing that p if r *explains why*

<hr />

[24] McDowell (1994a), p. 419, n.10.

A believes that *p*. And in the two cases that inform the argument from error, what explains why the subject believes that *p* seems to be the same in both cases. McDowell's contention is what explains the subject's belief is *not* the same in these cases. In one case a fact is made manifest to the subject, who is thereby in a state of informedness, whereas the other case is merely subjectively indistinguishable from this. However, according to traditional internalist thinking, if these two cases are subjectively indistinguishable, then whatever explanation holds for one must hold for the other, and they must thereby be the same with respect to the reasons they make cognitively available. McDowell's reconciliatory thought runs as follows.

There is something gripping about the 'internalism' that is expressed here. The root idea is that one's epistemic standing on some question cannot intelligibly be constituted, even in part, by matters blankly external to how it is with one subjectively. . . . But the disjunctive conception of appearances shows a way to detach this 'internalist' intuition from the requirement of a non-question-begging demonstration. When someone has a fact made manifest to him, the obtaining of the fact contributes to his epistemic standing on the question. But the obtaining of the fact is precisely not blankly external to his subjectivity.[25]

McDowell's claim here is that the internalist demand is satisfied because states of informedness are reason-giving *mental states* that make the world apparent to a subject in both an epistemic and a phenomenal sense. The epistemic sense is that the state is inconsistent with the world being other than the state represents it as being, and so gives a conclusive reason for belief. The phenomenal sense is that the state represents the world as being a certain way through it phenomenally appearing to the subject to be this way. It is this phenomenal sense that is crucial to satisfying the internalist demand because it explains why the subject's being in a state of informedness is a good explanation of the subject's belief.

The first problem is then that these claims are off-kilter in the case of testimony because the phenomenology of testimony is very different to the phenomenology of perception. This phenomenological point could be put in terms of the non-parallel of the contrast between perception and the imagination on the one hand, and between being told something and being told a fiction on the other hand. There is a significant phenomenological

---

[25] McDowell (1982), pp. 390–1.

difference between perceiving something and imagining it; this difference is shown by the fact that we are inclined to believe what we see in a way that we are not inclined to believe what we imagine. However, there is no significant phenomenological difference between being told something (by a speaker who knows what she tells) and being told a fiction. To illustrate this consider case 31.

Case 31. Let me—the author, Paul Faulkner—tell you something about myself. When I was schoolboy I was a member of Phoenix Athletic Club. And I came third in the school senior cross-country race.

One of these claims is true, and in telling you it I put you in a position to know it. The other claim is a lie. But you, the reader, before you knew that one claim was a lie, would be inclined to either believe both the things I told you or neither. In particular, hearing from me that something was the case does not activate the inclination to believe in a way that hearing the lie does not. There is no phenomenological difference between reading the true testimony and reading the fiction. Indeed were you to believe me in either case phenomenology would not figure as any part of the explanation of your belief. The testimonially presented fact just does not 'impress itself' in the way that perceptually presented facts do. As such, it is just not plausible to suppose the knowledge of my high school years that the former testimony makes available to you makes it reasonable for you to believe that I am telling the truth with this statement. Thus even if the corollary of uptake principle (R) for perception is trivially satisfiable, (R) is not.

Second, the deeper philosophical motivation for the principle of reasonable uptake (R) is not the brute fact that we, as audiences, can be in error in the testimony we believe, but that testimony itself can be in error because it was not produced with the intention of getting us, as audiences, to believe truly. Giving testimony is something we, as speakers, do for reasons, and our reasons need not put our audiences' informational needs first. Thus, what is required for warranted uptake is paradigmatically some reason for thinking that a speaker's purpose in utterance is informative. Not because testimony is often not made with this purpose, though there is some truth to that claim, but because being made with this purpose does not define giving testimony as a practical activity. Insofar as (R) is grounded on these practical considerations, which make up the argument from cooperation, a constraint is thereby placed on what reasons can satisfy (R).

Reasons for uptake must make uptake reasonable. And the reason McDowell proposes does not satisfy this requirement.

There is no short way to dispense with the condition on warranted uptake imposed by (R); and, in particular, it is not to be satisfied by the mere affirmation of the content of the speaker's testimony, even if that content is the making manifest of facts which could in principle give a conclusive reason to believe that a speaker is indeed telling what she knows.

5.5 Conclusion: the distinctiveness of testimony

The non-reductive theory of testimony recognizes the distinctiveness of testimony as a source of knowledge and warrant in that it proposes that testimony, like perception and memory, is a source of knowledge and warrant in its own right. A belief can be warranted, or amount to knowledge, merely by being based on testimony that is warranted or known because the uptake of testimony can allow the transmission of knowledge and warrant. However, given this comparison of testimony to perception and memory, it is perhaps unsurprising that when Burge considers our entitlement to rely on testimony, it turns out that

Many of the differences between content passing between minds and content processed by a single mind derive from differences in modes of acquisition and in necessary background conditions that do not enter in the justification force underwriting entitlement.[26]

Similarly, when McDowell considers the state of informedness generated by non-deceptive cases of testimony, it turns out that

[S]ensory confrontation with a piece of communicative behaviour has the same impact on the cognitive state of a perceiver as sensory confrontation with the state of affairs which the behaviour, as we may say, represents.[27]

Testimony, it seems, is not merely a distinctive epistemic source like perception and memory, it is fundamentally similar to both.

---

[26] Burge (1993), p. 474.

[27] McDowell (1980), p. 45. The 'as we may say' clause is inserted because McDowell is considering communication broadly construed. I consider the point of McDowell's doing this in 7.4.3.

In some ways this is true. We are irredeemably epistemically reliant on all these sources, for instance. And testimony can be interestingly compared to both memory and perception: from the social perspective it is, like memory, a way of retaining old knowledge; and from the individual perspective it is, like perception, a way of acquiring new knowledge. However, there are important differences between these sources. The crucial difference is that testimony paradigmatically involves two agents. This distinguishes testimony because it makes the deliverances of testimony qua epistemic source a practical matter with a practical rationality. This changes the epistemology. In particular, a problem that is practical in its origins—the problem of cooperation—determines the falsity of the non-reductive uptake principle. We do not possess a general entitlement to believe what people tell us, but must support testimonial uptake with reasons.

In not recognizing how giving testimony is a practical activity, the non-reductive theory does not adequately recognize the distinctiveness of testimony as an epistemic source. In this respect it shares a failing with the reductive theory. But whereas this failure leads the reductive theory to wrongly deny that testimony transmits knowledge and warrant, it leads the non-reductive theory to wrongly propose an entitlement to testimonial uptake. The correct theoretical position on testimony is to combine something like the reductive uptake principle, but liberally interpreted, with the non-reductive idea that testimony transmits knowledge and warrant. It is to combine uptake principle (R) with transmissions principles (TK) and (TW)—stated in 5.2 and 3.2 respectively.

Moreover, this failure of the non-reductive and reductive theories is related to another: neither theory properly recognizes the problem of cooperation. This philosophical mistake in the case of the non-reductive theory is manifest in the assumption that the demand that testimonial uptake be supported with reasons is motivated by the same argument that institutes the demand that believing the deliverances of memory and perception be supported with reasons, namely the argument from error. But it is not: this uptake principle for testimony is motivated by considerations that are distinctive to testimony, and which inform the argument from cooperation. Whilst in the case of the reductive theory this philosophical mistake is manifest in the reductive theory only providing a sceptical solution to this problem of cooperation.

In the next chapter, I will offer the foundations of a non-sceptical solution to the problem of cooperation. Cooperation, I will claim, can be rationalized by an attitude of trust. And this same attitude can thereby supply an audience with a reason for testimonial uptake, which can warrant uptake. In arguing this, I hope to discharge the promissory notes I gave in 3.1 and 5.1 and begin to fill in the detail of the trust theory of testimony this monograph aims to present.

6

The Assurance Theory

Giving testimony—asserting something or telling someone something—is an action, something we do for reasons. This fact about testimony, that its production is a practical activity, establishes that we need reasons for accepting a piece of testimony. When acceptance is uptake these reasons then need to be of a certain kind. More precisely, confronted by testimony to p, an audience A is warranted in believing that p if and only if A's other attitudes make it reasonable for A to believe that p. In 5.2, I labelled this the principle of reasonable uptake or (R). If (R) is correct, the question is: what attitudes make it reasonable for A to believe that p on the basis of testimony to p?

In answer to this question consider the contrast between *believing a speaker* and merely *believing what a speaker says*. This contrast suggests that when we acquire a belief on the basis of testimony there can be two different explanations of this fact. According to the second explanation testimonial uptake is a matter of judging that a bit of testimony is true. The belief that testimony to p is evidence for p, or reliably indicates that p, would supply a good reason for this judgement. The substance of the reductive theory then details the extent of the grounds we can have for such a belief. This answer is good insofar as it explains how testimonial uptake can be warranted. However, if our reasons for uptake are limited to our reasons for believing that a bit of testimony is evidence for its truth, then what is missed is the possibility of the first explanation. That is, our reason for testimonial uptake can be simply that we believe a speaker, or trust a speaker for the truth.

Believing a speaker, Richard Moran argues, is the appropriate response to a speaker *telling* one something. This is because in telling an audience something, a speaker does not present his utterance as something to be judged as evidence for its truth, but as *assurance*.

Telling someone something is not simply giving expression to what's on your mind, but is making a statement with the understanding that here it is your word that is to be relied on.[1]

[W]hen someone tells me it's cold out I don't simply gain an awareness of his beliefs, I am also given his *assurance* that it's cold out. This is something I could not have gained by the private observation of his behaviour. When someone gives me his assurance that it's cold out he explicitly assumes a certain responsibility for what I believe.[2]

The aim of this chapter is to outline and develop the *assurance theory of testimony*. In doing so I hope to explain how believing a speaker, or the attitude of trusting a speaker for the truth, can provide an audience with a reason for testimonial uptake. And a reason that satisfies the condition on warranted uptake placed by principle (R).

6.1 The assurance theory of testimony

Consider the restricted domain of testimony that is a conversation whose ostensible purpose is the giving and receiving of information—a 'conversation as to the facts'.[3] Consider the Testimony Game where a speaker S tells an audience A that p, ostensibly in response to A's need to know whether p. As the reductive theory makes clear it is ordinarily the case that A will have ample grounds for judging whether S's telling is evidence for p, and so for judging whether p, given S's testimony. However, if A's reasons for testimonial uptake are restricted to these grounds the reductive theory confronts the *problem of intentionality*.

[I]f we are considering speech as evidence, we will have eventually to face the question of how recognition of its intentional character could ever *enhance* rather than detract from its epistemic value for an audience. Ordinarily, if I confront something as evidence (the telltale footprint, the cigarette butt left in the ashtray), and then learn that it was left there deliberately, and even with the intention of bringing me to a particular belief, this will only discredit it as evidence in my eyes. It won't seem *better* evidence, or even just as good, but instead like something fraudulent, or tainted evidence.[4]

---

[1] Moran (2006), p. 280.   [2] Moran (2006), p. 278.
[3] The phrase is Welbourne's, see Welbourne (1986).
[4] Moran (2006), p. 277. And see 3.3.

The problem for the reductive theory is that S's telling A that p can seem to add epistemic value. The issue is explaining how this could be the case. How could S's act of telling A that p alter A's epistemic position other than through providing A with evidence for p?

Moran approaches this question by way of Paul Grice's contrast between 'deliberately and openly letting someone know' and 'telling', where Grice illustrated this difference with the cases of (i) showing 'a photograph of MrY displaying undue familiarity to MrsX', and (ii) drawing 'a picture of MrY behaving in this manner'.[5] The photograph lets MrX know the facts and would do so even if he discovered it accidentally. Its epistemic value is independent of its being shown. This is not true of the drawing, which could produce belief *only* through MrX recognizing that it was produced with just this intention. The drawing, considered as an utterance, is a 'telling', in that it is produced 'with the intention of inducing belief by means of the recognition of this intention'.[6] Similarly, S's telling A that p provides more than doctored evidence, it provides A with a reason to believe that p because and insofar as it is made with this intention. That is, an act of telling adds epistemic value because the intentions constitutive of this act determine certain reasons for belief.

The question, of course, is how is it that A's recognizing that S intends A to believe that p, by means of this very intention or not, gives A reason to believe that p? As Moran observes, the mere recognition that someone 'wants me to do X does not, in general, provide me with much of any reason at all for complying'.[7] So how is A's recognition of S's intention meant to give A reason to comply? The answer, Moran suggests, and what needs to be added to Grice's original formulation, is that telling is an *assumption of responsibility*.

The speaker intends not just that the recognition of his intention play a role in producing belief that P, but that the particular role this recognition should play is that of showing the speaker to be assuming responsibility for the status of his utterance as a reason to believe P.[8]

In telling A that p, S assumes responsibility for her telling being a reason for belief. It is this assumption of responsibility that makes the difference.

---

[5] Grice (1957), p. 218. Moran (2006), p. 285.   [6] Grice (1957), p. 219.
[7] Moran (2006), p. 287.   [8] Moran (2006), pp. 289–90.

In the background here is an analogy with promising. In promising one assumes certain responsibilities, in particular one assumes the responsibility of undertaking to do what one promised to do. Similarly, so the assurance theory claims, telling involves the assumption of certain responsibilities. The next question is then: what is it one assumes responsibility for? Moran's suggestion, I think, is that in telling A that p, S assumes the responsibility of guaranteeing the truth of A's belief.

[T]he speaker, in presenting his utterance as an *assertion*, one with the force of *telling* the audience something, presents himself as *accountable* for the truth of what he says, and in doing so he offers a kind of guarantee for this truth.[9]

This suggestion echoes Robert Brandom's idea that in asserting that p, a speaker S 'undertakes the conditional task responsibility to justify the claim [that p] if challenged'.[10] And S assumes the same responsibility for challenges to A's assertion that p, which A may legitimately defer to S, when A's assertion is a reassertion of S's.[11] The problem with this assumption of responsibility, Gary Watson observes, is that it is too onerous. 'We would be hard pressed', he rightly says, 'actually to defend many of the things we are prepared to assert.'[12] Watson's counter-proposal is that, in asserting p, S assumes responsibility for the 'defensibility' of p.[13] And this assumption of responsibility still acts as a guarantee because it carries the secondary commitment to respond to both justificatory challenges and deferred justificatory challenges.

There are, I think, two things that need to be clarified here. First, 'defensibility' needs to be restricted to 'epistemic defensibility'. It is possible to defend a belief on the basis of the practical good of holding it, which is the case with Pascal's Wager. But this is not the kind of defensibility that is a commitment of assertion. However, to say that p is epistemically defensible is, I assume, just to say that p is warranted. Second, the (secondary) commitment to respond to justificatory challenges, Watson claims, is 'discharged in the limiting case just by acknowledging that an objection is

---

[9] Moran (2006), p. 283.   [10] Brandom (1983), p. 641.

[11] 'That A's assertion of p has the social significance of authorizing B's reassertion of p consists in the social appropriateness of B's deferring to A the responsibility to respond to justificatory challenges regarding B's claim. B's justificatory responsibility is discharged by the invocation of A's authority, upon which B has exercised the right to rely. Further challenges are appropriately addressed to A rather than B.' Brandom (1983), p. 642.

[12] Watson (2004), p. 68.   [13] Watson (2004), p. 68.

prima facie relevant, or needs to be met'.[14] However, this is to undertake too little. In asserting, one undertakes some commitment to back up what one says, even in the limiting case. Recall here Burge's definition of extended warrant as including those warrants 'that are possessed or indicated by interlocutors on whom the recipient depends for this knowledge'.[15] So to capture testimonial dependence, and the idea of a guarantee, I suggest the (secondary) commitment to respond to justificatory challenges is a commitment either to justify what is asserted or to indicate where such a warrant might be found.

The assurance theory of testimony, I propose, can then be stated in these terms. That is, *in telling A that p, S assumes responsibility for his utterance being a reason for belief in that S undertakes the responsibility of responding to justificatory challenges to p's being warranted, and to deferred challenges made to the belief A acquires by the uptake of S's telling, either by justifying p or by indicating where such warrant might be found.* Call this S's *assurance*. In telling A that p, S offers a 'kind of guarantee' in that S offers A the assurance that p in this sense.

Where an audience A has a speaker S's assurance that p, A has a distinctive reason for believing that p, which defines testimony as distinctive route to knowledge and warranted belief. Assurance thereby supplies another interpretation of transmission: where an audience A has a speaker S's assurance that p, A is warranted in believing that p without having to establish whether p because, by means of uptake of S's testimony, A transfers this epistemic responsibility to S. In short, knowledge and warranted belief are transmitted in one direction as epistemic responsibility is transferred in the other. Call this the *assurance explanation*.

When all goes well, in testimony a speaker gives his audience a reason to believe something, but unlike other ways of influencing the beliefs of others, in this case the reason the audience is provided with is seen by both parties as dependent on the speaker's making himself accountable . . . Whether this counts as a good or sufficient reason for belief is *not* a matter of the speaker's illocutionary authority, but will depend both on his sincerity and on his having discharged his epistemic responsibilities with respect to the belief in question.[16]

Transmission principles (TK) and (TW) state that where A believes that p through uptake of testimony to p, A *testimonially* knows that p or is

---

[14] Watson (2004), p. 69.   [15] Burge (1998), pp. 5–6, and see 4.3.
[16] Moran (2006), p. 295.

testimonially warranted in believing that *p* only if a prior speaker knew that *p* or was warranted in believing that *p*. The assurance explanation of transmission implies these principles because it implies the stronger necessary condition that *A* can acquire knowledge and warranted belief from a speaker *S*'s testimony only if the relevant warrant can be articulated or indicated *by S*; that is, only if the immediate speaker *S* is in a position to discharge the responsibilities she assumes in telling.

What of uptake principle (R), which states that an audience *A* is warranted in the uptake of testimony to *p* if and only if *A*'s other attitudes make it reasonable for *A* to believe that *p*? If the assurance theory endorses (R) in addition to (TK) and (TW) it would be a trust theory of the type this monograph aims to defend. As it stands, the assurance theory does not endorse (R). Confronted by *S* telling him that *p*, *A*'s reason for testimonial uptake is simply meant to be *S*'s telling and not *A*'s other attitudes; *A* is not meant to need a reason over and above *S*'s assurance. Now *in a sense* I think this is right, and I will explain why in 6.4, but, in order to get to this explanation, I first need to say why I think that strictly speaking this is wrong.

What is wrong with the assurance theory, as so far presented, is that it is missing an account of testimonial uptake. In telling an audience something, Moran notes, 'the speaker aims at being believed'.[17] And the speaker's telling then presents to the audience 'an invitation to trust'.[18] These things are directly connected since, as Anscombe observes, 'we can see that believing someone (in the particular case) as *trusting him for the truth*—in the particular case'.[19] The crucial missing element, then, is that it is trust, or belief in a speaker, which is needed to receive the speaker's assurance, and so take the speaker's telling as something other than a piece of evidence. This is a dynamic that Welbourne has stressed.

The mechanism by which knowledge is transmitted is *belief*. More precisely, in the simplest kind of case where you address me directly, it is sufficient and necessary for the transmission of your knowledge that *p* to me that I *believe you* when, speaking (or writing) from knowledge, you tell me that *p*.[20]

The need for a particular non-evidential account of testimonial uptake—the need for some account of trust as it is involved in believing a speaker—can

---

[17] Moran (2006), p. 299.   [18] Moran (2005), p. 17.
[19] Anscombe (1979), p. 151. My emphasis.   [20] Welbourne (1979), p. 3. See 3.4.

then be put by observing that without it the assurance theory faces a dilemma.

The dilemma starts with the observation that a speaker can have the aim of being believed—the speaker can *tell* an audience something—even if the speaker does not intend to convey knowledge. We tell one another what we know but we also tell lies. Moreover, in lying a speaker equally intends an audience accept what is told because the audience recognizes that this is what the speaker intends. Consequently, that an audience A recognizes that a speaker S intends A to believe that p will not by itself suffice to move A to believe that p. Moran, as described, realizes this and so adds that in telling A that p, S further intends A to take the intention that A believe that p as a reason to believe that p *because* A construes S's telling as assuring that p. The problem is that lies purport to be sincere and in doing so equally purport to offer assurance.[21] Thus A gains the kind of reason for belief the assurance theory is at pain to describe *only if* A takes S's intentions at face value, believes S, or trusts S to tell the truth.

At this juncture the dilemma is faced since the question then raised is, what warrants A's attitude of trust? And in response to this question reductive and non-reductive views seem to be exhaustive: an audience's trust would seem to be either entitled or justified by evidence. That is, either A is warranted in uptake because A lacks counter-evidence and is entitled to trust in the absence of such evidence, or A is warranted in uptake because A has positive evidence for believing S to be trustworthy. And either way there ceases to be a distinctive assurance position.

The way out of this impasse is to see that the reductive and non-reductive theories of testimony do not exhaust the options available. It is true, strictly speaking, that telling itself does not suffice to give an audience a reason for belief. But what needs to be added is simply trust, not an entitlement to trust or any belief in trustworthiness. To make sense of this claim what is needed is some account of the nature of trust. I attempt this next.

6.2 An analysis of trust and trustworthiness

'Trusting' can describe both an attitude and an action. I can trust you to turn up on time by displaying a certain attitude towards your turning up

---

[21] I give a definition of lies in Faulkner (2007b). And see Simpson (1992).

on time, and by arranging to meet you in a place where it would be very inconvenient to have to wait. With respect to testimony, the act of trusting is the uptake of testimony. The question I want to consider is, what is the *attitude* of trust that determines this action?

Since trust as an action involves depending on someone or something doing something, the attitude presupposes this dependence and is then characterized as an attitude towards this dependence. Often the dependence is practical: we might only get to the film on time, for instance, if we both arrive at the arranged place on time. And equally often we depend in more ways than one: in trusting you to arrive on time, I might also put my good feelings towards you at risk. In general, to say that person A depends on S ϕ-ing is just to say that S's ϕ-ing is necessary for A pursuing some good or holding some attitude. With respect to our relation as audiences to speakers, the dependence at issue is epistemic: the starting point is the Testimony Game, which involves an audience depending on a speaker for information and so depending, at the very least, on the speaker telling the truth.

In this situation, we can distinguish two different ways of trusting: we can trust speakers to tell the truth, and we can trust testimony to be true. And we can trust in the latter way without trusting in the former way. We can judge that a speaker's testimony is evidence for its truth and so trust this bit of testimony to be true, even if we do not trust the speaker to tell the truth—indeed even if we judge the speaker to be quite untrustworthy. Were this the case, we would believe what is said, but we would not believe the speaker or take the speaker's telling as assurance. So explaining how believing someone amounts to trusting them for the truth requires attention to the differences between these ways of trusting.

These two different ways of trusting, I suggest, actually manifest two distinct attitudes of trust—the attitudes I labelled *predictive trust* and *affective trust* in 1.3.7. Predictive trust is simply a judgement of reliability made in a situation of dependence. It is described in Hollis's remark that

we trust one another to behave predictably in a sense that applies equally to the natural world at large. I trust my apple tree to bear apples, not oranges. I trust its boughs to bear my weight, if they look strong and healthy. I trust my reliable old alarm clock to wake me tomorrow, as it did yesterday.[22]

---

[22] Hollis (1998), p. 10.

To say an audience A trusts a speaker S's telling him that p, on this understanding, is just to say that A is dependent on S for the information as to whether p, knows that this is so, and judges that p is probably true, given S's testimony. This attitude of trust might then be defined thus:

A trusts S to ϕ (in the predictive sense) if and only if (1) A depends on S ϕ-ing and (2) A expects S to ϕ (where A expects this in the sense that A predicts that S will ϕ).

Trust is a combination of dependence (condition 1) and expectation (condition 2).

The dependence condition (1) should be understood factively: A depends on S ϕ-ing only if S's ϕ-ing really is necessary for A pursuing some good or holding some attitude. The expectation condition (2) by contrast is merely a matter of belief; it is a matter of a belief about the future, a prediction. Remove the expectation and all that remains is reliance, which is to say that A relies on S to ϕ if and only if A depends in some respect on S ϕ-ing. Remove the dependence and all that remains is a certain expectation, which is like trust in the same way that justified false belief is like knowledge. It is like trust in that it has the same mental component, but it is not the same attitude because trust is an attitude that one can only have in circumstances of dependence. By way of illustration consider Hollis's example of trusting a bough to hold one's weight. If one can see the bough is rotten, one doesn't trust it because one doesn't expect it to hold, though circumstances might still force one to rely on it. And if the bough is resting on the ground and one is idly balancing, one doesn't trust because there is no sense in which one is dependent—in particular *one is not exposed to any risk* were the bough not to hold one's weight.

Trust in this broad predictive sense is a matter of dependence and expectation: it is a willingness to rely because one predicts reliance will be profitable. One reason we can have for relying on a bit of testimony—for testimonial uptake—is that we think that this bit of testimony is true. So talk of trust in this predictive sense sits happily with a reductive theory of testimony. And with the reductive solution to the problem of cooperation: predictive trust is reasonable just when there are grounds for judging a cooperative outcome; and what makes the act of trusting reasonable is these grounds.

However, this attitude of trust is not sufficient for belief in a speaker. In 1.3.7 I illustrated this with case 15—Coady's case of hypnosis. To repeat this case, suppose an audience knows that Jones has been hypnotized by a master criminal and knows that this hypnotism is in effect when Jones blurts out something the audience knows the master criminal has an interest in his knowing. In this case, the audience can put all this background knowledge together and regard Jones's testimony as evidence for its truth, and so believe what Jones's says on this basis. The audience thereby trusts Jones's testimony to be true in the predictive sense, but there is little trust. He certainly does not *believe Jones* or *trust Jones for the truth*. So what is involved in trust in this sense?

There is a more normative notion of trust, what I have called *affective trust*. When we trust in this sense we expect things *of the trusted*, and not merely that something will happen. And that this expectation is more than a statement of our subjective probabilities is shown by the fact that we are susceptible to various reactive attitudes when these expectations are disappointed.[23] Trust is something that can be betrayed, and its being so would leave the trusting party open to feelings of betrayal. This thicker normative sense of trust may then be defined as follows.

A trusts *S* to ϕ (in the affective sense) if and only if (1) *A* depends on *S* ϕ-ing; and (2) *A* expects (1) to motivate *S* to ϕ (where *A* expects this in the sense that *A* expects it *of S* that *S* be moved by the reason to ϕ given by (1)).[24]

Trust in both the affective and predictive senses implies dependence. In both senses of trust *A* depends on *S* ϕ-ing; condition (1) is constant. And in both senses of trust there is an expectation condition (2); in both cases, *A* expects *S* to ϕ.[25] However, the *nature and grounds* of the expectations

[23] '[T]o hold someone to an expectation is essentially to be susceptible to a certain range of emotions in the case that the expectation is not fulfilled, or to believe that the violation of the expectation would make it appropriate for one to be subject to those emotions.' Wallace (1994), p. 21.

[24] This differs from the definition given in Faulkner (2007a), p. 882, which stated: '*A* trusts *S* to ϕ (in the affective sense) if and only if (1) *A* knowingly depends on *S* ϕ-ing; and (2) *A* expects *S*'s knowing that *A* depends on *S* ϕ-ing to motivate *S* to ϕ (where *A* expects this in the sense that he expects it of *S*).' The 'knowingly' has been dropped from (1) because it was meant to capture the two facts: of dependence, and of *A* having a perspective on dependence. But the former fact is still captured by (1), the latter is entailed by (2). And the 'knowing' has been dropped from (2) because I think it is the fact of *A*'s dependence that it is meant to move *S*, not *S*'s knowing this fact. Finally, the reason claim is added to (2) to clarify how *S* is meant to be motivated.

[25] It is also worth noting that the analysandum in both predictive and affective trust is the narrow '*A* trusts *S* to ϕ' rather than the broader '*A* trusts *S*'. This is because one can trust someone to do something without trusting them in general. However, it is arguable that trusting someone in general is accountable in terms of trusting them to do something. '*A* trusts *S*' could be read as 'For some significant range of ϕ, *A* trusts *S* to ϕ'.

stated in condition (2) differ across these senses of trust and it is important to make these differences clear.

Condition (2) describes the *nature* of *A*'s expecting *S* to be motivated to ϕ in terms of *A* expecting this *of S*. The contrast here is with the expectation that is constitutive of predictive trust. The contrast is between expecting *that something will happen* and expecting *something of someone*. When we expect something of someone we are susceptible to certain reactive attitudes if they do not do what is expected. Thus *A*'s expectation of *S*, stated in condition (2) of affective trust, needs to be understood in terms of *A* being susceptible to certain reactive attitudes were *S* to show no motivation to ϕ. The general reactive attitude in play here is *resentment*: in affectively trusting *S* to ϕ, *A* will be prone to resentment were *S* to show no motivation to ϕ. This reactive attitude is the hallmark of the defeat of normative expectations. Thus, were *S* to show no inclination to ϕ, *A*'s susceptibility to resentment shows that *A*'s expectation of *S* was that *S should have* been moved by his, *A*'s, depending on *S* ϕ-ing. To clarify the normative nature of *A*'s expectation, consider the connecting notion of *trustworthiness*.

Let me say that a trusted party *S* is trustworthy in a circumstance where *A* trusts *S* to ϕ if and only if *S* fulfils the expectation that *A* had in trust. This gives two notions of trustworthiness corresponding to the two notions of trust. With respect to testimony, and for the case of predictive trust where an audience *A*'s expectation is just that a speaker *S*'s testimony be true, the associated notion of trustworthiness is merely that *S* tell the truth. However, that we can demand more from a speaker if we are to regard the speaker as trustworthy is shown by Williams's example—case 32—of being told 'Someone's been opening your mail', when it is the speaker who has been doing so.[26] This speaker has said something she believes to be true, but what she has said is misleading because it implicates the falsehood that someone else has been opening the mail. To be informative and communicate a truth, she'd have to say more: 'Someone has been opening your mail and that someone is me' (or 'I've been opening your mail'). So despite telling the truth, the mail-opener is not trustworthy because she does not tell the truth informatively. However, this is what her audience would expect of her in testimonially depending on her: that she

---

[26] Williams (2002), p. 96.

regards his need for the truth as a reason to tell the truth informatively, or non-misleadingly. Generalizing this, one may say that a trusted party S is trustworthy, in a circumstance defined by A's trusting S to ϕ, if and only if S sees A's depending on his ϕ-ing as a reason to ϕ and is moved to ϕ for this reason.

The normative dimension of the expectation held in affective trust is then that the trusted party *should be* trustworthy. Thus, in trusting S to ϕ, A presumes that S *ought to* ϕ and, other things being equal, that S will ϕ for this reason. *De re* this is the presumption that the situation defined by A depending on S ϕ-ing is structured by a *norm of trustworthiness*. That the attitude of trust involves this presumption is shown in A's reactive attitudes; it is shown by the fact that A will be liable to resent S if S doesn't ϕ, or doesn't ϕ for this reason, since it is this norm which provides the content of A's reactive attitude. Thus, A's expectation is normative in that the resentment A would be susceptible to were S to show no inclination to ϕ is that S *did have* a reason and *ought to have acted on it*. This is the reason described by the norm, which is meant to prescribe behaviour irrespective of subjective motivation.

What the assurance account of telling then makes plain is that in the testimonial situation as it is found in the Testimony Game there is also a paired *norm of trust*. In telling A that p, S expects to be believed, where this involves more than A merely believing what S says, it involves A trusting S for the truth. And we can now see that this is a matter of A presuming that the reason S tells him, A, that p is just because he, A, depends on S for this information. That is, it is to presume something about S—how S sees the testimonial situation—and S's reasons for utterance. In this regard, Moran approvingly quotes Anscombe's observation that '[i]t is an insult and it may be an injury not to be believed'.[27] A speaker's susceptibility to this reactive attitude shows this expectation of being believed to be normative; and the norm gives the content of the speaker's reactive attitude were she not believed.

This norm of conversational trust, I suggest, is an instance of a general norm dictating that in circumstances where A could choose to trust S to ϕ, A ought to trust, other things being equal. That is, A *should* act on the presumption that if he depends on S ϕ-ing, S will be motivated by this to

---

[27] Anscombe (1979), p. 150. Quoted in Moran (2006), p. 301.

ϕ, and if S ϕs in a context where it is salient that A depends on S ϕ-ing, then A *ought to* explain S's ϕ-ing as a response to his, A's, need for S to ϕ. The operation of this general norm of trust might be illustrated by considering a variation of case 17, which sees a shopkeeper employ a recently discharged convict and leave him alone with the till. Suppose now, as case 33, that the shopkeeper installs CCTV and focuses it on the till. In these circumstances, where the shopkeeper could choose to trust her new employee with the till, we could imagine the employee resenting the shopkeeper taking these measures. Equally, the shopkeeper might feel shame at this behaviour and others judge that if she has gone so far as employing the ex-convict, when she need not have done, she ought to give him a chance.[28]

This is to say something about the *nature* of the expectation constitutive of affective trust, and with respect to the *ground* of this expectation two things need to be remarked. First, it is different from the ground of the expectation had in predictive trust, which is a background assessment of the probabilities of S ϕ-ing or the evidence for this, in that it is *reflexive*: affective trust is partly grounded by A's belief that S can recognize something about his situation, namely that he, A, depends on S ϕ-ing.[29] However, second, A's belief that S recognizes his, A's, depending on S ϕ-ing is only part of the ground of A's expectation because this expectation is further that S will be motivated to ϕ *because* he, A, depends on S ϕ-ing. Thus A's expectation is fully grounded by the belief that S recognizes that A's dependence on S ϕ-ing *and* the presumption that this will move S to ϕ.[30] This marks another difference with the grounds of the expectation constitutive of predictive trust. In the case of predictive trust, these grounds are A's general background of belief as applied to the trust situation. This is something fixed (for A at a time). So a potential trust situation will be conceived by A either as a situation where A can trust S or as one where A must merely rely on S; A does not have the liberty to decide to trust S. But we do have the liberty to decide to trust, and we do so because we have the liberty to decide to affectively trust. This is possible

---

[28] I consider the norms of trust and trustworthiness in more detail in 7.3.

[29] Compare Hardin's encapsulated interest model of trust. See Hardin (2002).

[30] In presuming that the trusted will see one's dependence as a reason to be trustworthy, the idea of affective trust is directly at odds with definitions of trust which make recognition of a truster's dependence a reason for untrustworthy behaviour. See Bacharach and Gambetta (2001), p. 3, Dasgupta (1988), p. 51.

only because of the way affective trust is grounded. It is possible because we can choose to depend on others doing things and have a certain liberty in the presumptions we make.

This feature of how affective trust is grounded has an important consequence. If one believes that p and presumes that p implies q, one will thereby come to presume that q. So in believing that S recognizes his, A's, dependence on S ϕ-ing and presuming that S will see his dependence as a reason to ϕ, A thereby presumes that S will recognize that she, S, has a reason to ϕ. So A will presume, other things being equal, that S will ϕ for this reason. This implied presumption that S will ϕ because A depends on S ϕ-ing is just the presumption that S will satisfy the expectation that A holds S to. It is the presumption that S will prove trustworthy.[31] Thus taking an attitude of affective trust involves presuming that the trusted will prove trustworthy.

This feature of affective trust has epistemic implications: it implies that the attitude of trust can warrant testimonial uptake. I argue this in the next section.

6.3 The rationality of trust

Trusting someone to do something is an action. Leaving one's closed diary on a desk where one knows one's partner will see it. Not asking for a second quote when a mechanic says one's car needs lots of work. Shaking on a deal. Following a stranger's directions. Purchasing a good that will be delivered later. These are examples of trust, and we trust in these cases by acting one way rather than another. So the rationality of trust, in the first instance, is practical. And the first question is, how does the attitude of trust practically rationalize an act of trusting?

6.3.1 The practical rationality of trust

Where trust is predictive its practical rationality is straightforward. It is reasonable for A to rely on S ϕ-ing if A predicts that S will ϕ. However, a

---

[31] The idea that trust involves a presumption that the trusted will be moved is also suggested by Jones, who states that in trust A has 'the expectation that S will be directly and favourably moved by the thought that A is counting on her'. Jones (1996), p. 6. Similarly Horsburgh identifies a notion of trust, therapeutic trust, which 'presupposes a belief in the possibility of stirring someone's conscience to an extent sufficient to affect his conduct'. Horsburgh (1960), p. 346.

key feature of affective trust is that it is not grounded by any belief about outcome. Again this can be illustrated by case 17—the shopkeeper case. The shopkeeper knows that her new employee has a history of theft, and this is evidence that there is some significant chance that he will steal from her. So, short of further evidence, it would be unreasonable for her simply to believe that things will work out favourably. However, one could suppose that she has no further evidence and yet not attribute any naïvety or false belief in explaining her trust. All that needs to be considered is how she, as a trusting person, will see things.

Keeping this case in mind but using the more general schema, in trusting S to ϕ, the grounds of A's attitude of trust are the belief that S can recognize his, A's, depending on S ϕ-ing, and the presumption that this will move S to ϕ. Thus, A will perceive the situation defined by this act of trust as one wherein S has a reason to ϕ. So other things being equal A will presume that S will ϕ. If this turns out to be true and S acts as A expects, S will have proved trustworthy. So in affectively trusting S to ϕ, A presumes that S will prove trustworthy just as in predictively trusting S to ϕ, A would believe this. This is not to suggest that trust involves A reasoning to this conclusion but is rather to claim that in trusting S to ϕ, A makes this presumption. However, the presumption that S will ϕ rationalizes A's act of trust in the same way that the belief that S will ϕ would do so. Consequently, the act of trust is rationally *self-supporting* in that it is based on an attitude of trust, which through implying the presumption that the trusted is trustworthy, gives a reason for trusting.

It might seem odd that trust can bootstrap itself into reasonableness in this way. However, this oddness should be lessened once it is clear that trust is both an attitude and an action and that what is being offered is an account of the interaction of these two aspects of trust. The dynamic by means of which reasons for trusting are generated can then be clarified by separating out the temporal stages wherein an act of trust follows a decision to trust.

The intention to do something, Bratman claims, involves a commitment to act and reason. Suppose that at t_0, A decides to trust S to ϕ, this decision involves commitments to act and reason. It implies a commitment to depend on S ϕ-ing at some later time t_1 and a commitment to act as if S has ϕ-ed at t_2, some later time still. In deciding to trust her new employee with the till the shopkeeper commits to leaving him alone with the till and acting as if he has behaved honestly subsequent to that. The decision to trust also involves a commitment to reason, or think about the trust situation, in a characteristic way. It involves a commitment to accept various things for the purposes of further practical reasoning. Acceptance here need not involve belief: the set of things accepted in adopting an attitude of trust may *bracket* certain beliefs or *posit* certain things that are not believed.[32] So in trusting her new employee the shopkeeper brackets her belief that he might well prove undesirable and thereby gives him the benefit of the doubt. And, in general, in deciding to trust S to ϕ, at t_0, A accepts 'S will be able to see that I depend on his ϕ-ing' and 'S will see this as a reason to ϕ'. Antecedent to the decision to trust S to ϕ, A may or may not have believed this about S, but adopting the attitude of affective trust commits A to accepting these propositions about S. Having accepted this at t_0, at t_1, when the context is one of depending on S ϕ-ing, A is thereby committed to accepting, 'S can see my dependence on his ϕ-ing', 'S sees that he has a reason to ϕ', and so to accepting: 'S will ϕ for this reason, other things being equal'. Then at t_2, and assuming that S did ϕ, A is committed to accepting 'S ϕ-ed, at least in part, because I depended on his ϕ-ing'.

Of course, this set of commitments can be overturned by the evidence: in deciding to trust S to ϕ, A does not decide to trust come what may. But if any of these propositions were not accepted, it would cease to make sense to say that A trusted because accepting this set of propositions is an expression of A's attitude of trust and so a commitment of A's decision to trust. This is not to suggest that trusting someone to do something involves explicitly committing to these propositions in one's reasoning. The claim is rather that the acceptance of these propositions partly defines how it is that the attitude of affective trust involves seeing things in a certain light.[33]

This comes out in the phenomenology. It is part of the phenomenology of trust that the adoption of an attitude of trust involves a certain insensitivity to the possibility that one's trust will be let down.[34] So if the shopkeeper trusts her new employee, she will not worry about the possibilities of theft her leaving him alone with the till opens. And this

---

[32] See Bratman (1999), p. 30, n.20.

[33] 'Partly' because 'seeing things in the light of trust' is also a matter of seeing the testimonial situation in the way it would be seen by one who has internalized the norms of trust, and what this involves I describe in 7.3.1.

[34] See Möllering (2009).

phenomenological point flags a constitutive one: if the shopkeeper really does worry about the various possibilities, and, as described in case 33, installs CCTV to guard against them, then the shopkeeper's attitude ceases to be one of trust. To trust, Elster observes, 'is to lower one's guard, *to refrain from taking precautions against an interaction partner*, even when the other, because of opportunism or incompetence, could act in a way that might seem to justify precautions'.[35] In trust one lowers one's guard because the possibilities of one's trust being betrayed are excluded by what must be accepted in holding an attitude of trust. This background of acceptance then specifies a way of thinking about the trust situation, which yields the presumption that the trusted is trustworthy that provides a reason for trusting.

One case of trust, and the case that I am centrally interested in, is trusting a speaker for the truth. In this case, the act of trust is the acceptance of testimony, but acceptance on trust is uptake. So even if it is allowed that trust can practically rationalize the acceptance of testimony, and so make acceptance reasonable, it remains a further question whether trust can provide an epistemic reason for belief, and so make uptake reasonable. Whether it can do so I consider next.

6.3.2 *The epistemic rationality of trust*

The intuitive contrast between an epistemic and a practical reason for belief is that an epistemic reason is a consideration that counts in favour of a belief being true, whereas a practical reason is a consideration that counts in favour of holding a belief irrespective of its truth. This idea can be taken at face value and explicated in terms of *subjective probability*: a consideration r is an epistemic reason for a hypothesis h if and only if the probability of h given r is greater than the probability of *not-h*. Now consider Pascal's Wager: it is better to believe in God than not because the cost of not believing so far outweighs the cost of believing falsely. This is a practical reason for belief: it is an argument for holding a belief, or system of beliefs, irrespective of the truth of the matter. And it is not an epistemic reason on this understanding: the hypothesis that there is a God, heaven and hell etc. is no more probable given Pascal's Wager than not. So this probabilistic definition provides a simple way of understanding what an epistemic reason is.

---

[35] Elster (2007), p. 344.

On this minimal understanding, the attitude of affectively trusting a speaker for the truth provides an epistemic reason for believing the speaker's testimony. For suppose A trusts S for the truth as to whether p and S tells A that p. Then A's attitude of trust, I argued in the last section, involves A accepting various propositions about S and the trust situation, where the acceptance of these propositions defines what it is to see depending on S for information as to whether p in the positive light of trust. So in affectively trusting S for the truth, A accepts that S will see his, A's, depending on S for information as to whether p as a reason to tell A the truth on this matter. So trust involves A accepting that S has a reason to tell him the truth, and accepting that S will act on this reason, other things being equal. (And if A believed that other things were not equal, then trust would become as psychologically problematic as bracketing this belief.) In accepting these things about S and the trust situation, A thereby presumes that S is trustworthy, or that S will tell him the truth and will do so for the reason that he, A, depends on S for this. This presumption need not amount to the belief that S is trustworthy since its ground is things which need be merely accepted in the trust situation. However, this presumption, like the belief with the same content, makes it probable for A that p is true given that this is what S tells him. So A's attitude of trust raises the probability of p, when this is what S tells him. So A's trusting S for the truth, in a situation where S tells A that p, provides A with an epistemic reason to believe that p.

Nevertheless, this might be taken to suggest that more is needed for a consideration to be an epistemic reason. Thus consider the Bayesian conception of evidence, which has been given the same definition *viz.*, e is evidence for h iff prob$(h/e) \rangle$ prob(h); or, more accurately, e is evidence for h iff prob$(h/e\&b) \rangle$ prob(h/b), where 'b' is one's background information.[36] One problem with this conception of evidence, according Peter Achinstein, is that it fails of sufficiency. Some fact might raise the probability of a hypothesis without being evidence. 'When I walk across the street', Achinstein observes, 'I increase the probability I will be hit by a 1970 Cadillac; but the fact that I am walking across the street is not evidence that I will be hit by a 1970 Cadillac.'[37] It is not evidence that I will be hit by a 1970 Cadillac, Achinstein thinks, *because it does not warrant*

---

[36] See Horwich (1982), pp. 51–2.
[37] Achinstein (1978), p. 152.

me in believing this.[38] However, if one cannot similarly identify a notion of epistemic reasons independent of reason's normative dimension, there is the murky issue of how good a reason has to be in order to be a reason. Rather than try and resolve this, let me, for the sake of argument, run the connection the other way. It is surely true that a consideration that epistemically warrants belief must by that very fact be an epistemic reason. And that a belief is epistemically warranted if it is based on the evidence.[39] So if a consideration *r* is evidence for a hypothesis *h*, then *r* is an epistemic reason for *h*. The question, then, is whether trust can be conceived as a form of evidence.

To answer this question, a concept of evidence is needed. A well-articulated, and defended, definition is that proposed by Achinstein:

e is potential evidence that *h*, given *b*, if and only if (a) *e* and *b* are true, (b) *e* does not entail *h*, (c) prob(*h*/*e*&*b*) $\rangle k$, (d) prob(there is an explanatory connection between *h* and *e*/*h*&*e*&*b*) $\rangle k$.[40]

Applied to the present case, where *A* trusts *S* to tell him the truth and *S* tells *A* that *p*, *e* is *A*'s attitude of trust, or, more precisely, the fact that *A* trusts *S* to tell him the truth, *b* is the background of propositions *A* accepts in holding this attitude, and *h* is the proposition that *p*. Are conditions (a) to (d) then satisfied in this case?

Let me consider condition (a) last. Condition (b) is satisfied: it is always possible for *A* to trust and for *S* to be untrustworthy, or for *A* to trust *S* to be trustworthy but just to be wrong as to whether *p*. So the fact that *A* trusts *S* to tell the truth when *S* tells *A* that *p* does not entail that *p* is true.

The probability at issue in conditions (c) and (d) is objective.[41] So the questions are respectively whether the fact that *A*'s trusts *S* to tell the truth whether *p* makes it more objectively probable that *p* is true? And whether there is some objective probability of an explanatory connection between the truth of *p* and the fact that *A* trusts *S* to tell the truth as to whether *p*?

---

[38] So one defence of the Bayesian conception: deny the assumed connection between evidence and warrant. See Kronz (1992), p. 160.

[39] Note: this is not a claim about the nature of warrant; though it has been proposed as such. See Feldman and Conee (1985).

[40] Achinstein (1978), p. 162. Achinstein (2001) changes this definition by dropping condition (c), making the probability stated in condition (d) as relative to *e*&*b*, not *h*&*e*&*b*, and specifying *k* as equal to ½, see p.170. The argument that follows is indifferent to this change.

[41] See Achinstein (1978), p. 159.

These conditions can be taken together since both would be satisfied if either of the following two things were objectively probable: (1) the fact of A's trust explains S's trustworthiness; (2) some further feature of the trust situation explains both the fact of A's trust and S's trustworthiness. (I take it for granted that S's trustworthiness can explain the truth of p.) Both of these things, I will now contend, ordinarily hold.

With respect to (2), the feature of the trust situation that explains both the fact of A's trust and S's trustworthiness is its being a situation where norms of trust apply. According to these norms S should take A's dependence on her for information as a reason to tell A what he needs to know. And A should explain S's telling him that p in terms of S being motivated by this reason. So if both interlocutors were to have internalized these norms of trust, S would see that she has a reason to tell A the truth and would feel the force of this reason; whilst A would see that S has this reason and presume it to be what motivates S's telling. The operation of these norms can thereby explain A's trust and S's trustworthiness. So *if our society is such that there are norms of trust*, then it is objectively probable that this explanation will apply. Here I must issue a final promissory note: I will only complete the argument that this antecedent is true in the next chapter, in 7.3.2. However, this argument has already been started. Our conversations as to the facts, I've argued, are structured by normative expectations: we can expect others to tell us the truth, and can expect others to presume that we do so when we tell them things. And, I have claimed, these normative expectations, and the reactive attitudes that they render interlocutors susceptible to, can only be properly specified by reference to the norms that guide our conversational practices.

With respect to (1), the fact of A's trust would explain S's trustworthiness if it gave S reason to be trustworthy. And this it does do. In trusting S to tell the truth, A takes an evaluative stance towards S which gives S two types of reason to be trustworthy, yielding two different explanations of S's trustworthiness. First—explanation (1a)—A's evaluative stance is expressed positively in A's presumption that S will take the same view of his, A's, dependence on S for information, as he, A does. It is expressed positively in A's presumption that S will see his need for the truth as a reason to tell the truth. And even if this is not true prior to the trust situation, this situation gives S the opportunity to make it true by responding to A's dependence as A expects. In this way, acts of trust can create as well as sustain trusting relations.[42] So if S thinks about the trust situation in the same way as A does in trust, or if S proves sensitive to A's trust, then S will take herself to have a reason to be trustworthy where this reason is intrinsic to the logic of trust. Second—explanation (1b)—the evaluative stance that A takes in trusting S is expressed negatively in A's willingness to resent S were S not to try and tell the truth. And were S to let A's trust down in this way, S's behaviour would, in all probability, equally elicit the judgement of third parties. So A's trust gives S an instrumental reason to be trustworthy.[43]

There is a split between these explanations of S's trustworthiness. The instrumental reason, described in explnation (1b), is a reason for anyone, to the extent that everyone desires to avoid the resentment and disapproval of others. So, to the extent that S can imagine the responses untrustworthiness would provoke, rational deliberation over how to respond to A's trust should lead S to the conclusion that she has some reason to be trustworthy. The split is that this practical reason is not that prescribed by the norm; it is extrinsic to the logic of trust, it is *a mere side-effect*. This is shown by the fact that this motivation can be self-defeating. Suppose that S only tells A the truth because she knows A will be provoked if she does not. If A finds this out, A might yet be provoked: that S was inattentive to what should have been S's reason for telling, which is his, A's, need to know whether p. Jon Elster makes a related point in claiming that trustworthiness is *essentially a by-product*.[44] He cites Montaigne who gives a case much like case 17—the case of the shopkeeper: his trusting his servant with 'full charge of [his purse] without supervision'.[45] The servant, Montaigne observes, 'could cheat me just as well if I kept accounts, and, unless he is a devil, by such reckless trust I oblige him to be honest'.[46] However, this obligation would vanish if Montaigne's reason for giving his servant full charge of his purse was simply to make the servant behave well. To say that trustworthiness is an essential by-product, is then to say that 'it cannot be realized by actions motivated only by the desire to realise [it]'.[47] The reason for this, I suggest,

---

[42] 'Not only does trust build on trust . . . trust can also build on nothing and can help to establish such relationships in the first place. It can create *de novo*.' Pettit (1995), p. 218.

[43] See Pettit (1995).

[44] Elster (2007), p. 351.

[45] Montaigne (2004), p. 1078.

[46] Montaigne (2004), p. 1079, cited in Elster (2007), p. 350.

[47] Elster (2007), p. 86.

is that in trusting his servant, Montaigne makes manifest a positive presumption about his servants trustworthiness; whereas Montaigne would make manifest that he believes the quite contrary proposition that his servant is not trustworthy, if his trust were meant to secure its end by way of the threat of his resentment or others' disapproval.

Nevertheless, the fact of A's trust gives S two types of reason to be trustworthy. And if S then responds to either of these reasons, A's trust will be an essential premise in an explanation of S's trustworthiness. And given that our society is such that we think about trust in the ways that the norms of trust prescribe, and desire to avoid others' resentment and judgement, there is some objective probability of such an explanation. Thus conditions (c) and (d) are satisfied.

So the fact that A trusts S to tell the truth is potential evidence that p is true when S tells A that p if and only if condition (a) is satisfied. This condition states that e and b are true. Note that it is not required that e and b be known by A to be true, or that A be justified in believing that e and b true. But merely that e and b are true. Now, by hypothesis e is true since it is A's attitude of trust that is under consideration, in fact A does trust S to tell the truth. However, the background of propositions that A accepts in adopting this attitude of trust—that is, b—will be true in some trust situations and false in others. If b is false then S would not see A's dependence as a reason to tell A the truth, or would not be motivated by this reason. Consequently, the fact that A trusts S to tell the truth *would not be* potential evidence that p is true, when S tells A that p. However, in many trust situations b will be true. In these cases S will see A's need for the truth as a reason to tell A the truth and be motivated by this reason to try and tell the truth. Consequently, the fact that A trusts S to tell the truth *would be* potential evidence that p is true, when S tells A that p.

So there are two situations, in both of which A's attitude of trusting S to tell to the truth, when S tells A that p, provides an epistemic reason to believe that p, in the minimal sense described that it makes it subjectively probable for A that p. But only in one case does the fact of A trusting in this situation provide potential evidence that p is true. However, this is an epistemological commonplace. Take the case of perception where e is the fact that A confronts the perceptual appearance of p and b is the background belief that in this case the perceptual appearance is caused in the ordinary way that perceptual appearances are caused, namely by the objects and events it seems to A to be a perception of. Then consider the two cases defined by *b* being true in one and false in the other (where these are the two cases that form the starting point of an argument from perceptual error). In both cases, the perceptual appearance provides *A* with an epistemic reason to believe that *p*, in the minimal sense described. But only in one case does the fact that things appear to *A* as they do provide potential evidence that *p* is true. Nevertheless, we do not hesitate to regard the perceptual appearance of *p* as an epistemic reason for believing that *p*. And, arguably we do not hesitate because we know that when our background belief about the causal structures in which the perceptual appearance of *p* is embedded are true, the fact that *A* confronts this perceptual appearance is potential evidence that *p* is true. And the very same thing goes for testimony, or, more specifically, for trusting a speaker's telling.

This is to say two things. First, given that *A*'s attitude of trusting *S* to tell to the truth, when *S* tells *A* that *p can be* evidence that *p*, we should not hesitate in regarding it as providing *A* with an epistemic reason to believe that *p*. Second, ultimately what determines that the attitude of trust provides an epistemic reason is the existence of the causal structures that ensure the attitude of trust can be potential evidence. This is to say that trust supplies an epistemic reason for belief because the substantive conditions (c) and (d), in Achinstein's definition of evidence, can be satisfied. And that is, because it is objectively probable that explanations (1) and (2) hold good. The difference with perception is then that the causal structures that underwrite these explanations concern the reasons we have for telling audiences things and believing what speakers tell us. Thus, ultimately, the attitude of trust provides an epistemic reason because there are norms of conversational trust shaping the nature of the reasons we have, for utterance and for belief, in conversations as to the facts. Again, I will return to this in 7.3.

6.4 Trust and assurance

The assurance theory of testimony, I argued in 6.1, faces a dilemma. Suppose that *A* trusts *S* for the truth as to whether *p* and *S* tells *A* that *p*. What warrants *A*'s testimonial uptake? To the extent that it considers this question, the assurance theory answers: the fact that *A* recognizes the intentions constitutive of *S*'s telling, and so regards this as offering *S*'s assurance that *p*. The problem is that *A* will take *S*'s intentions at face value, and regard *S*'s telling in this way, if and only if *A* trusts *S* for the truth. But this then raises the question, what warrants A's attitude of trust? And here the options can seem to be exhausted by the reductive and non-reductive theories; that is, either A's trust must be entitled, or it must be warranted by the reasons that A has for believing that S is trustworthy.

It is now possible, I think, to resolve this dilemma through adding an account of trust-based testimonial uptake to the assurance account. In trusting S for truth as to whether p, A trusts in the affective sense. This is the attitude of trust that S invites in telling A that p: to view her, S's, telling as an intentional response to A's need to know whether p. But while predictive trust can be equated with the belief that the trusted is trustworthy, this is not true of affective trust, which is constituted by a different expectation. So the dilemma is shown to be a false one. What warrants A's testimonial uptake is neither some general entitlement to trust, nor the grounds that A has for believing S to be trustworthy (for trusting in the predictive sense). Rather, what warrants A's testimonial uptake is simply A's attitude of affective trust. In the context of S telling A that p, this trusting attitude provides A with an epistemic reason for believing that p.

With this account of trust added to the assurance theory of testimony, this theory can be seen to be of the trust type this monograph aims to defend. That is, it can be seen to endorse both uptake principle (R) and transmission principles (TK) and (TW). It endorses all three principles because it endorses a narrower principle in each case. With respect to the latter transmission principles, (TK) and (TW) are endorsed for the reason described in 6.1: in telling A that p, S's telling transmits knowledge, or warranted belief, only if S *herself* is in a position to discharge the responsibilities assumed in telling; that is, only if S can articulate the knowledge supporting grounds or warrant for p, or is able to indicate the source of this. And given that A's uptake of S's telling requires that A trust S for the truth as to whether p, what is required is that A have a particular reason warranting testimonial uptake. This implies satisfaction of the requirement on warranted uptake imposed by (R).

Nevertheless, there is a sense in which the assurance theory is right to claim that it is S's telling that provides A's reason for belief. To see this the trust-based account of testimonial uptake should be compared and contrasted to the reductive account. When S tells A that p, what is A's reason for believing that p? According to the reductive theory, A's reason is the conjunction of S's telling and the belief that S's telling is a bit of evidence. According to the trust-based account, A's reason will be the conjunction of S's telling and A's attitude of trust. So in both cases A's reason for believing that p will be S's telling him that p plus some uptake-warranting attitude. But in the case of the reductive theory the epistemic status of A's resulting testimonial belief is determined by the warrant that A has for this attitude: it is determined by A's grounds for believing that S's telling is evidence. However, according to the assurance theory, the epistemic status of A's resulting testimonial belief is determined by S's epistemic standing. But then, with regards to the epistemic status of A's testimonial belief, A's attitude of trust is, in this sense, epistemically invisible. Through testimony A gains knowledge, or warranted belief, *on trust* as it were. Thus, it is natural, if a little infelicitous, to say simply that it is S's telling that supplies A's reason for belief.

6.5 Lackey's objections to the assurance theory

In her monograph *Learning from Words* (not people) Jennifer Lackey devotes a chapter to criticizing root and branch the assurance theory, which she calls 'the interpersonal view of testimony'. In this section I hope to clarify and defend my conception of the assurance theory by developing and responding to Lackey's arguments.

Lackey's central objection takes the form of a dilemma: 'either the view of testimony in question is genuinely interpersonal but epistemologically impotent, or it is not epistemologically impotent but neither is it genuinely interpersonal'.[48] Lackey's argument for the first horn of the dilemma runs as follows:

Suppose, for instance, that I have counter-evidence for Hubert's testimony that albatrosses have the largest wingspan among wild birds—say, a respectable colleague called into question his credentials as an ornithologist. . . . Suppose, also, that you tell me Hubert is one of the best in his field. According to the Assurance View . . . certain non-evidential features of our interpersonal relationship provide me with a *reason* for believing that Hubert is one of the best ornithologists in the field, one that is entirely different in kind than a reason provided by evidence. Now, if this is a reason *in an epistemic sense*, it should clearly be capable of functioning as a defeater-defeater for the original counter-evidence I had against Hubert's competence as an ornithologist. But here is the problem: if, on the one

---

[48] Lackey (2008), p. 222.

hand, the epistemic value of your testimony is conceived in wholly non-evidential terms... then it is entirely unclear how a purely non-evidential reason could function as a defeater-defeater.... On the other hand, if... the non-evidential reason provided by your testimony simply cannot function as a defeater-defeater, then this amounts to a concession to the epistemological irrelevance of the reasons provided by testimony.[49]

So Lackey concludes that in believing you, or trusting you for the truth, I *must* gain a defeater-defeater. But this requires that further conditions must be satisfied. It is not enough that you *tell* me that Hubert is one of the best in the field because we know that very unreliable speakers tell us things and give their assurance. Thus, we must further suppose at least that a speaker satisfies a reliability condition. The second horn of the dilemma is then the challenge of stating why the epistemic nature of the reason provided by a speaker's testimony remains 'certain non-evidential features of the interpersonal relationship' once this further condition is added. This is a challenge Lackey thinks cannot be met.

This dilemma, in my opinion, fails at the first horn. If you tell me that Hubert is one of the best in his field and I believe you, then I come to form a belief—namely that Hubert is one of the best in his field—that functions as a rebutting defeater of my counter-evidence.[50] It is entirely clear how a belief can function as a defeater.

Nevertheless, Lackey's objection could be pushed back a level: in coming to this belief about Hubert I must weigh up the non-evidential reason provided by your testimony against the contrary evidence provided by my colleague's testimony. In order to do this, I must weigh the evidence of my colleague's testimony against my reasons for trusting you. And the problem here is that the kinds of consideration that go into explaining acts of trust will frequently be non-epistemic. Trusting someone to do something is an action, so the reasons we can have for trust will be firmly in the practical sphere. One might trust, for instance, in anticipation of future reward or out of fear of sanctions. The decision to trust you might come down to the fact that not doing so will evoke your ire. This reason is genuinely interpersonal but it is not an epistemic reason for belief. And here is Lackey's dilemma: if my reasons for trusting you are only practical reasons, then trust does not provide an epistemic reason for

---

[49] Lackey (2008), p. 225.
[50] For the distinction between rebutting and under-cutting defeat see Pollock (1986).

belief; but if my reasons for trusting you are evidential, then adding that my uptake of what you tell me is nonetheless based on trust merely adds an interpersonal layer that contributes nothing epistemic.

Now as Lackey's criticism observes, our reasons for trusting can be merely practical. But this in itself does not imply that the reason for belief that trust provides is merely a practical reason. What motivates trust—its psychological background—is one question, whether or not trust can provide an epistemic reason for belief is another. So the question is, can the reason for testimonial uptake that trust provides be an epistemic reason? If it can, Lackey's dilemma fails at its first horn, as claimed. Hopefully, 6.3.2 persuaded that the attitude of trust does indeed provide an epistemic reason, or more precisely that A's attitude of trusting S for the truth, when S tells A that p, provides A with an epistemic reason for believing that p. The nub of the argument for this claim is that A's attitude of trust provides an epistemic reason because, when it is true that p, it is objectively probable that the truth of p is not accidental relative to A's trust.

However, Lackey has a further argument against the idea that trust gives an epistemic reason because of these kinds of explanatory connections. In her terms the 'reasons generated by trust argument', or 'RGTA', fails because one cannot justifiably believe *of anyone* that they will prove trust-responsive. Moreover, we only believe this of *some* people and in *some* circumstances. Consequently, 'when I decide to trust S with respect to x, my trust moving S with regards to x depends, at the very least, on S's character, S's regard for others, S's regard for me, S's attitude towards x, and S's current situation or context'.[51] What this means is that either I have reasons to believe that S will prove trust-responsive on the basis of believing these things about S's character etc., in which case my testimonial belief will be justified but 'not on the basis of an awareness of trust's generative nature'; or I do not have any basis for believing that S will prove trust-responsive 'in which case beliefs acquired on the basis of her testimony are clearly not epistemically justified'.[52]

At this juncture Lackey is wrong to suppose that 'the thesis put forth . . . is: a hearer's awareness of the generative feature of trust—as it is characterized in the RGTA—can render the belief that she forms on the basis of a

---

[51] Lackey (2008), p. 245.   [52] Lackey (2008), p. 248.

speaker's testimony epistemically justified'.[53] The audience A's reason for believing that p, when this is what S tells him, is not the belief that S will prove to be trust-responsive, it is simply the fact that S told him that p (and A trusts S for the truth on this matter). And S's telling is seen to provide a reason, I argued, because in trusting S for the truth A accepts certain things about S and the testimonial situation which yield the presumption that S is trustworthy. However, this mistake does not address Lackey's major objection, which is that we are discriminating in whom we trust, and it is the background of belief that informs our discriminations that matters epistemically. So, and in short, the reason ostensibly provided by affective trust in fact reduces to a more ordinary probabilistic reason.

In reply, it can be conceded that we are always in a position to form some judgement of the truth of a piece of testimony. This is what makes a reductive theory of testimony theoretically viable. Suppose then, for the sake of argument, that it is allowed that for every case where testimonial uptake is warranted, an audience possesses proprietary reasons that could account for this warrant. This is not yet to concede that these reasons are the grounds of testimonial uptake, and so what matters epistemically. Rather, it might be that these reasons play a merely psychological role—even a necessary psychological role—of getting an audience into a position where trust becomes psychologically possible. If this were their function, it would be to enable testimonial uptake. But testimonial uptake would then be warranted by its being grounded on trust. Thus, proprietary reasons for uptake might be ever present, and even psychologically necessary, but they need play no essential epistemic role insofar as they are not an epistemic pre-condition of trust and so are not necessary for uptake to be warranted.

We can have evidence that a piece of testimony is true and yet base testimonial uptake on trust rather than this evidence. And it could be allowed, for the sake of argument, that for every actual case of testimonial uptake based on trust, the propositions that we accept in adopting an attitude of trust we also have evidence for, and that this evidence is psychologically necessary for trust.[54] However, what cannot be allowed is that the attitude of trust be based on this evidence, as the objection

---

[53] Lackey (2008), p. 242.

[54] In fact, in many actual cases of testimonial uptake on the basis of trust the dictates of an audience's proprietary reasons would not be so clear. See, for instance, case 17 and 3.1.

suggests, as then it would not be trust (or it would be merely trust in the predictive sense). In this respect, a too thorough assessment of the risk is inimical to trust.[55] This point is subtle because it is not clear at what point trust ceases; it is not always clear when thinking about whether to trust becomes the ground of uptake rather than merely the fixation of trust. But there is a point at which one merely believes what is said and not the person.

Equally subtle is the point at which evidence undermines the reasonableness of trust. The objection is right to claim that trust can be unwarranted, and right to assign a central justificatory role to the proposition that the trusted will respond to being trusted in a certain way. The key proposition, in trusting a speaker S for the truth as to whether p, is that: S will view A depending on S for the truth as a reason to tell A the truth. However, just as it is the case that it is not a pre-condition of trust that A have evidence for the truth of this proposition, A's trust is not rendered unreasonable by evidence that this proposition is false. In trust we can, and do, give the trusted the benefit of the doubt, and in part because extending trust can be a way of creating the conditions for this proposition's truth. When would evidence of this proposition's falsity determine that trust is unreasonable? If the evidence *obliged* A to believe that this proposition is false, then trust would certainly be unreasonable. And, in most cases, it would no doubt be unreasonable *before* this limiting point. But at what point it would be so is not something that can be specified by a rule: the reason provided by trust is not subject to any simple logic of defeat.

This is illustrated by Lackey's Hubert case, quoted above. Let me simplify this case slightly, and let this be case 34:

Hubert tells A that albatrosses have the largest wingspan, and A is trying to decide whether or not Hubert knows what he is talking about—A is trying to decide whether p. X tells A that Hubert has no credentials as an ornithologist, and A has good reason to believe X. Y tells A that Hubert is one of the best ornithologists in his field, and A is inclined to trust Y on this matter.

What should A think about Hubert? Should A believe that Hubert knows what he is talking about? That is, should A believe that p? Certainly, this question can be difficult to answer. It is unclear how we weigh up evidence on the one side against our trust in a person on the other. However, this lack of clarity is not peculiar to the idea that trusting a person for the truth can give a reason. Suppose that A does not trust Y on this matter but has simply observed Y's testimony to have often proved true. In this case A has two straightforwardly conflicting bits of evidence— Y's testimony that p and X's that not-p—and it is equally often quite unclear how we should proceed in these circumstances. Of course, we can specify what A should do in trivial manner: A should form belief on the basis of the better item of evidence. But this triviality cannot be specified into anything that might inform A's decision as to whether or not to believe that p; it cannot be specified into anything like a rule. And short of something like a rule, what A would actually do is either make some kind of educated guess, or choose to trust one or other of X and Y.

Suppose that A then chooses to trust Y. In believing Y, A will come to believe that p. Lackey's question about defeat may then put as: can A's trust warrant the uptake of Y's testimony in the face of the counter-evidence provided by X's testimony that not-p? As with the case where A confronts conflicting bits of evidence, the answer to this question depends on how strong the evidence is. And this can be hard to judge. But it is certainly not the case that A's warrant for the uptake of Y's testimony is defeated by any counter-evidence. Is the contrary evidence provided by X's testimony of the belief obliging sort? I suppose not, and on this supposition, I take it that A's trust could warrant the uptake of Y's testimony to p.[56]

Thus, in a testimonial situation defined by S telling A that p, evidence that p is true, and evidence that p is false, has a bearing on the warrant that A has for the uptake of S's testimony, but it need not have the direct bearing that Lackey presumes. This is because when A acquires the belief that p on the basis of S's telling him that p there can be two different explanations of this fact. According to the first explanation A's testimonial uptake is grounded on the belief that S's testimony is evidence for p, or A's opinion of the truth of the telling. According to the second explanation A's testimonial uptake is grounded on A's trusting S for the truth as to whether p, or A's believing S. These explanations are not exclusive in that

---

[56] Or consider the boy who cried wolf. By the third cry he was no longer believed. But suppose a trusting villager managed to reason himself into a position where he did trust the boy in his cry—'he wouldn't lie a third time!' In this case, could the villager get to know on trust that a wolf was amongst the flock? I think so.

in many cases both options are live. We can trust or not. We can regard a speaker's telling as evidence or assurance. But these explanations are exclusive in that each determines a different explanation of the warrant we have for testimonial uptake. The mistake made by Lackey's criticism, and the mistake made by the reductive theory quite generally, is then that it fails to recognize that there are more ways of being warranted in the uptake of testimony than by way of the evidence.

6.6 Conclusion: the limits of assurance

The assurance theory of testimony gives a good account of the epistemology of what Welbourne calls 'the simplest cases', where an audience is addressed and belief in a speaker is an option.[57] It is good for the conversations as to the facts, which are the focus of the Testimony Game. After considering these cases, the argument from cooperation concludes that an audience must have a reason for believing that p, when this is what a speaker tells him. The assurance theory then provides a statement of a reason that an audience can have, which is simply that the speaker told him that p, and he trusts the speaker for the truth on this matter. In trusting the speaker for the truth, the audience will regard the speaker's telling as offering the speaker's assurance that p; and this is what the speaker intends in telling the audience that p. This reason is then available in nearly any given case. In particular, the attitude of trust can rationalize testimonial uptake even in a one-off game played under conditions of ignorance. So the assurance theory provides a non-sceptical solution to the problem of cooperation. I will return to develop this point in 7.3.

The assurance theory of testimony, as here presented, is also a trust theory insofar as it implies both the principle of reasonable uptake (R) and transmission principles for testimonial knowledge and warrant, (TK) and (TW). However, the assurance theory is *not the trust theory* this monograph aims to defend. The assurance theory *fails as a theory of testimony*. The problem is one of scope.

---

[57] '[I]n the simplest kind of case where you address me directly, it is sufficient and necessary for the transmission of your knowledge that p to me that I *believe you* when, speaking (or writing) from knowledge, you tell me that p.' Welbourne (1979), p. 3.

168 KNOWLEDGE ON TRUST

The problem is that the assurance explanation of transmission is not entirely general. It cannot explain the conditions on any given occasion under which one can acquire testimonial knowledge or testimonially warranted belief. Tellings, according to Moran, are assertoric speech acts, which intend to be informative through belief in the speaker.[58] However, many intelligible utterances either do not allow such recognition of intention, or are not made with this specific intention. The anonymity of much that is written ensures it is difficult to uncover intentions beyond the writer's presenting something as true; whilst in illicitly eavesdropping we do not recognize any intention that we be informed of things. Similarly, it does not make sense to regard the illicit eavesdropper as affectively trusting the speaker for the truth. It would certainly be unreasonable for the eavesdropper to presume that the speaker said what she did in order to tell *him*, the eavesdropper, something. However, writings and overheard conversations can be highly informative. So identified as *sources of knowledge* writings and overheard conversations are testimony in a broad sense. Consequently, when it is identified as a source of knowledge, a natural way of understanding 'testimony to *p*' is 'an intelligible utterance that presents that *p* as true', where this was the definition of testimony offered in 1.3.2. Tellings are testimony in this latter sense, but they also constitute a specific class of testimony in their own right. The scope of assurance views is therefore that they merely provide an account of the *epistemology of tellings*.

It is possible, of course, to hold fast and equate a theory of testimony with a theory of tellings. The epistemological interest in testimony lies in the identification of testimony as a unique source of knowledge. So it is possible to hold that testimony is a unique source of knowledge because it is knowledge-based-on-tellings. This seems to be what Hinchman has in mind when he contrasts 'tellings' with 'mere assertions'; *only* in explicitly telling something does a speaker assume responsibility for having given, or standing able to give, a reason for belief. This is illustrated, Hinchman claims, by the difference in the epistemic position of someone who merely overhears a speaker's telling an audience something and the audience who is told this thing: the telling makes an entitlement available to the audience but the eavesdropper must get away with whatever evidence this

---

[58] 'Finally, within the class of assertions whose aim *is* informative, some of these have the aim that the speaker himself *be believed*, and these have the force or intent of *telling* the audience something.' Moran (2005), p. 347.

provides.[59] The epistemic contrast between these cases is thereby a contrast between two different explanations of an audience's acquisition of knowledge. When an audience is told that p the assurance explanation of the audience's getting to know p is possible. By contrast, when an audience merely overhears another being told that p, or merely understands an utterance that asserts that p, the explanation of the audience's acquisition of the knowledge that p is the reductive explanation.

This division of the epistemic domain is right in principle: there are two distinct ways of acquiring knowledge and warranted belief from testimony. However, it is wrong in its extension. We can acquire *testimonial* knowledge from overheard testimony, and are not limited to acquiring inductive knowledge from it. This is illustrated by case 18 (the gossip case) wherein it is testimonial knowledge that is acquired, but where the assurance explanation of this knowledge is not possible.

Case 18. A speaker S tells a gossip T that p knowing that p. The gossip T doesn't believe S but knowing that p will upset audience A maliciously tells A that p.[60]

In this situation, it seems that A can acquire knowledge that p provided only that S knows that p. In this case it seems as if S's knowledge has been transmitted to A, skipping the link in the chain that is T. However, T does not believe S and does not stand responsible for what he tells A. Thus, testimonial knowledge seems to be broader category than knowledge-transmitted-by-assurance.

The assurance theory does not suffice for an adequate epistemological theory of testimony. But this is not to say that it cannot be part of such a theory. The part it plays, I want to argue in the next chapter, is in providing a solution to the problem of cooperation. And this solution shows how we have a social institution of testimony defined by the existence of social norms of conversational trust. The correct description of this institution then takes testimony out of the simplest cases, where tellings are offered as assurance, and reveals testimony to be a general mechanism for the transmission of knowledge and warrant.

---

[59] 'As I've argued, only these hearers *eo ipso* gain access to an entitlement to believe what the speaker tells them; other hearers—overhearers—gain access to the same kind of warrant to believe what she asserts as they would if she'd manifested her belief in some other kind of way.' Hinchman (2005), p. 576.

[60] A similar case was offered by Hintikka in criticism of Austin's proto-assurance theory. See Hintikka (1962), p. 48.

7

Trust and the Institution of Testimony

Consider the Testimony Game, where an audience A, who wants to know whether p, is told that p by a speaker S who knows that p. It might be possible for A to treat S's testimony as a piece of evidence and believe that p on this basis. This would be possible if A has grounds for believing that S's testimony is evidence for p. In this case, it is these grounds that determine the epistemic status of A's testimonial belief. This is the route to knowledge described by the reductive theory of testimony. However, it might also be possible for A simply to believe S, or trust S for the truth. In this case, A would take S's telling as giving S's assurance that p, and the epistemic status of A's testimonial belief would be determined by the fact that S, in knowing that p, is in a position to offer this assurance. This is the route to knowledge described by the assurance theory of testimony. So a single piece of testimony might offer two different routes to knowledge. How is this possible?

A reductive theory of testimony is possible, I concluded in 2.3, insofar as testimony can be presumed to be reliable in various ways. The foundation of the reductive theory is a presumption of testimonial reliability, so a philosophically satisfying reductive theory would supply some justification of this presumption. The facts that this justification must advert to are then facts about the motivations we have, as speakers, in giving testimony. Meanwhile, what makes an assurance theory of testimony possible, I argued in 6.4, is that we, as audiences, can take a speaker's assurance on trust. This philosophical foundation, I now want to argue, is one and the same. Our ability, as audiences, to see testimony in the light of trust comes down to the fact that we have internalized social norms of trust. And it is these same social norms that shape the motivations we have, as speakers, in giving testimony, and which determine that testimony is the reliable source of knowledge that it is.

The possibility of treating a piece of testimony as both evidence and assurance is determined by the fact that our testimonial practices are shaped by norms of trust. These social norms determine the nature of testimony as a source of knowledge. In this chapter I want to argue this and the starting point is Bernard Williams's genealogical justification of the reductive theory of testimony.

7.1 Truth and truthfulness

In *Truth and Truthfulness* Bernard Williams proposes a reductive theory of testimony. The non-reductive claim that testimonial uptake is entitled in the absence of a supporting belief Williams simply describes as 'a piece of bad advice'.[1] Rather, he says,

It may be said that a hearer never has a reason for believing that P which lies just in the fact that a given speaker has told him that P. He has to believe also that the speaker (on such matters, and so on) is a reliable informant.[2]

An audience can always reflect on whether or not to accept what a speaker tells him; and, Williams claims, '[t]hese reflections are appropriate just in virtue of the fact that assertions are direct expressions of belief'.[3] Thus,

[a]ssertions play their role in the transmission of knowledge just because they are taken to be direct expressions of belief *and the speakers are taken to be reliable*.[4]

What Williams aims to do in *Truth and Truthfulness*, amongst many other things, is to provide a philosophical explanation of how testimonial knowledge is possible, given this reductive characterization of it. This amounts to a philosophical justification of the presumption of testimonial reliability.

Williams's argument takes the form of an imaginary genealogical account of what he calls the *virtues of truth*: *Accuracy* and *Sincerity*. A genealogical account of some phenomenon explains this aspect of human life by showing how it could have come about. Evolutionary accounts are genealogies: they explain particular aspects of human life in terms of the circumstances of our

---

[1] Williams (2002), p. 111.   [2] Williams (2002), pp. 77–8.
[3] Williams (2002), p. 79.   [4] Williams (2002), p. 79, my emphasis.

Pleistocene ancestors and the forces of natural selection. An *imaginary* genealogy then explains some aspect of human life by showing how it follows from an imagined *State of Nature*, where this is abstractly character- ized in terms of basic human limitations and needs. Such imaginary genea- logies can be justificatory, Williams claims, because they can show how some phenomenon is necessary for human life being as it is. Thus, in *Truth and Truthfulness* Williams sets out to show how our valuing the dispositions to care about the truth of one's beliefs and to come out with what one believes—our valuing Accuracy and Sincerity—is necessary for testimony being a source of knowledge (reductively conceived).

Williams's genealogy starts by imagining a State of Nature consisting of a group of human beings who share a common language but have limited technology and no writing. If this group is to form anything like a society, there will need to be cooperative engagements which demand informa- tion be communicated between individuals. Given that an individual can only be at one place at one time, individuals will often gain what Williams calls *purely positional advantage*; that is, by virtue of their location at a time, one individual can come to possess information that another individual needs.[5] It follows that even in the State of Nature Accuracy and Sincerity are desirable from the social point of view: they will be socially valued because pooled information is a social good necessary for cooperative endeavour, itself necessary for society.

However, possessing the disposition of Sincerity need not always be in an individual's best interest. Williams gives the example—case 35—of the hunter who has found prey that he would rather keep for himself and his family. This raises the problem that:

> The value that attaches to any given person's having this disposition [Sincerity] seems, so far as we have gone, largely a value for other people. It may obviously be useful for an individual to have the benefits of other people's correct information, and not useful to him that they should benefit of his. So this is a classic example of the 'free-rider' situation.[6]

The problem is that the collective valuing of Sincerity does not itself give an individual a reason to value Sincerity, or be sincere. Whilst it is always in an audience's interest to be informed, sincerity need not best serve a speaker's interest and as audiences we know that this is the case. This fault

---

[5] Williams (2002), p. 42.   [6] Williams (2002), p. 58.

line is the basis of the problem of cooperation, described in 1.1, which Williams thus identifies.

The reductive solution to this problem, described in 3.1, is straightforward: as audiences we often have grounds for predicting that a piece of testimony is true. This solution, I also argued in 3.1, is a sceptical solution in that it takes the problem of cooperation to suggest limits on when it is possible to acquire knowledge from testimony. In particular, it implies that testimonial uptake in a one-off encounter set against a background of ignorance is unwarranted. It is unwarranted because in this testimonial situation there are no grounds for predicting the truth of testimony. As such it is not clear whether the reductive solution to the problem of cooperation is available when this problem is confronted in the State of Nature. It all depends. It depends on whether or not the social group is imagined to have stable and ongoing interactions. And it depends on whether or not the social group is already imagined to be a genuine society with roles and relationships that could be indicators of truth. If the social group in the State of Nature is imagined to be either stable or fully social, the reductive solution could get a grip, and if not, then not.[7]

However, Williams's solution to the problem of cooperation is not the reductive solution. The source of this problem, Williams argues, is that Sincerity has only been given *instrumental value*: its value is given by that good which follows from knowledge being communicated, such as the good brought about by cooperative endeavour. And when it is only valued in this way there will always be the possibility of a fissure between speakers' and audiences' interests; speakers who have the disposition of Sincerity will always be potentially exposed to 'free-riders'. An adequate solution must not allow the realization of this possibility to be systemic. And since the State of Nature is meant to be socially basic, what this shows, Williams claims, is 'that no society can get by . . . with a purely instrumental conception of the values of truth'.[8] What any society requires, if testimony is to be a source of knowledge, is that Sincerity be *intrinsically valued*. The problem with the reductive solution is that it is a 'game-theoretical' solution and 'no line of argument which sets out from a game-theoretical formulation of the problems of trust could possibly

---

[7] Were interactions ongoing, interest would become encapsulated. See Hardin (2002) and Axelrod (1984).

[8] Williams (2002), p. 59.

show that trustworthiness had an intrinsic value'.[9] A non-sceptical solution—or one that is based on the idea of intrinsic value—is what is wanted.

Something's having intrinsic value, Williams then goes on to argue, can be understood in terms of the satisfaction of two conditions. For something, X say, to have intrinsic value in a society: first X must be 'necessary, or nearly necessary for basic human purposes and needs'; and second X must 'make sense to them [the society members] from the inside, so to speak'.[10] The first of these desiderata is established by the imagined genealogy. If Sincerity is not given intrinsic value, then any conversation that purports to be one of giving and receiving information will generate the problem of cooperation. This threatens potentially to stymie both the conversation and any further cooperation. It threatens, ultimately, to undermine the possibility of society. However, our conversations as to the facts run smoothly. We tell one another what we know and we have a society wherein testimony is a source of knowledge. So whatever needs to be in place to avoid the problem of cooperation structuring communication must be in place, and that is that we intrinsically value Sincerity. We must be motivated to be Sincere as an end in itself.

The second desideratum is then giving an account of how this motivation is made sense of. Here 'the fictional history of genealogy, which aims to bring out the necessary, structural features, is replaced by the real history of specific cultural determinations'.[11] A society will make sense of Sincerity through its relation to other values. So how a society gives intrinsic value to Sincerity can be philosophically unearthed through conceptual analysis. What conceptual analysis shows about *our* social history is that *we* understand Sincerity through its relation to trust and our valuing trustworthy behaviour. *Sincerity is trustworthiness in speech.* It is through taking its place amongst the nexus of concepts and values that centre on trust that Sincerity comes to have intrinsic value for us.

This conjunction of imagined genealogy and conceptual analysis, Williams then claims, will be justificatory: it will explain why it is right that Sincerity is intrinsically valued in the way that it is. It is right because it enables a non-sceptical solution to the problem of cooperation as this is found in the State of Nature. And so it is necessary for explaining how testimony is the source of knowledge that it is.

---

[9] Williams (2002), p. 90.   [10] Williams (2002), p. 92.
[11] Williams (2002), p. 93.

What Williams's genealogical argument thereby provides is a justification of the grounding presumption of the reductive theory of testimony: the presumption of testimonial reliability. Since if we by necessity value Sincerity and Accuracy, it follows that testimony will be reliable in various ways. So, given that we value these virtues of truth, we have an explanation of how it is that testimony can be the source of knowledge that reductive theory takes it to be.

7.2 The value of trust

Williams's genealogical justification of the reductive theory suffers two problems. Both of these problems centre on Williams's claim that the solution to the problem of cooperation confronted in the State of Nature is given by an intrinsic valuation of Sincerity. The first problem is one of theoretical fit: this claim does not fit with Williams's reductive theory of testimony. The second problem is one of clarity: this claim is simply mysterious. I consider these two problems in the next two sections respectively, and propose solutions. The solution to the first problem is simply to abandon the reductive theory; it is mistaken. The solution I propose to the second problem is a way of demystifying intrinsic value.

7.2.1 Sincerity and accuracy

In developing his assurance theory, Richard Moran criticizes the reductive theory for putting 'speaker and audience into disharmony with each other'.[12] This criticism, I think, is well made, and the reductive theory can be seen to generate this disharmony as follows. In telling an audience A that p, a speaker S intends that A believe that p because A believes her, S. But the reductive theory requires for warrant that A believe that p because A believes that S's telling is evidence for p. However, in telling A that p, S does not intend her telling to be taken as a piece of evidence, even if it is this.

This disharmony is equally present in Williams's genealogical justification of the reductive theory. Williams's official solution to the problem of cooperation, as it is encountered in the State of Nature, is that a speaker will be sincere because of the intrinsic value found in trust and Sincerity as

---

[12] Moran (2006), p. 301. See 6.1.

a species of trustworthiness. However, what makes it rational for an audience A to cooperate in conversation, and believe a speaker S's testimony to p, will be whatever supplies the grounds for the belief that S 'is a reliable informant'.[13] The disharmony is then that if A believes that p on the basis of S's testimony only because A believes S is reliable, A does not really trust S. Or, otherwise put, A merely trusts in the predictive sense that A expects p to be true given S's testimony. And the problem here is that the value of such predictive trust is solely instrumental: its value lies in the benefit dependence brings, which in the case of communication, will be simply that S's testimony might be a source of information as to whether p. Consequently, this account of what makes it reasonable for *audiences* to cooperate in conversation is at odds with Williams's claims that we cooperate *as speakers* because we give Sincerity intrinsic value.

The problem of theoretical fit could then be put as follows. Williams wants to claim (a) that the problem of cooperation is resolved through an intrinsic valuation of Sincerity as a species of trustworthiness. And (b) that warranted testimonial uptake requires a judgement of speaker Accuracy or reliability. And these claims do not fit in that if (a) is true, then (b) is false. Or, at least this follows insofar as trustworthiness is meant to be a thick evaluative notion.

We give Sincerity intrinsic value, Williams claims, by its connections with trust and our valuing trusting relations. These connections, I now want to claim, are to trust in the thick affective sense defined in 6.2. Thus, Williams observes that where relations are trusting, discovered insincerity would provoke 'recriminations and a retreat from these relations'.[14] This would not be so if our willingness to rely were merely grounded by a belief about reliability. But it would be the case if it were grounded by the presumption that the trusted will respond in a certain way to our dependence, where such a presumption is characteristic of trust in the affective sense. However, if we think a speaker is trustworthy in the sense that the speaker fulfils the expectation constitutive of affective trust, then this thought provides a sufficient reason for testimonial uptake. For suppose that a speaker S tells an audience A that p and A thinks that S is trustworthy in this sense, then A thinks that S's telling that p is best explained by the fact that S intends to let A know that p. Trust is sufficient to explain A's

[13] Williams (2002), p. 78, quoted above.   [14] Williams (2002), p. 112.

uptake of S's testimony to p, just as it is sufficient to explain cooperation more generally. (Notoriously, we can cooperate for no other reason than that we trust: witness case 17 of the shopkeeper.) So if trust is a locus of intrinsic value—such that audiences are motivated to trust just as speakers are motivated to be sincere or trustworthy—then that one is told something can itself be seen as a sufficient reason for belief.

Thus I propose that Williams's official solution to the problem of cooperation—claim (a)—should be endorsed and the ill-fitting reductive theory—claim (b)—should be abandoned. On this proposal, the resolution of the problem of cooperation, as it is encountered in the State of Nature, will be provided by an account of our attitude of trust which shows this attitude to be sufficient to make cooperation reasonable. This is the account outlined in 6.3 and 6.4. In short, and to recall, in trusting S for the truth as to whether p, when S tells A that p, A presumes that S is trustworthy. This presumption suffices to give A reason to cooperate in conversation and does not need the backing of a belief in Accuracy or reliability. And A cooperates by taking S's telling at face value as the assurance it purports to be.

7.2.2 The intrinsic value of sincerity

To say that Sincerity is given intrinsic value by a social group is to say members of that group will be motivated to act in sincere ways merely because these ways of acting would be described as sincere. The problem, as Williams is aware, is that this claim about intrinsic value faces a dilemma. Left like this it is mysterious as a claim. Why should the description of an act as sincere be a motivation to act this way? But if the mystery is explicated—Sincerity must be internalized as a disposition if cooperation is to be generally secured—the account of Sincerity's value appears reductive, or instrumental.

Williams's two condition account is meant to address this problem; genealogy is meant to achieve 'explanation without reduction'.[15] According to this account Sincerity has intrinsic value because it is 'necessary, or nearly necessary for basic human purposes and needs' that individuals generally have this disposition, and their having this disposition 'makes sense to them from the inside, so to speak'.[16] However, it is not clear how

---

[15] Williams (2002), p. 90.   [16] Williams (2002), p. 92.

this resolves the dilemma. Either it remains a mystery how the intelligibility of Sincerity should supply a motivation to act sincerely. Or this claim about intelligibility can be interpreted as a claim about preferences: the speakers who find Sincerity intelligible in this way have a preference for acting Sincerely. In this case the valuation of Sincerity can be simply added to such a speaker's set of preferences. And if the audience is then allowed knowledge of the speaker's values, and so preferences, the problem of cooperation can be simply resolved. But this resolution is the reductive or game-theoretical resolution. And if the audience is ignorant of these preferences, the threat to cooperation and the rationality of testimonial uptake remains.

Nevertheless, I think that Williams's strategy can be pursued. It is possible to demystify the connection between the fact that Sincerity makes sense from the inside to a speaker and the fact that this speaker will be motivated to act in sincere ways. To achieve this what is needed is an account of how the testimonial situation is structured by norms of trust that shape our understanding of it. I attempt this account in the next section.

7.3 Norms of trust and trustworthiness

Norms are instructions how to act. Their form is the imperative or hypothetical imperative: 'do X', 'don't do X', or 'if Y, then do X'. The attitudinal hallmark of norms is that they are associated with, and sustained by, 'feelings of embarrassment, anxiety, guilt and shame that a person suffers at the prospect of violating them, or at least at the prospect of being caught violating them. Social norms', Jon Elster continues, 'have a *grip on the mind* that is due to the strong emotions their violations can trigger.'[17] There are three attitudinal dimensions that can be individuated. Violation of the norm will provoke emotions of shame or guilt in the 'wrongdoer'; it will provoke the reactive attitude of resentment in the 'wronged'; and it will provoke punitive attitudes of disapproval or anger in third parties.[18] And these hallmark emotions are found in our attitudes towards truth-telling and believing others.

---

[17] Elster (1989), p. 100.   [18] See Sripada and Stich (2006).

We are liable to resent speakers who deceive us, and audiences who do not believe us. And we are liable to feel guilt in misleading audiences, and feel pressure to believe what speakers tell us. These feelings suggest that we have something like a norm of truth-telling and credulity. So the first question is what is the content of these two norms? And since these norms must be available in the State of Nature, if they are to be part of a solution to the problem of cooperation as it is encountered there, let me keep the restricted focus on the Testimony Game, which is a simple conversation as to the facts.

The norms of trust for the Testimony Game are roughly the norms of truth-telling and credulity. But only roughly. Suppose one needs to know whether p, then ideally one would find a speaker who would tell one that p if p and tell one that not-p if not-p.[19] However, since it is not always plain what is true, the most one might think one could hope for is a speaker who would tell one that p if the speaker had good evidence for p and believed that p, and tell one not-p otherwise. However, we should, and do, hope for more than this. In 6.2, I argued this point by reference to case 32: Williams's mail-opener.[20] The audience who is told 'Someone's been opening your mail', when it is the speaker who has been doing so, is liable to resent being misled into thinking that someone else has been opening his mail. This speaker tells the truth, but is not trustworthy and does not demonstrate the disposition of Sincerity. So if our situation is one of wanting to know whether p, then, in addition to wanting a speaker to try and say what is true, we also want the speaker to be as informative as is required for our not being misled. Ideally the speaker's contribution would also be appropriately relevant and lucid. And if it is all of these things, the speaker's contribution has been guided by Grice's maxims of Quality, Quantity, Relation and Manner respectively. Given our conversational goal of learning whether p, and a conversation that is one as to the facts, a reply that is guided by these maxims is cooperative.

On the other side, the norm of believing others is less one of credulity and more the paired norm of presuming cooperation. Grice's claim is that we can presume conversation to be cooperative and guided by 'the Cooperative Principle'.

---

[19] Compare Williams (1978), p. 38.   [20] Williams (2002), p. 96.

NORMS OF TRUST AND TRUSTWORTHINESS 181

We might then formulate a rough general principle which participants will be expected (ceteris paribus) to observe, namely: make your conversational contribution such as is required, at the stage at which it occurs, by the accepted purpose or direction of the talk exchange in which you are engaged. One might label this the Cooperative Principle.[21]

For Grice, it is the presumption that participants are following this principle that makes a 'talk exchange' into a 'conversation', where each understands what the other means. What Williams's example, case 32, illustrates is that not all talk exchanges are cooperative, or conversations in Grice's sense. In this case, the speaker S seems to be telling the audience A something and on the presumption that S is following the Cooperative Principle, A will understand S to be telling him that someone other than S has been opening his mail. If it were claimed that this is what S does tell A, then S's telling is a lie, but it is open to S to claim that she did not tell A *that* so has been misunderstood. Grice's point is then that the presumption that one's interlocutor is following the Cooperative Principle is necessary for understanding what it is one's interlocutor is saying. And in this case the audience A was right to 'misunderstand' S's utterance for two reasons. First, S's utterance did not appear to flout the Cooperative Principle or any of its associated maxims. Second, this principle is a *normative* principle in effect prescribing that if one is having a conversation with an accepted purpose and one wants to be understood, then one should make one's conversational contribution such as is required by this accepted purpose.

The norms of trust in the Testimony Game, I suggest then, are that the speaker should follow the Cooperative Principle and its maxims and the audience should presume that the speaker has done this. And since the accepted purpose of the conversation in the Testimony Game is the giving and receiving of information, these norms of trust are: *tell the truth informatively*; and *presume the speaker is telling the truth (informatively)*. These norms of trust then describe a standard that we expect interlocutors to live up to when engaged in a certain practice: that of having a certain type of conversation. On this standard if another depends on you for information, then you should try to say what is true informatively; and if another purports to tell you that something is so, then you should presume that they are telling you the truth.

<hr/>

[21] Grice (1967), p. 26.

This *norm of trustworthiness* and *norm of trust*, respectively, have already been encountered in the analysis of trust and trustworthiness given in 6.2. This analysis needed to refer to these norms in order to give the correct *theoretical* characterization of the expectation that a trusting party has, and the reactive attitude a trusting party is vulnerable to, in affective trust. In affectively trusting a speaker S for the truth as to whether p, an audience A expects S to tell him, A, the truth because he, A, depends on S for this. The normative character of this expectation is then shown by the fact that A will feel wronged by any deception; and the content of this reactive attitude is stated by the norm of trustworthiness: A's feeling is that S ought to have told him, A, the truth as to whether p in this testimonial situation. Similarly, what the assurance theory shows is that in telling A that p, S will expect to be believed. That this expectation is equally normative is then revealed by the fact that S will feel wronged by any disbelief; and the content of this reactive attitude is stated by the norm of trust: S's feeling is that A ought to have presumed that she, S, was telling the truth or letting A know whether p.

With this statement in hand, the questions that need to be considered are: how do these norms of trust bear on the mystery of intrinsic value? And considering 'the real history of specific cultural determinations' can it be claimed that these norms are our social norms?

7.3.1 Internalized norms of trust

Suppose, then, that the Testimony Game is governed by these norms of conversational trust. On the face of it this still does not help with the dilemma Williams faces. It appears relevant only if the audience can judge it is in the speaker's interest to follow these norms, (otherwise put: only if the speaker cares about not being misunderstood). So if the audience is ignorant or uncertain as to the speaker's motivations, the audience will by this very fact be ignorant or uncertain as to whether their exchange is governed by these norms, or is a conversation in Grice's sense. This quick rebuttal, however, misconceives how these norms of trust guide behaviour. Explaining this misconception then reveals how the hypothesis of these norms of trust provides a bridge between how a situation 'makes sense' to us and what we are motivated to do in it.

The misconception is the assumption of a teleological account of norm guidance. On this account, norm guidance is mediated by a desire to follow the norm. A speaker should think, 'in these circumstances (defined by the audience trusting me for the truth as to whether p) the norm of trustworthiness dictates that I tell the truth informatively, I want to follow this norm, so I should tell the audience what I know'.[22] The problem is that this reason for telling the truth makes no reference to the audience's need for the truth. So the motivating desire could, for instance, be based on a further desire to avoid sanctions. Consequently, telling the truth for this reason is not sufficient for trustworthiness.

Similarly, an audience is supposed to think 'in these circumstances (defined by the speaker telling me that p) the norm of trust dictates that I presume the speaker to be telling the truth, I want to follow this norm, so I should believe what the speaker tells me'. And the corresponding problem here is that this reason for presuming the speaker to be telling the truth does not make any positive presumptions about the speaker. As a motivating desire it could be mediated merely by the belief that the speaker's telling is evidence for its truth. And believing what is told for this reason is not sufficient for believing the speaker or trusting the speaker for the truth. The problem, in short, is that this account of norm following merely produces the 'right' behaviour, but behaving in the 'right way' is not sufficient for following these norms of trust.

It might help to illustrate this point with the pair of cases considered in 3.3.

Case 21. Having just discovered clear evidence of his wife's long-suspected infidelity, the anxious husband confronts her. She confesses to the affair.

Now suppose it is added that the wife's motivation is this: she realizes that she can no longer hide her affair and judges that if she allows her husband to work things out for himself the outcome will be worse. If a certain simple-mindedness is allowed, it should be clear that despite cooperating in their conversation—that is, telling the truth informatively—the wife's reason for utterance is not that of the trustworthy person because her husband's need for information has nothing to do with it.

The second illustration, case 22, is the mirror of this; in it the wife employs a different strategy.

---

[22] Boghossian (2008), p. 485, calls this the 'intention view' of norm following. And, following Kripke (1982), argues that since it makes norm following inferential it cannot offer an account of inference, which is itself an instance of norm following. This general problem does not afflict the view I am about to describe.

Case 22. Having just discovered clear evidence of his wife's long-suspected infidelity, the anxious husband confronts her. She denies the affair but he observes reliable indicators that her denial is a lie.

The husband's good evidence does not *oblige* him to disbelieve his wife's denial. So what she hopes in lying is that he will put this good evidence to one side—bracket it. The point of the lie—part of the reason she lies directly rather simply tries to cover things up—is then to (re)assure her husband and so draw his attention away from this evidence; it is to affirm trust by getting him to believe her on the basis of trust. If the wife then gets away with the lie, her husband's testimonial uptake is not to be explained in terms of a prediction of truth: it is not rationalized by a belief about her reliability. He presumes she is telling the truth, right enough, but makes this presumption because of an attitude of trust. As such the husband conforms to the norm of trust: he behaves in the right way—he works on the presumption that his wife is telling him the truth—for the right reason—he trusts her for the truth on this matter. In doing so, he believes her denial, as she hopes, *out of trust*.[23]

There are two points being made here. The first point should be familiar from H. A. Prichard's discussion of moral motivation.[24] One could motivate someone to behave in the same way as a moral person by showing this action to be in that person's interest, but this reason for acting morally is not the reason that would motivate the moral person. Moreover, any attempt to substantively motivate someone to behave in the same way as the moral person—to offer motivation for an action beyond it being the moral thing to do—would, Prichard argued, face the same issue. The parallel is that acting as the trustworthy or trusting person acts similarly requires one to have certain motivations. The second point is then that these motivations are not best described in terms of a desire to follow some norm of trust or trustworthiness, and the belief that such a norm applies.

The norms of conversational trust describe certain ways of acting, but in order to be an action of the prescribed sort, the way of acting described must have a distinctive motivation. In the circumstances of the Testimony Game, what is prescribed is that S should tell A that p, *and do so for the reason that A needs this information*. And what is prescribed is that A should presume that S tells the truth, *and presume this on the basis of the presumption*

---

[23] See Stocker (1981), p. 747.   [24] Prichard (1912).

that S's telling is motivated by his need to know whether p. To tell the truth for this reason is to be trustworthy, and to presume that a speaker has this motivation is to trust them for the truth. To say that we are guided by these norms is then to say that we see the Testimony Game, a situation wherein the norms apply, in terms of these norms. This claim must, of course, be understood *de re* and not *de dicto.* The norms of trust are theoretical denizens. Our thinking about the Testimony Game does not refer to these norms of trust—and in this respect the teleological account of norm guidance is mistakenly legalistic. This point may be put using a sociological term of art: we have *internalized* these norms.[25] This idea that norms of trust and trustworthiness guide behaviour through being internalized can, I suggest, be defined along three axes.

First, it is a quasi-perceptual matter because where the norms of trust are internalized, the subject's perception of a situation wherein the norms apply, such as the Testimony Game, will be structured by the prescriptions of the norms. This situation will be *seen in a certain light.* Thus, if S can see that A depends on her telling the truth as to whether *p*, this will be *seen by S as* a reason to do so. And if S tells A that *p*, this will be *seen by A as* an assurance that *p*, and so as a reason to believe that *p*. That is, the subject's perception of a situation wherein the norms apply will contain within it a judgement about what ought to be done.[26]

Second, it is a claim about how rational deliberation proceeds, or ought to proceed. The norm of trust prescribes that A's practical reasoning should be framed by the presumption that, in telling him that *p*, S has certain reasons for utterance, namely that he, A, depends on S for this information. And the norm of trustworthiness prescribes that S's practical reasoning should be framed by the perception that A depends on her, S, for the truth as to whether *p*. Insofar as these norms are internalized this presumption and perception of dependence will frame practical reasoning through supplying a reason for belief and utterance respectively.[27] How we deliberate in the Testimony Game, or think we should deliberate, then determines what explanations and justifications of action we find plausible.

---

[25] See Sripada and Stich (2006).

[26] Compare McDowell (1978), particularly pp. 100–1.

[27] Since, on one conception of value, to value X is to treat X as a justifying consideration in one's practical reasoning, this way in which internalized norms shape rational deliberation expresses value. See Bratman (1996), p. 39 and Bratman (2000).

Having internalizing the norms of trust, we explain and justify our own and others' behaviour in terms of the descriptions the norms articulate. Asked why she told A that p, S might simply respond, 'A trusted her for the truth'. And asked why he believes that p, A might equally respond that he 'trusted S for the truth'. No further facts need to be adduced.

Third, rational deliberation in the trust situation is in part an imaginative matter. Violations of the norms of trust are associated with distinctive emotions. This association is two-way. The particular nature of these emotions is defined by their association with a scenario itself specified in terms of the breach of a norm of trust. But insofar as these norms are internalized, these norms of trust also ground our imagined emotional responses to scenarios real and imagined. An ability to imagine the Testimony Game complete with the spectrum of emotional responses that non-compliance with the norms of trust would elicit is then part of what it is to think about this situation in terms of these norms.[28]

Through internalizing the norms of trust, we think about the Testimony Game, and any situation wherein the norms apply, in the terms articulated by the norm. And this, I have just suggested, can be explicated along the three axes just sketched. Through thinking about a potential trust situation in these terms our having the dispositions that follow from internalizing the norms of trust and trustworthiness makes sense to us from the inside. This is what the idea of internalization delivers: the prescription of the norm captures the way the subject thinks about the action prescribed. Thus one could say that to have internalized a norm of trust is to be motivated to conform to a certain pattern of behaviour for no other reason than that this pattern is valued in itself or intrinsically valued.[29] And this, I hope, makes it non-mysterious how an intrinsic valuation of Sincerity, as a species of trustworthiness, delivers the motivation to be sincere.

7.3.2 That these norms are our norms

The argument that the norms of trust and trustworthiness are our social norms has been entirely given in its substance. It consists in the plausibility

---

[28] What determines the nature, and so appropriateness, of the emotions generally, de Sousa argues, is their location in circumstances that resemble a scenario which is a paradigm for feeling this emotion. Sousa (1987), p. 184.

[29] Sripada and Stich (2006) uses the notion of intrinsic value.

of the conceptual analysis of trust and the assurance theory of testimony, given in the previous chapter. And the data that this analysis and theory appeal to. In particular, explananda of this conceptual analysis and theory—respectively our tendency to resent deceptive speakers and disbelieving audiences—support the contention that there are norms of trust and trustworthiness operative in our society, which we have internalized. However, the argument that these norms are socially operative can be completed by reference to two further facts.

First, the hypothesis of these norms is just the hypothesis that our conversations as to the facts are guided by Grice's Cooperative Principle and associated maxims. And this hypothesis, Grice persuasively argued, is necessary for our understanding what a speaker means by what they say. Earlier I illustrated this with Williams's mail-opener (case 32). In this example, the hypothesis that the conversation is guided by the Cooperative Principle is necessary for uncovering the implication that someone else has been opening one's mail. And if this hypothesis is not available, the cost is a failure to understand what it is the speaker means by what she says. Since we easily and happily understand implicatures, the implication is that we presume that our conversations are guided by the Cooperative Principle, as Grice claimed.

Second, the hypothesis that our conversations as to the facts are guided by the norms of conversational trust also explains why we find it so hard to judge when we are being lied to. Two recent studies have shown that, when shown a series of videos of speakers, subjects easily identify a couple of clues to deceit (namely whether a speaker looks to be having to think hard about what she says and whether a speaker looks comfortable in saying what she does). And yet subjects found it extremely hard to identify which speakers were lying, despite there being a very high correlation between these clues and speakers who were lying.[30] Arguably subjects found this hard because our background sentiment is that we ought to believe what people tell us, and so feel that we ought not to accuse someone of lying. Moreover, I would argue that part of this explanation of our poor judgement has to be that lies are active. In lying a speaker purports to be sincere and so invokes an audience's trust and intentionally

---

[30] O'Sullivan (2009), p. 79.

engages these norms. By doing so lies demand belief and we, as audiences, feel constrained to believe lies.[31]

Taking this altogether, I conclude that the hypothesis of these norms of trust is a good one. However, this needs to be reconciled with the fact that, in many cases, the idea that we should trust a speaker and believe what they say merely because they say it, is, as Williams observes simply 'a bad piece of advice'. We feel some obligation to believe speakers, but not all speakers on all occasions. In many cases, our testimonial uptake is based on a careful consideration of the evidence, and not anything like trust; and in some cases we would be culpable if this were not so. The assurance theory, I argued in 6.6, thereby suffers the problem that it is not a complete account of testimony as a source of knowledge. What I want to show in the next section, is then how Williams's genealogy of Sincerity can be adapted to give a genealogy of testimony, which explains how testimony is the source of knowledge it is where all these things are true of it.

7.4 A genealogy of testimony

Commenting on Grice's discussion of implicature, Williams observes the following.

> Implicatures...look to the use of language under favourable social conditions which enable it to be indeed co-operative. They are *conversational* implicatures, but not everyone who is talking with someone else is engaged, in the required sense, in a conversation. What is required for that to be so are certain understood levels of trust.[32]

We have achieved these levels of trust because we intrinsically value trustworthiness in speech, which is the disposition of Sincerity. And this is just to say, I suggest, that the norm of trustworthiness, which is the prescription that speakers follow the cooperative principle and its maxims, is internalized as a norm. In learning to have conversations one learns this norm and the paired norm of trust, and the presumption prescribed by the latter then allows us to uncover implicatures or what people mean by what they say. Since we can tell people what we know by implication as much as by bald statement, these norms of trust are necessary for testimony being the source of knowledge that is. The genealogical justification that Williams

---

[31] I outline this mechanism in Faulkner (2007b).   [32] Williams (2002), p. 100.

offers for our having the disposition of Sincerity can thereby be presented as a genealogical justification of these norms. And, most importantly for the present concern, this same genealogical account can provide an explanation of how testimony is the source of knowledge that it is.

There are two properties of testimony as a source of knowledge that require explanation. First, testimony is a source of transmitted knowledge and warrant, but it is possible to give different explanations of transmission. What I have labelled the assurance (6.1), evidential (3.7), and same-state (4.5) explanations are all possible. Second, testimony is a source of transmitted knowledge and warrant, but it is also possible to give a reductive explanation of the knowledge that we acquire from testimony. An explanation of how testimony is the source of knowledge that it is should account for these two features of testimony.

The genealogical account I develop in this section has three parts. The first part concentrates on testimony in the State of Nature and develops, in the way suggested, Williams's official solution to the problem of cooperation confronted there. The second part elaborates on Williams's forward extension towards a society like our own. The third extends this genealogy backwards into an imagined pre-history of the State of Nature.

7.4.1 The State of Nature

In the State of Nature we frequently suffer positional disadvantage and so have to rely on others' reports. Trust is then demonstrated in 'the willingness of one party to rely on another to act in certain ways'.[33] Since this dependence can be exploited, the pooling of information generates 'game-theoretical problems about securing assurance'.[34] We confront, what I have called, the problem of cooperation. Williams's official solution to this problem is that it is resolved through an intrinsic valuation of the disposition of Sincerity. As a society, we then give Sincerity intrinsic value through taking it to be a form of trustworthiness and giving value to trust and relations structured by trust. And this claim, I argued in 7.3.1, is best understood in terms of the idea that as a society we have certain norms of trust, which we have then internalized as individuals.

Where norms of trust and trustworthiness are internalized, the social background will be one of 'certain understood levels of trust'. It will be

---

[33] Williams (2002), p. 88.   [34] Williams (2002), p. 89.

such that if an audience A depends on a speaker S for information, this will give S a reason to tell A what he needs to know; and if S tells A something, this gives A reason to accept what S tells him. The idea that conversation can be structured by presumptions of trust then allows for the following explanation of what goes on, or should go on, in a conversation as to the facts. A speaker S's reason for telling an audience A what she does—the explanation of S's testimony—will be S's perception that the audience depends on her for this information. In this case, if S tells A that p, it will be because S believes herself to know that p, and assumes responsibility for letting A know that p. And in recognizing that S intends that he, A, come to believe that p and trusting S, A will then take S's telling him that p as an assurance that p is true. Testimony then functions to transmit knowledge from S to A because it transmits the responsibility for justifying belief from A to S. This is the assurance explanation outlined in 6.1 and 6.4. Thus, we have a way of life wherein testimony is a source of knowledge because we tell others what we know, and in doing so offer our assurance, and take the assurance of others' tellings on trust.

Where there are social norms of trust and trustworthiness, there will also be significant consistency in speakers' motivations—whether because they have internalized these norms, or are sensitive to the sanctions that follow from these norms being socially operative. This will establish the possibility of a reductive theory of testimony since it will ensure that it is possible to have good evidence for testimonial reliability. Consequently, this genealogy can be used as a vindication of the reductive theory, and it is used in this way by Williams. However, it should be clear that this genealogy does not justify this theory because this reductive explanation is only possible given that testimony is already established as a source of knowledge that can be given an assurance explanation. Testimony must be offered and taken as assurance before it can be treated as evidence.

7.4.2 History

The assurance theory of testimony, I argued in 6.6, offers a good account of what Welbourne calls 'the simplest cases'—where an audience is addressed and belief in a speaker is an option—and this is the testimonial situation in the State of Nature where there is no writing and limited technology. But our society is quite different to this imagined State.

This difference can be illustrated by defining an *epistemic community* as a group of two or more individuals who share knowledge through testimony.[35] In the State of Nature members of an epistemic community would additionally be members of a social community and connected by the many social ties that allow for a local group identity. It is this identity, I suppose, which ensures that the presumptions made in affective trust come out largely true, and that the responsibilities speakers take on in offering assurance, speakers are generally in a position to discharge. However, history separates us from this State. It is now true that we share knowledge with a much wider social group; the epistemic community has become detached from its origin in a local social community, and the 'social community' has lost its deeply local identity.

Thus, in the State of Nature an audience would almost certainly know the speaker—and if a chain of testimony was relevant to the audience's possessing testimonial knowledge, then the audience would in all probability know the members of this chain too. Now it is as frequent for us that we are at the end of a testimonial chain where *all* the other members are unknown. Recall case 2, reading in the Sunday paper that the distance from the Earth to the Sun is one Astronomical Unit or 149,597,870.69 kilometres. This testimony pools knowledge, but it is essentially anonymous: there is no affective trust or assurance.

In the last section, 7.4.1, I argued that the hypothesis of social norms of trust and trustworthiness makes it possible to treat testimony as evidence. This possibility, I now want to suggest, can be seen as part of a shift to a more objective way of thinking about epistemic value, which ends with our present way of thinking about testimony, not as a piece of evidence, but as a means of basing belief on the evidence. This *evidential explanation* of transmission, introduced in 3.7, can then be regarded as an objectification of the assurance explanation. On the assurance account, in a one-link testimonial chain, an audience A gets to know that p on the basis of trusting a speaker S who tells him that p insofar as S knows that p and shoulders the responsibility for A's knowing that p. In order to explain A's knowing that p, S must thereby be able to articulate knowledge supporting reasons for believing that p. Call these reasons e. The assurance account of A's knowing that p is then that A's belief that p is backed by S's willingness

<hr />

[35] This is Welbourne's definition of a *community of knowledge*. See Welbourne (1986), p. 25. Also note: it is not sufficient for an epistemic community that individuals know the same thing because two individuals could coincidentally come to know the same thing, even for the same reasons, as sometimes happens in mathematics.

to articulate *e*. The evidential account objectifies this by relieving *S* of any active epistemic role: *A* knows that *p* because *S*'s testimony to *p* allows *A*'s believing that *p to be based on e*. This account thereby involves a shift to a third person view of reasons for belief: *e* is no longer a matter of articulated, so accessible, reasons for belief but simply what could constitute a reason for belief—in short evidence, or an extended body of warrant.

What the possibility of a reductive theory of testimony shows is that audiences, as well as speakers, can articulate knowledge-supporting justifications of testimonially presented propositions. This fact determines that the extended body of warrant must be a conjunction of the justification possessed by the original speaker together any further warrant provided by the chain(s) of communicators (see 1.3.5). The extended body of warrant can be added to, supplemented, and otherwise changed through communication. This possibility is then demonstrated in the collaborative production of scientific knowledge.[36] A good illustration of this is the experiment recording charm events and measuring the lifespan of charm particles, which was cited by Hardwig and referred to in case 29. The results of this experiment are stated in an article with ninety-nine co-authors. Clearly no one individual could accomplish such an experiment, so the evidence that this experiment constitutes for its conclusion—that the charm cross-section is calculated to be such and such—can but be a collaborative assemblage. Thus the treatment of testimony as evidence is part of a shift towards a scientific, or evidence-based, way of viewing the world.

The shift to an evidential explanation of knowledge transmission and a reductive explanation of the knowledge acquired from testimony are then different moments and expressions in the development of our scientific outlook.[37] We speak of scientific knowledge in objective terms; for instance, we speak about the current state of physics, and in doing so we consider current theory as an epistemological product rather than as an item of belief.[38] And when we thereby consider current theory what we

---

[36] 'All work in science is work directed towards the growth of objective knowledge. We are workers who are adding to the growth of objective knowledge as masons work on a cathedral.' Popper (1968), p. 121.

[37] Shapin (1994) shows how the reductive, or Humean, theory of testimony emerged with the birth of modern science.

[38] This perspective on knowledge was pursued by Karl Popper who labelled knowledge thus conceived the 'third world of objective knowledge'. See Popper (1968) and Faulkner (2006).

are really interested in is its content and warrant—scientific theory and its supporting evidence—and not its genesis in the thinking of the specific individuals. Science is knowledge that has outgrown its original knowing subject. Call the scientific body of evidence that has been articulated for a proposition's truth *its third-world warrant*. One way of knowing something would then be to have a true belief appropriately based on its third-world warrant. The evidential explanation of transmission proposes that testimonial uptake creates this basing-relation: testimony is a route to knowledge, and warranted belief, because it is a way of basing belief on an *extended body of warrant*. Where the belief formed is a scientific one, the extended body of warrant will equal its third-world warrant provided the epistemic community and the scientific communities are co-extensive.[39]

In terms of the example that is case 2, there is a body of scientific work involving bouncing radar waves off Venus and doing some trigonometry, which determines the distance of Earth to Sun to be 149,597,870.69 kilometres. It is this body of scientific work that the reporter refers to and whose credential determines the epistemic status of the newspaper report. On reading this report, the audience can then get to know this fact because uptake of this report is a way of basing belief on this scientific evidence. The reader knows at second-hand because the scientists have worked out the sums at first-hand. Thus, we can think of our acquisition of testimonial knowledge in the terms articulated by the evidential explanation of transmission.

7.4.3 Origins

The evidential explanation of transmission, I observed in 4.5, has the advantage of generality. It can be applied to any case where knowledge or warrant is transmitted through testimonial uptake. However, being applicable to any case of transmission is an advantage only if one can understand the evidential explanation independently of the other explanations. One consequence of the genealogy given so far is that testimony needs to be treated as assurance before it can be treated either as evidence or indeed as a way of basing belief on the evidence. (The latter consequence follows from the fact that the evidential explanation of transmission presupposes that testimony can be treated as evidence, since its being so can be necessary for

---

[39] This will be the case provided there are effective communication channels. A counter-example would be the arms-race at the end of World War Two and the start of the Cold War.

the development of the extended body of warrant.) And there is still the question of how it is that testimony is fit to transmit knowledge in the first place?

John McDowell answers this question, and argues for a same-state interpretation of transmission, by way of a speculation about evolution.[40] We can find non-intentional creatures that possess in their behavioural repertoire a propensity to visibly respond to certain features of the environment *and* a propensity to manifest a comparable reaction to the exhibition of such responses by other animals of the same species. For instance perception of danger or the perception of a behavioural response provoked by danger, such as squawking, might similarly prompt flight. This is primitive communication, and it functions like testimony to inform its recipient.

When the communicative process functions properly, sensory confrontation with a piece of communicative behaviour has the same impact on the cognitive state of a perceiver as sensory confrontation with the state of affairs which the behaviour, as we may say, represents; elements of the communicative repertoire serve as epistemic surrogates for the represented states of affairs.[41]

It is then possible to answer the question about how our utterances could be fit to communicate information by hypothesizing that the assertoric use of language is 'a descendant, now under intentional control' of such pre-linguistic communication.

The linguistic repertoire retains, through the alteration of nature involved in the onset of self-consciousness, a form of the characteristic that was essential to its pre-linguistic ancestor: in suitable circumstances . . . its exercises are cognitive stand-ins for the states of affairs that they represent.[42]

As such, testimony transmits knowledge because it can create in an audience the same state of informedness with regard to the facts that the speaker enjoys. This is the same-state explanation described in 4.5.

As stated, McDowell presents this hypothesis as a speculative proposal about the course of evolution.[43] A problem for this proposal is the issue of how much continuity exists between this kind of pre-linguistic communication and our putting another in a position to know that p by telling them that p. McDowell argues that there is continuity in the following sense: once we understand that this is the ancestral communicative

---

[40] See McDowell (1980).   [41] McDowell (1980), p. 45.
[42] McDowell (1980), p. 46.   [43] See McDowell (1980), p. 47 n.17.

function of assertion, we can see that only assertions that convey information are *genuinely communicative*.

Now this is surely true of the imagined ancestral bird squawks: if a bird,
which ordinarily squawks only when there is a predator, squawks when
there is none, then something has gone wrong and at one level there does
seem to be a failure of communication. Since the squawk functions 'to
furnish information about the environment to birds that witness it', in this
case 'there has been a malfunction of a natural process'.[44] Once communication is under intentional control, things are remarkably different in
that speech acts are now 'publications of intentions' so that there is
communication whenever there is mutual awareness of the intentions a
speech act publicizes, which may be just to say that *p*. However, irrespective of communicative success at this level, McDowell claims that '[a]t the
first level, communication takes place, as before, only when information is
actually transmitted about the topic of discourse'.[45] So if a speaker were to
say that *p* and lie, there would be the same failure in communication as
there is when a bird, which ordinarily squawks only when there is a
predator, squawks when there is none.

Certainly, lies do involve a failure of communication in one sense: a lie
does not produce the same belief in audience and speaker. However, the
intentionality of the successful case—the case of a knowledgeable speaker telling what she knows—cannot be so easily stripped away. It is not
just another communicative level. Rather, the intentions a speaker has in
utterance determine the nature of the speaker's speech act. The problem
with McDowell's equation is that malfunction requires there be some
proprietary cause. It is the fact that a bird's squawk is *properly caused* by the
presence of a predator that makes it into a reliable sign of the whereabouts of the predator, which can then inform other members of the
same species. However, while a speaker might be prompted to utterance
by something in her environment, a bird predator say, the resulting
utterance is not a natural sign in the way that the squawk might be. It
is not to be explained as a causal response to this feature of the environment. Speakers say things for reasons, and once communication operates
within 'the space of reasons' everything is different because utterance

---

[44] McDowell (1980), p. 45.   [45] McDowell (1980), p. 42.

ceases to have a proper function but serves whatever function a speaker intends.[46]

Suppose a speaker's reason for assertion was to crack a joke; or, put more laboriously, suppose the speaker intended to get an audience to laugh by saying something funny, and succeeded in this. The speaker's assertion in this case is not a malfunction, and nor would it be so if the speaker's intention in asserting was to misinform. This raises the question of how the intentionality of testimony changes its epistemic value as a source of information. And it changes it, I argued in 1.1, in that once it is allowed that communication serves many more functions than the transmission of information, there is the possibility that there can be a divergence in communicative interest. This is to say that once communication is under intentional control the problem of cooperation emerges. This problem must be addressed once testimony is taken out of the primitive domain and into the social domain. It must be resolved in the State of Nature. It is resolved, I argued in 7.4.1, by considering how it is that we can trust one another for the truth. As audiences we need reasons for testimonial uptake, and the most basic way of getting these reasons is to trust and so presume things about a speaker's reasons for utterance. Only given this intentional story can the problem of cooperation be resolved, and an explanation of the transmission of knowledge be given.

McDowell's speculation about the primitive origins of testimony cannot explain how testimony, conceived as an intentional product, is a source of knowledge. Linguistic communication generates a problem that has no counterpart within instinctive communicative behaviour, and whose resolution requires an account that operates at the intentional level. Nevertheless, McDowell's speculation about the primitive origins of testimony could explain how it is that testimony has certain features as a knowledge source. In particular, it can explain how testimony is fit to transmit knowledge and how, on some occasions, a same-state explanation of transmission can be given. Thus we are to imagine that someone's telling us something is fit to transmit knowledge, understood as some state of informedness, about our environment because its primitive communicative ancestors had just this as an essential function. How this

---

[46] As McDowell says elsewhere, 'language, in initiating subjects into the space of reasons, puts them in possession of the world, which needs to be distinguished from the mere ability to live competently in a habitat'. McDowell (1994a), p. 433.

function survived once communication became intentional then requires the intentional story that is given above.

7.5 Conclusion: testimony as a source of knowledge

The aim of this chapter has been to explain how it is that testimony has certain characteristics as a source of knowledge. The explanation offered has been a development of Bernard Williams's genealogy of Sincerity. This genealogy explains how it is that testimony is the transmissive source it is that can yet be treated in reductive terms.[47]

One of the features of testimony as a transmissive source is that it is possible to give three quite different explanations of transmission. Of these, the evidential explanation has the advantage of being general enough to cover all cases of the transmission of knowledge and warrant, whilst the assurance and same-state explanation only happily cover certain cases. The assurance explanation is not entirely general because not all cases of testimony involve a speaker giving assurance. We can acquire testimonial knowledge, for instance, from illicitly reading someone's diary. Or take case 2, the example of reading that the Sun lies 149,597,870.69 kilometres distant from the Earth. It much more natural to describe the journalist who reported this scientific result as shouldering responsibility for reporting the scientific result accurately than for shouldering responsibility for a reader's belief. But it then seems that it is the evidence upon which this result was based, and which neither the reader nor the journalist possesses, that explains the reader's coming to knowing what the journalist reports. This example is also problematic for the same-state explanation, which best fits cases where a speaker reports something seen. In this case, by contrast, the journalist's testimony is to a scientific result which, in all probability, will have been a collaborative effort. So it seems wrong to represent the transmission of this knowledge in terms of testimony recreating a starting state of informedness.

---

[47] It is worth observing that this genealogy is also one of knowledge in that it traces the emergence of our concept of knowledge from that of a primitive state of informedness to a state identified by its association with an ability to justify—a standing in a social space of reasons, of giving and asking for reasons—and finally to a state defined theoretically by its relation to the evidence—a standing in a space of reasons more abstractly conceived.

The evidential explanation is not similarly limited: in general, testimony can be conceived of as a way in which belief can be based on external evidence. In simple cases, the evidence is a speaker's, this evidence supports the speaker's belief, which is the proposition presented by the speaker's testimony, and this evidence then continues to supports this proposition when it is believed by an audience. In more complex cases the evidence need not be the speaker's and the proposition presented by the speaker need not be believed by them. However, the same mechanism operates throughout: *the warranted uptake of testimony provides a way in which belief may be based on external evidence or evidence an audience does not possess.*

The proposal is this. We have a way of life whereby testimony is a source of knowledge because it is a way of transmitting knowledge and warrant that can be conceived in these evidential terms. The story of how we have come to have this way of life must see believing a speaker, in the sense of trusting them for the truth, as a way of getting to know things. And it must start from the idea that communication can function, in its most basic instances, to convey information. Testimony needs to be able to recreate states of informedness before it can be treated as assurance, and it needs to be treated as assurance before it can be treated as evidence or as a way of basing belief on the evidence. A consequence is that it is now possible to give different and potentially overlapping explanations of how testimony transmits knowledge and warrant.

And it is possible to give different explanations of how we can acquire knowledge and warranted belief from testimony. In this respect, it is as if we inhabit two different worlds in that we find both the assurance and the reductive explanations of the acquisition of knowledge and warrant right in their own domain. Equally, when it comes to explaining why it is that we trusted in the Testimony Game—in the broad sense of showed a 'willingness to depend'—we find that both the trust-based and reductive, or game-theoretical, explanations of action have their own spheres of application. The key claim is then that our society is such that we can find the more normative trust-based explanation of action a good one; and we are sensitive to the kinds of reasons that the norms of trust prescribe that we be sensitive to. Certainly, this does not always capture the rationality of behaviour, but it is a distinctive feature of our society that it can do so.

Relatedly, it is possible to give different solutions to the problem of cooperation. The reductive solution is sceptical in that it implies that opportunities of acquiring knowledge and warranted belief from testimony are more limited than might have been thought. But it is also a straight solution: it accepts the terms of the problem and shows how it can be resolved. This is not true of the trust-based solution, which rather dissolves the problem of cooperation through showing how it rests on a restricted conception of what reasons we can have for trusting and being trustworthy. In this way, it is a non-sceptical solution because it shows how trust need not be conceived as problematic. It would not be conceived as problematic were norms of trust and trustworthiness internalized. Then the Testimony Game would simply be perceived by interlocutors as a situation wherein each had a reason to trust and be trustworthy.[48]

However, the question of whether a speaker is cooperating in conversation, or indeed cooperating more generally, can be problematic. A testimonial situation can be characterized by *distrust*. For such situations, the trust-based solution offers no resolution at all. If we genuinely worry about whether relations are trusting, it would not be reasonable to adopt an attitude that presumes that they are! Consider case 3, the case of the anxious would-be purchaser of a used car. This individual might only ever be persuaded by the evidence, and given a sceptical background of belief this is how things should be rationally. As observed in 6.5, the attitude of affective trust is not always reasonable, and it would not be reasonable if one believed someone would attempt to exploit one's dependence on them. Thus, the trust-based solution to the problem of cooperation is not proposed as a strategy for resolving sceptical worries, or removing a background of distrust: it is not a straight solution. Rather, the claim that we intrinsically value trust and trustworthiness is part of a philosophical explanation as to why such distrust is not pervasive. This explanation is genealogical.

Finally, it is worth clarifying that this genealogy offers some support to the assurance theory, and indirectly to the reductive theory, only insofar as these theories of testimony offer solutions to the problem of cooperation. The problem of cooperation can be posed as the demand that an audience have reasons for testimonial uptake. And both the assurance theory, as presented in 6.4, and the reductive theory of testimony, as argued in 3.1, articulate grounds for testimonial uptake and so define solutions to this

---

[48] Analogously, Prichard (1912) does not provide a straight solution to the question, why must I be moral?

problem of cooperation. The non-reductive theory, I argued in 5.2, offers no solution to this problem, and so could not be justified by this genealogical argument. Moreover, the norms of trust that this genealogy supports are *social norms*, they are not general or universal epistemological principles.[49] Whilst every society confronts the problem of trust, since it is confronted in the State of Nature, securing the necessary motivations through a valuation of trust is but one solution to this problem. Other norms are possible.[50]

---

[49] I argue in Faulkner (2010) that these norms cannot be generally justified.

[50] And other norms undoubtedly exist. Velleman (2010) cites ethnographic data of societies that do not seem to follow Grice's Cooperative Principle and maxims. For instance, see Keenan (1976), Harris (1996), and Sweetser (1987).

pg.187

8

The Trust Theory

An epistemological theory of testimony is adequately given by a conjunction of three statements: a statement of what makes testimonial uptake warranted; a statement of what it is that warrants testimonial belief; and an explanation of how it is that this warrants testimonial belief. I propose the following.

(A) Confronted by testimony to p, an audience A is warranted in testimonial uptake if and only if A's other attitudes make it reasonable for A to believe that p.

(B) Where A believes that p through uptake of testimony to p, A is *testimonially* warranted in believing that p only if a prior speaker was warranted in believing that p.

(C) If A's uptake of testimony to p is warranted and a prior speaker was warranted in believing that p, then the extended body of warrant that supports the proposition that p, comes to support A's belief that p.

Call this conjunction the *trust theory of testimony*.[1] By way of conclusion, let me say a little about each component thesis, and consider an objection.

Thesis (C) states the *evidential explanation* of transmission. This thesis was first presented in 3.7, and the genealogy of testimony as a source of knowledge given in 7.4 concluded that we conceive of testimonial knowledge and warrant in these evidential terms: the warranted uptake of testimony provides a way in which belief may be based on evidence an audience does not possess—the extended body of warrant. This thesis, to use Goldberg's term, is *anti-individualist* since whether or not a testimonially presented proposition comes with the support of an extended body of warrant is a social fact. And, as defined in 4.5, it is socially externalist in

---

[1] This develops the statement given in Faulkner (2000).

that the holding of this social fact is not something that is discernible to an audience by 'searching reflection alone'.[2]

Thesis (B) states the *transmission principle for warrant* formulated in 3.2. It identifies the warrant that an audience has for a testimonial belief as distinctively *testimonial* in character. According to this thesis, the testimonial relationship is one of epistemic dependence: an audience's acquisition of testimonial knowledge or testimonial warrant necessitates that a prior speaker knows or is warranted. This prior speaker need not be the immediate speaker and, as observed in 3.5, this transmitted warrant might be a collaborative product, so the claim put forward is that there must be warrant in the testimonial chain (see cases 23 and 29). This thesis, like (C), is socially externalist and anti-individualist.

Thesis (A) states the *principle of reasonable uptake* formulated in 5.2 and supported by the *argument from cooperation* given in 1.1. This thesis is *individualist* in that it concerns reasons that an audience can articulate by 'searching reflection alone'. And it is *internalist* in that it makes the acquisition of warranted testimonial belief depend upon an audience's possession of reasons for uptake. The goodness of these reasons is given by whether they rationalize dependence rather than ground knowledge. The attitude of affective trust, 6.3 argued, can thereby give an audience a good reason for uptake. And once it is recognized that these reasons need not ground an audience's knowledge any belief that allows a prediction of truth will do. All that is needed is that the reason for uptake be an *explanatory epistemic reason*, and reasons that could not suffice for the reductive project may still be this.

An audience's reasons for uptake also play the role of warranting the audience's testimonial belief. Hence (A) states necessary and *sufficient* conditions. However, this is not the essential epistemic role of an audience's reasons for uptake, which is rather to make the extended body of warrant available. As such, thesis (A) is open to different interpretations (we live in 'two worlds' as 7.5 argued). What is necessary for warrant is that uptake be reasonable in the light of an audience's other attitudes. To the extent that an audience's reasons are good ones *in the sense that they could play the role the reductive theory demands* they suffice for the acquisition of *warranted belief from testimony*. But what is needed for *testimonial warrant*, as

---

[2] Goldberg (2007), p. 135.

(B) states, is that there be an extended body of warrant. So to the extent that an audience's reasons are good ones *in the sense that they epistemically rationalize dependence* they suffice to put the audience in a position to inherit what extended body of warrant is available.

One could put things this way: in the central cases, *one needs to possess reasons to be warranted in testimonial uptake but it is reasons one does not possess that warrant one's testimonial beliefs*. Since the reasons one needs are reasons for thinking that a bit of testimony is true, and these reasons could be delivered by an attitude of affective *or* predictive trust, one could equally say that testimony transmits knowledge and warrant by means of trust. Or simply that *testimonial knowledge is knowledge on trust*.

An objection to this theory of testimony might be taken to be implied by the claim that children can acquire testimonial knowledge. Children, it might be claimed, do not have the capability to satisfy the principle of reasonable uptake, (A) above, since both the attitude of affective trust and the ability to make predictions require a sophistication that children do not possess. So it would seem that this theory puts testimonial knowledge beyond children and thereby gets the 'epistemology of under elevens' wrong.

This objection gets the trust theory wrong, and trades on an equivocation. A threefold response, I think, is possible. First, whilst it is true that both the attitude of affective trust and the ability to make predictions require some sophistication, it is not true that the satisfaction of the principle of reasonable uptake requires much sophistication. All that is needed is some reason to think that a piece of testimony is true. It must merely be the case that there is an epistemic reason available as an explanation of an audience's testimonial uptake. Second, it is arguable that this is true of children, and that children have the sophistication necessary for possessing a reason for uptake.[3] Third, if it is nevertheless claimed that children are lacking in this respect, then, I suggest, the judgement that they are equally not in a position to acquire testimonial knowledge is the correct one.

There is a vague domain here, and the objection should not illicitly exploit it. There is clearly an age at which children lack any kind of sophistication, and an age when they just as clearly are in a position to

---

[3] Harris (2002), for instance, argues that children have a sensitivity to a speaker's communicative intentions.

acquire testimonial knowledge. And Brandom's remarks on assertion seem to the point with respect to the latter.

As we grant socially the sorts of responsibility and authority characteristic of adulthood only gradually and in proportion to a child's mastery of the demands and the skills required to fulfill those demands, so it is with assertion.[4]

Finally, even considering the age at which children lack the sophistication necessary for the acquisition of testimonial knowledge, things are not epistemically all bad. Children tend to inhabit micro-social environments that protect them from falsehood just as they protect them from falls and other mishaps.

---

[4] Brandom (1983), p. 644.

References

Achinstein, Peter. 1978. 'Concepts of Evidence'. In *The Concept of Evidence*, ed. P. Achinstein. Oxford: Oxford University Press.

——2001. *The Book of Evidence*. Oxford: Oxford University Press.

Adler, Jonathan E. 1994. 'Testimony, Trust, Knowing'. *Journal of Philosophy* 91 (5): 264–75.

——1996. 'Transmitting Knowledge'. *Noûs* 30 (1): 99–111.

——2002. *Belief's Own Ethics*. Cambridge, MA: MIT Press.

Anscombe, G. E. M. 1979. 'What Is It to Believe Someone?'. In *Rationality and Religious Belief*, ed. C. Delaney. London: University of Notre Dame Press.

Audi, R. 1997. 'The Place of Testimony in the Fabric of Knowledge and Justification'. *American Philosophical Quarterly* 34 (4): 405–22.

Austin, J. L. 1946. 'Other Minds'. In *Philosophical Papers*, ed. J. Urmson and G. Warnock. Oxford: Clarendon Press.

Axelrod, R. 1984. *The Evolution of Cooperation*. New York: Basic Books.

Bacharach, M., and D. Gambetta. 2001. 'Trust as Type Detection'. In *Trust and Deception in Virtual Societies*, ed. C. Castelfranchi and Y.-H. Tan. Dordrecht: Kluwer.

Bezuidenhout, Anne. 1998. 'Is Verbal Communication a Purely Preservative Process?'. *The Philosophical Review* 107 (2): 261–88.

Blackburn, S. 1984. 'Knowledge, Truth, and Reliability'. *Proceedings of the British Academy* 70: 167–87.

Blais, M. 1987. 'Epistemic Tit for Tat'. *Journal of Philosophy* 82 (7): 335–49.

Boghossian, Paul. 1996. 'Analyticity Reconsidered'. *Noûs* 30 (3): 360–91.

——2008. 'Epistemic Rules'. *Journal of Philosophy* 105 (9): 472–500.

Bond, Charles F. and Bella M. DePaulo. 2006. 'Accuracy of Deception Judgements'. *Personality and Social Psychology Review* 10 (3): 214–34.

Brandom, Robert. 1983. 'Asserting'. *Noûs* 17 (4): 637–50.

Bratman, Michael. 1996. 'Identification, Decision and Treating as a Reason'. In *Faces of Intention: Selected Essays on Intention and Agency*, ed. M. Bratman. Cambridge: Cambridge University Press.

——1999. 'Practical Reasoning and Acceptance in a Context'. In *Faces of Intention: Selected Essays on Intention and Agency*, ed. M. Bratman. Cambridge: Cambridge University Press. Original edition, *Mind* 1992.

——2000. 'Reflection, Planning and Temporally Extended Agency'. In *Structures of Agency*, ed. M. Bratman. Oxford: Oxford University Press.

Burge, Tyler. 1993. 'Content Preservation'. *Philosophical Review* 102 (4): 457–88.

——1996. 'Our Entitlement to Self-Knowledge'. *Proceedings of the Aristotelian Society* 96: 91–116.

——1997. 'Interlocution, Perception, and Memory'. *Philosophical Studies* 86: 21–47.

——1998. 'Computer Proof, A Priori Knowledge, and Other Minds'. *Philosophical Perspectives* 12 (Language, Mind and Ontology): 1–37.

——2003. 'Perceptual Entitlement'. *Philosophy and Phenomenological Research* 67 (3): 503–48.

Coady, C. A. J. 1973. 'Testimony and Observation'. *American Philosophical Quarterly* 10 (2): 149–55.

——1992. *Testimony: A Philosophical Study.* 1st edn. Oxford: Clarendon Press.

Cohen, L. J. 1992. *An Essay on Acceptance and Belief.* Oxford: Clarendon Press.

Connee, E. and R. Feldman. 1998. 'The Generality Problem for Reliabilism'. *Philosophical Studies* 89 (1): 1–31.

Dasgupta, P. 1988. 'Trust as a Commodity'. In *Trust: Making and Breaking Cooperative Relations*, ed. D. Gambetta. Oxford: Basil Blackwell.

Davidson, D. 1973. 'Radical Interpretation'. In *Inquiries into Truth and Interpretation*, ed. D. Davidson. Oxford: Clarendon Press.

——1974a. 'Belief and the Basis of Meaning'. In *Inquiries into Truth and Interpretation*, ed. D. Davidson. Oxford: Clarendon Press.

——1974b. 'On the Very Idea of a Conceptual Scheme'. In *Inquiries into Truth and Interpretation*, ed. D. Davidson. Oxford: Clarendon Press.

——1975. 'Thought and Talk'. In *Inquiries into Truth and Interpretation*, ed. D. Davidson. Oxford: Clarendon Press.

——1977a. 'The Method of Truth in Metaphysics'. In *Inquiries into Truth and Interpretation*, ed. D. Davidson. Oxford: Clarendon Press.

——1977b. 'Reality without Reference'. In *Inquiries into Truth and Interpretation*, ed. D. Davidson. Oxford: Clarendon Press.

——1983. 'A Coherence Theory of Truth and Knowledge'. In *Truth and Interpretation: Perspectives on the Philosophy of Donald Davidson*, ed. E. LePore. Oxford: Basil Blackwell.

——1991. 'Three Varieties of Knowledge'. In *Subjective, Intersubjective, Objective*, ed. D. Davidson. Oxford: Clarendon Press.

——1996. 'The Folly of Trying to Define Truth'. *Journal of Philosophy* 93 (6): 263–78.

——ed. 1984. *Inquiries into Truth and Interpretation.* Oxford: Clarendon Press.

DePaulo, Bella M., James J. Lindsay, Brian E. Malone, Laura Muhlenbruck, Kelly Charlton, and Harris Cooper. 2003. 'Cues to Deception'. *Psychological Bulletin* 129 (1): 74–118.

Dummett, M. 1993. 'Testimony and Memory'. In *The Seas of Language*, ed. M. Dummett. Oxford: Clarendon Press.

Ekman, Paul. 1985. *Telling Lies: Clues to Deceit in the Marketplace, Marriage, and Politics*. New York: W. W. Norton.

——2009. 'Lie Catching and Microexpressions'. In *The Philosophy of Deception*, ed. C. Martin. Oxford: Oxford University Press.

Elgin, Catherine Z. 2002. 'Take It from Me: The Epistemological Status of Testimony'. *Philosophy and Phenomenological Research* 65 (2): 291–308.

Elster, Jon. 1989. *The Cement of Society: A Study of Social Order*. Cambridge: Cambridge University Press.

——2007. *Explaining Social Behaviour: More Nuts and Bolts for the Social Sciences*. Cambridge: Cambridge University Press

Evans, Gareth. 1982. *The Varieties of Reference*, ed. J. McDowell. Oxford: Clarendon Press.

Faulkner, Paul. 2000. 'The Social Character of Testimonial Warrant'. *Journal of Philosophy* 97 (11): 581–601.

——2006. 'Understanding Knowledge Transmission'. *Ratio* 19 (2): 156–75.

——2007a. 'On Telling and Trusting'. *Mind* 116 (464): 875–902.

——2007b. 'What is Wrong With Lying?'. *Philosophy and Phenomenological Research* 75 (3): 535–58.

——2009. 'Review: Jennifer Lackey: *Learning from Words: Testimony as a Source of Knowledge*'. *Mind* 118 (470): 479–85.

——2010. 'Norms of Trust'. In *Social Epistemology*, ed. D. Pritchard, A. Haddock, and A. Millar. Oxford: Oxford University Press.

Fehr, Ernest, Urs Fischbacher, and Simon Gachter. 2002. 'Strong Reciprocity, Human Cooperation, and the Enforcement of Social Norms'. *Human Nature* 13 (1): 1–25.

Feldman, R. and E. Conee. 1985. 'Evidentialism'. *Philosophical Studies* 48 (1): 15–34.

Foley, R. and R. Fumerton. 1985. 'Davidson's Theism?'. *Philosophical Studies* 48: 83–9.

Frank, Mark G. 2009. 'Thoughts, Feelings, and Deception'. In *Deception: From Ancient Empires to Internet Dating*, ed. B. Harrington. Stanford: Stanford University Press.

Fricker, E. 1994. 'Against Gullibility'. In *Knowing from Words*, ed. B. K. Matilal. Dordrecht: Kluwer.

——1995. 'Telling and Trusting: Reductionism and Anti-Reductionism in the Epistemology of Testimony'. *Mind* 104 (414): 393–411.

——2006. 'Martians and Meetings: Against Burge's Neo-Kantian Apriorism about Testimony'. *Philosophica* 78: 69–84.

Gettier, E. 1963. 'Is Justified True Belief Knowledge?'. *Analysis* 23: 121–3.

Gilbert, Daniel T., Douglas S. Krull, and Patrick S. Malone. 1990. 'Unbelieving the Unbelievable: Some Problems in the Rejection of False Information'. *Journal of Personality and Social Psychology* 59 (4): 601–13.

Gilbert, Daniel T., Romin W. Tafarodi, and Patrick S. Malone. 1993. 'You Can't Not Believe Everything You Read'. *Journal of Personality and Social Psychology* 65 (2): 221–33.

Goldberg, S. and D. Henderson. 2007. 'Monitoring and Anti-Reductionism in the Epistemology of Testimony'. *Philosophy and Phenomenological Research* 72 (3): 576–93.

Goldberg, Sanford. 2001. 'Testimonially Based Knowledge From False Testimony'. *Philosophical Quarterly* 51 (205): 512–26.

——2007. *Anti-Individualism: Mind and Language, Knowledge and Justification*. Cambridge: Cambridge University Press.

Goldman, Alvin. 1976. 'Discrimination and Perceptual Knowledge'. *Journal of Philosophy* 73: 771–91.

——1979. 'What Is Justified Belief?'. In *Epistemology: An Anthology*, ed. E. Sosa and J. Kim. Oxford: Blackwell. Original edition, Pappas ed., *Justification and Knowledge*.

Graham, Peter J. 2000a. 'Conveying Information'. *Synthese* 123 (3): 365–92.

——2000b. 'The Reliability of Testimony'. *Philosophy and Phenomenological Research* 61 (3): 695–709.

Grice, P. 1957. 'Meaning'. In *Studies in the Way of Words*, ed. P. Grice. Cambridge, MA: Harvard University Press.

——1967. 'Logic and Conversation'. In *Studies in the Way of Words*, ed. P. Grice. Cambridge, MA: Harvard University Press.

Hardin, R. 2002. *Trust and Trustworthiness*. New York: Russell Sage Foundation.

Hardwig, J. 1985. 'Epistemic Dependence'. *The Journal of Philosophy* 82 (7): 335–49.

——1991. 'The Role of Trust in Knowledge'. *The Journal of Philosophy* 88 (12): 693–708.

Harris, P. L. 2002. 'Checking Our Sources: The Origins of Trust in Testimony'. *Studies in the History and Philosophy of Science* 33: 315–33.

Harris, Rachel M. 1996. 'Truthfulness, Conversational Maxims and Interaction in an Egyptian Village'. *Transactions of the Philological Society* 94: 31–55.

Hinchman, E. 2005. 'Telling as Inviting to Trust'. *Philosophy and Phenomenological Research* 70 (3): 562–87.

Hintikka, J. 1962. *Knowledge and Belief: An Introduction to the Logic of the Two Notions*. London: King's College Publications.

——1989. *The Logic of Epistemology and the Epistemology of Logic: Selected Essays*. Dordrecht: Kluwer.

Hobbes, T. 1651. *Leviathan*. 1968 edn. Harmondsworth: Penguin.

Hollis, M. 1998. *Trust Within Reason*. Cambridge: Cambridge University Press.

Holton, R. 1994. 'Deciding to Trust, Coming to Believe'. *Australasian Journal of Philosophy* 72 (1): 63–76.

Horsburgh, H. J. N. 1960. 'The Ethics of Trust'. *Philosophical Quarterly* 10 (41): 343–54.

Horwich, Paul. 1982. *Probability and Evidence*. Cambridge: Cambridge University Press.

Hume, D. 1740. *A Treatise of Human Nature*, ed. L. A. Selby-Bigge. Oxford: Clarendon Press.

——1777. *Enquiries Concerning Human Understanding and Concerning the Principles of Morals*. 3rd edn. Revised and ed. P. H. Nidditch. Oxford: Clarendon Press.

Jones, K. 1996. 'Trust as an Affective Attitude'. *Ethics* 107 (1): 4–25.

Keenan, Elinor Ochs. 1976. 'The Universality of Conversational Postulates'. *Language in Society* 5: 67–80.

Knorr-Cetina, K. 1999. *Epistemic Cultures: How the Sciences Make Knowledge*. Cambridge, MA: Harvard University Press.

Kripke, Saul. 1982. *Wittgenstein on Rules and Private Language*. Oxford: Basil Blackwell.

Kronz, Frederick. 1992. 'Carnap and Achinstein on Evidence'. *Philosphical Studies* 67: 151–67.

Lackey, Jennifer. 1999. 'Testimonial Knowledge and Transmission'. *Philosophical Quarterly* 49 (197): 471–90.

——2008. *Learning from Words: Testimony as a Source of Knowledge*. Oxford: Oxford University Press.

Lipton, Peter. 1991. *Inference to the Best Explanation*. London: Routledge.

——1998. 'The Epistemology of Testimony'. *Studies in the History and Philosophy of Science* 29 (1): 1–31.

Lyons, Jack. 1997. 'Testimony, Induction and Folk Psychology'. *Australasian Journal of Philosophy* 75: 163–78.

Malmgren, Anna-Sara. 2006. 'Is There A Priori Knowledge by Testimony?'. *Philosophical Review* 115 (2): 199–241.

McDowell, J. 1978. 'Are Moral Requirements Hypothetical Imperatives?'. In *Mind, Value, and Reality*, ed. J. McDowell. Cambridge, MA: Harvard University Press. Original edn. 1978.

——1980. 'Meaning, Communication and Knowledge'. In *Meaning, Knowledge, and Reality*, ed. J. McDowell. Cambridge, MA: Harvard University Press.

——1981. 'Anti-Realism and the Epistemology of Understanding'. In *Meaning, Knowledge, and Reality*, ed. J. McDowell. Cambridge, MA: Harvard University Press.

——1982. 'Criteria Defeasibility and Knowledge'. In *Meaning, Knowledge, and Reality*, ed. J. McDowell. Cambridge, MA: Harvard University Press. Original edn. *Proceedings of the British Academy* 68.

——1994a. 'Knowledge by Hearsay'. In *Meaning, Knowledge, and Reality*, ed. J. McDowell. Cambridge, MA: Harvard University Press.

McDowell, J. 1994b. *Mind and World*. Cambridge, MA: Harvard University Press.

——1995. 'Knowledge and the Internal'. In *Meaning, Knowledge, and Reality*, ed. J. McDowell. Cambridge, MA: Harvard University Press. Original edn. *Philosophy and Phenomenological Research* 55.

Möllering, Guido. 2009. 'Leaps and Lapses of Faith: Exploring the Relationship Between Trust and Deception'. In *Deception: From Ancient Empires to Internet Dating*, ed. B. Harrington. Stanford: Stanford University Press.

Montaigne, Michel de. 2004. 'On Vanity'. In *The Complete Essays*, ed. M. A. Screech. London: Penguin Books.

Moran, Richard. 2001. *Authority and Estrangement: An Essay on Self-Knowledge*. Princeton: Princeton University Press.

——2005. 'The Problems of Sincerity'. *Proceedings of the Aristotelian Society* 105 (3): 341–61.

——2006. 'Getting Told and Being Believed'. In *The Epistemology of Testimony*, ed. J. Lackey and E. Sosa. Oxford: Clarendon Press.

O'Sullivan, Maureen. 2009. 'Why Most People Parse Palters, Fibs, Lies, Whoppers and Other Deceptions Poorly'. In *Deception: From Ancient Empires to Internet Dating*, ed. B. Harrington. Stanford: Stanford University Press.

Owens, D. 2000. *Reason without Freedom: The Problem of Epistemic Normativity*. London: Routledge.

Pettit, Philip. 1990. '*Virtus normativa*: Rational Choice Perspectives'. In *Rules, Reasons, and Norms: Selected Essays*, ed. P. Pettit. Oxford: Clarendon Press.

——1995. 'The Cunning of Trust'. *Philosophy and Public Affairs* 24 (3): 202–25.

Pettit, Philip and Michael Smith. 1990. 'Backgrounding Desire'. *The Philosophical Review* 94 (4): 565–92.

Plantinga, A. 1988. 'Positive Epistemic Status and Proper Function'. *Philosophical Perspectives: Epistemology* 2: 1–50.

Pollock, J. 1986. *Contemporary Theories of Knowledge*. Totowa, NJ: Rowman & Littlefield.

——1990. *Nomic Probability and the Foundations of Induction*. Oxford: Oxford University Press.

Popper, K. 1968. 'On the Theory of the Objective Mind'. In *Objective Knowledge: An Evolutionary Approach*, ed. K. Popper. Oxford: Clarendon Press.

Porter, Stephen and John C. Yuille. 1995. 'Credibility Assessment of Criminal Suspects Through Statement Analysis'. *Psychology, Crime and Law* 1 (4): 319–31.

Prichard, H. A. 1912. 'Does Moral Philosophy Rest on a Mistake?'. *Mind* 21 (81): 21–37.

Pryor, James. 2000. 'The Skeptic and the Dogmatist'. *Noûs* 34 (4): 517–49.

Reichenbach, H. 1949. *A Theory of Probability: An Inquiry into the Logical and Mathematical Foundations of the Calculus of Probability*. Berkeley: University of California Press.

Reid, T. 1764. 'An Inquiry into the Mind on the Principles of Common Sense'. In *The Works of Thomas Reid*, ed. W. H. Bart. Edinburgh: Maclachlan & Stewart.

Reynolds, Steven L. 2002. 'Testimony, Knowledge, and Epistemic Goals'. *Philosophical Studies* 110 (2): 139–61.

Ross, A. 1986. 'Why Do We Believe What we are Told?'. *Ratio* 28 (1): 69–88.

Schmitt, F. F. 1987. 'Justification, Sociality and Autonomy'. *Synthese* 73 (1): 43–85.

Shapin, S. 1994. *A Social History of Truth: Civility and Science in Seventeenth Century England*. Chicago: University of Chicago Press.

Shogenji, Tomoji. 2006. 'A Defense of Reductionism about Testimonial Justification of Beliefs'. *Noûs* 40 (2): 331–46.

Simpson, D. 1992. 'Lying, Liars and Language'. *Philosophy and Phenomenological Research* 52 (3): 623–39.

Sober, Elliott. 1994. 'The Primacy of Truth-Telling and the Evolution of Lying'. In *From a Biological Point of View: Essays in Evolutionary Philosophy*, ed. E. Sober. Cambridge: Cambridge University Press.

Sousa, Ronald de. 1987. *The Rationality of Emotion*. Cambridge, MA: MIT Press.

Sperber, D. 2001. 'An Evolutionary Perspective on Testimony and Argumentation'. *Philosophical Topics* 29 (1&2): 401–13.

Sripada, C. S. and S. Stich. 2006. 'A Framework for the Psychology of Norms'. In *The Innate Mind: Culture and Cognition*, ed. P. Carruthers, S. Laurene, and S. Stich. Oxford: Oxford University Press.

Stevenson, L. 1993. 'Why Believe What People Say?'. *Synthese* 94 (3): 429–51.

Stocker, Michael. 1981. 'Values and Purposes: The Limits of Teleology and the Ends of Friendship'. *The Journal of Philosophy* 78 (12): 747–65.

Sweetser, Eve. 1987. 'The Definition of Lie: An Examination of the Folk Models Underlying a Semantic Prototype'. In *Cultural Models in Language and Thought*, ed. D. Holland and N. Quinn. Cambridge: Cambridge University Press.

Undeutsch, Udo. 1989. 'The Development of Statement Reality Analysis'. In *Credibility Assessment*, ed. J. C. Yuille. New York: Kluwer.

Velleman, David. 2010. 'Regarding Doing, Being Ordinary'. Manuscript.

Vendler, Z. 1979. 'Telling the Facts'. In *Contemporary Perspectives in the Philosophy of Language*, ed. P. A. French. Dordrecht: Reidel.

Vermazen, B. 1983. 'The Intelligibility of Massive Error'. *Philosophical Quarterly* 33: 69–74.

Wallace, R. Jay. 1994. *Responsibility and the Moral Sentiments*. Cambridge, MA: Harvard University Press.

Watson, Gary. 2004. 'Asserting and Promising'. *Philosophical Studies* 117: 57–77.

Webb, M. O. 1993. 'Why I know about as much as you: A reply to Hardwig'. *The Journal of Philosophy* 90 (5): 260–70.

Weiner, Matthew. 2003. 'Accepting Testimony'. *Philosophical Quarterly* 53 (211): 256–64.

Welbourne, M. 1979. 'The Transmission of Knowledge'. *The Philosophical Quaterly* 29 (114): 1–9.

——1986. *The Community of Knowledge*. Aberdeen: Aberdeen University Press.

——1993. *The Community of Knowledge*. Aldershot: Gregg Revivals.

Williams, B. 1972. 'Knowledge and Reasons'. In *Problems in the Theory of Knowledge*, ed. G. H. von Wright. The Hague: Martinus Nijhoff.

——1978. *Descartes: The Project of Pure Enquiry*. Harmondsworth: Penguin.

——1988. 'Formal Structures and Social Reality'. In *Making Sense of Humanity and Other Philosophical Papers, 1982–1993*, ed. B. Williams. Cambridge: Cambridge University Press.

——2002. *Truth and Truthfulness*. Princeton: Princeton University Press.

Williamson, Timothy. 2000. *Knowledge and Its Limits*. Oxford: Oxford University Press.

Index

CPSIA information can be obtained
at www.ICGtesting.com
Printed in the USA
JSHW030103207021
1668OJS0000IB/18